OUTDOOR BUILDING PROJECTS

—— *Byron W. Maguire* ——

Prentice Hall, Englewood Cliffs, New Jersey 07632

Library of Congress Cataloging-in-Publication Data

MAGUIRE, BYRON W.
    Outdoor building projects / Byron W. Maguire.
        p.   cm.
    Includes bibliographical references.
    ISBN 0-13-643354-5
    1. Garden structures—Design and construction.   I. Title.
TH4961.M33   1991
690'.89—dc20   89-48416
                                                                                    CIP

Editorial/production supervision
  and interior design: *Claudia Citarella*
Cover design: *Lundgren Graphics, Ltd.*
Manufacturing buyer: *Kelly Behr*

The publisher offers discounts on this book when ordered
in bulk quantities. For more information, write:

  Special Sales/College Marketing
  Prentice Hall
  College Technical and Reference Division
  Englewood Cliffs, NJ 07632

Printed in the United States of America

10 9 8 7 6 5 4 3 2 1

ISBN   0-13-643354-5

PRENTICE-HALL INTERNATIONAL (UK) LIMITED, *London*
PRENTICE-HALL OF AUSTRALIA PTY. LIMITED, *Sydney*
PRENTICE-HALL CANADA INC., *Toronto*
PRENTICE-HALL HISPANOAMERICANA, S.A., *Mexico*
PRENTICE-HALL OF INDIA PRIVATE LIMITED, *New Delhi*
PRENTICE-HALL OF JAPAN, INC., *Tokyo*
SIMON & SCHUSTER ASIA PTE. LTD., *Singapore*
EDITORA PRENTICE-HALL DO BRASIL, LTDA., *Rio de Janeiro*

CONTENTS

Preface ix

───── SECTION 1 ─────
Patios and Decks

1

The Basic Design and Construction of a Concrete Patio 1

Background 2   Specifications 3   Materials Assessment 5   Ground Preparation 6   Layout 8   Forming 12   Pouring and Finishing 14 Landscaping and Cleanup 16   Materials Invoice 16

2

Modifications and Enhancements to the Concrete Slab Patio 19

Using Lumber in the Slab 20   Using Brick in the Slab 24   Using Tile in the Slab 29   Using Slate in the Slab 30   Using Exposed Aggregate as the Top Surface 32   Using Rock Salt to Create a Finish for the Slab 34 Using Coloring Agents in the Concrete for the Slab 35   Using Trowel and Broom to Create Surface Patterns 36

3

Concrete Patio on Top of a Foundation 37

Background 38   Specifications 38   Materials Assessment 38 Construction 39   Cleanup 50   Landscaping 50   Materials Listing 51 Protective Coating Techniques for Concrete Surfaces 52

4

Resurfacing an Old Concrete Slab Patio 53

Grinding the Surface of the Slab and Sealing It 54   Acid Cleaning of the Slab's Surface and Sealing It 55   Tiling an Old but Sound Patio Slab 57 Overbricking a Concrete Slab Patio 61

5

The Wood Deck Patio—Basic Design and Construction 66

Background 67   Specifications 67   Materials Assessment 68 Ground Preparation and Masonry Tasks 69   Building the Frame for the Deck 73   Decking the Wood Deck 75   Finalize the Materials Listing 77 Summary of the Project 78

6

Railings, Steps, and Perimeter Seating 79

Method of Construction of Wood Deck Railings and Materials Assessment 80   Method for Construction of Wood Deck Steps and Materials Assessment 84   Methods for Construction of Wood Deck Perimeter Seating and Materials Assessment 89

7

Finishing Techniques for Wood Decks 96

Protection Techniques and Materials for the Wood Deck 97   Materials Assessment 103

8

Repairing and Refurbishing Old Decks 105

Examining Decks for Defects 106   Determining the Extent of Repair 110 Repair of Framing Section 111   Repair of Deck Surface Materials 113 Repair of Add-On Features 114   Checklist 115

─────────────── SECTION 2 ───────────────
Porches

9

The Basic Design and Construction of the Porch Floor 118

Background 119   Specifications 120   Materials Assessment 122
Ground Preparation and Masonry Tasks 123   Building the Frame for
the Floor 125   Decking the Floor and Adding Trim 127
Materials Listing 129   Summarizing the Project 129

10

Design and Construction of the Porch Roof 131

Background 132   Specifications 136   Materials Assessment 136
Layout of Materials 137   Framing, Sheathing, and Shingling 139
Cornice and Ceiling 151   Safety 155   Cleanup 156   Materials
Listing 155

11

Design and Installation of the Porch Columns 157

Background 158   Specifications and Materials Assessment 158
Layout and Construction 158   Cleanup and Safety Concerns 165
Materials Listing 165

12

Screening the Porch 167

Background 168   Specifications 169   Materials Assessment 170
Panel Design and Construction 170   Panel Installation and Trim 176
Door and Header Installation 178   Painting 178   Materials Listing 180

13

Finishing Techniques for Porches 181

Maintain Architectural Style 182   Building Materials 183   Paints and
Other Finishes 186

──────────── SECTION 3 ────────────
Gazebos

14

Gazebos: Styles and Uses 191

Styling the Gazebo 192   Uses for Gazebos 201   Summary 202

15

Design and Construction Techniques for the Gazebo 203

Background 204   Specifications 204   Materials Assessment 204
Ground Preparation and Masonry Tasks 205   Floor Assembly 210
Wall (Column) Construction 212   Roof Construction 214   Step
Construction 220   Finishing Touches 221   Safety and Cleanup 223
Materials Listing 223

──────────── SECTION 4 ────────────
Trellises

16

Trellises: Styles, Uses, and Construction 226

Styles Created with the Use of Different Materials and Features 227
Uses for Trellises 230   Background 231   Specifications 232
Materials Assessment 233   Construction 234   Materials Listing 237

17

Enhancing the Trellis 238

Adding Gingerbread 239   Adding Electricity 240   Adding Sidewalls 241
Planting Vines and Shrubs (Landscaping) 244   The Floor 244

----------- SECTION 5 -----------
Terracing

18

Solving Landscaping Problems with Terracing 247

Topography 248   Surface and Subsurface Conditions to Contend
with 251   Uses of Terraces 252

19

Single-Material Approach to Terracing 258

Terracing with Brick 259   Terracing with Wood 265   Terracing with
Stone 269   Retaining Wall Variations 274

20

Different Construction Techniques for Terrace Stairs 276

Gentle Slope Stair Design 277   Steep Grade Stair Design 279

----------- SECTION 6 -----------
Fencing

21

Wood Fences 285

Background 286   Specifications 289   Materials Assessment 290
Construction Sequence 290   Materials Listing 294

22
Brick Columns in a Wood Fence 296

Background 297   Specifications 297   Materials Assessment 298
Construction Sequence 298   Materials Invoice 302

References 303

Index 304

PREFACE

This book is about enhancing outdoor living areas around your property. It deals with the skills of carpentry, painting, and masonry, and very lightly touches on electricity. There is so much that we can do to improve our outdoor living spaces that I organized the book in six sections that contain chapters that are related in some way to each other. Section 1, for example, covers patios and decks. Other sections deal with porches, trellises, gazebos, terracing, and fences.

Some projects are small and require simple planning and execution. Others are complex and require much greater understanding and use of more advanced skills. I have provided a set of specifications for each job, an initial materials assessment, which lists all types of materials used in and on the job, and a materials invoice at each chapter's end to show the materials consumed and rented. With these tools as well as construction task lists and descriptions we will create beautiful outdoor living spaces.

What you must do is adapt the generic project to fit your particular surroundings and conditions. Having a model to work with is much simpler than starting from scratch. You create your specifications by using and modifying the generic specifications. You make your materials assessment and you prepare your materials invoice by modifying the model. Further, you select and modify the tasks associated with your job from the various ones used in creating the generic project.

In the first section on patios we begin in Chapter 1 with designing and constructing a concrete patio at ground level. First we discuss the project in general terms and concepts in a background section. Then we set some specifications in Table 1.1 from which we will later construct the generic ground-level concrete patio. Just to be sure we are starting out right we next make up a table of materials assessment. In this table we list the direct materials such as concrete, reinforcement wire, and rebars. The table also includes indirect materials, which are those needed to build the form, erect batter boards, and such. The last part of the table lists support materials, which are carpentry and mason tools, workbenches, rental tools, and so on.

So far we know what we want and what it takes to build the slab. Now the next phase is the ground preparation where we plan and do the things associated with topography and land preparation. Then a series of task-related steps follow, including layout, forming, pouring and finishing, and landscaping and cleanup. We close out the chapter with Table 1.3, where we prepare a materials invoice in which a set of actual materials used is listed.

From this beginning we can enhance the basic design by using Chapter 2. In this chapter we learn to use brick, wood, and tile in patio design. We also discuss making the aggregate exposed, using rock salt for the surface effect and coloring the concrete.

Not all patios are at ground level, so in Chapter 3 we construct one above ground. In fact, we build a block foundation first. This teaches us about footings and block laying plus forming for a slab on foundation. It discusses mortar mixtures, joint striking, backfilling the foundation, and reinforcement.

We end the first part of Section 1 on concrete patios with Chapter 4, which has several ideas on repairing and refurbishing concrete slabs. Here we talk about cleaning the old surfaces, making patches, overtiling and overbricking a sound concrete slab. Information on calculating quantities is included.

Chapters 5 through 9 are also about patios, but those made from wood, which are commonly called *decks*. Chapter 5 provides a thorough study in basic design and construction. There are nine objectives to accomplish, beginning with the background and concluding with the materials invoice. This deck is mounted on and supported by block piers. Here we use the termite shield, joists and headers, deck planking, and designs for dead and live loads. In Chapter 6 we add railings, steps, and beautiful perimeter seating. In Chapter 7 we add finishing techniques such as wood protectors, treated lumber, stains, and sealers. We also discuss organisms and bugs that attack wood. Chapter 8 differs from the other three; its emphasis is on the repair and refurbishing of old decks. Subjects discussed include techniques best suited to removal and replacement of decayed or broken pieces, tricks that make repairs blend in with old materials, and so on. A nice feature in this chapter are the three checklists. These will aid you in identifying your deck problems as well as arriving at possible solutions or techniques.

Section 2, Chapters 9 through 13, discusses porches. Chapter 9 deals with design and construction of the porch floor. Since the porch will have a roof (Chapter 10), we need to prepare a foundation. In Chapter 9 we build brick piers for beauty. Later (Chapter 13), we build lattice assemblies between the piers. We also design the floor assembly for 40-lb live load. The chapters all have specifications, materials assessments, construction tasks and details, and a materials invoice. Since some of this work is off-the-ground (Chapter 10), safety is discussed too. In Chapter 10 we design and build a truss roof that ties into the slope of the main roof. Terms are explained with illustrations to show clearly what they mean. Overhangs, cornices, lookouts, and such are all part of roof construction. We also discuss valleys, header construction, and squaring techniques.

It may seem strange, but columns are built and installed after the roof is built. Chapter 11 describes how to build on-site columns and install them.

In Chapter 12, "Screening the Porch," we use a really unique method of screen paneling to create a beautiful porch free of bugs. An ample number of illustrations shows us the way to do things such as making panels, screening them, and adding molding. Others show how to divide the long expanses with 2-in. stock and how to secure panels with quarter round.

In the event that we elect not to screen the porch, trims and other techniques such as adding gingerbread add beauty and distinctiveness to the porch. But we need to maintain architectural integrity. To help you with your designs I have provided a basic description of the six styles of homes—southern colonial, colonial, cape cod, ranch, modern and ultra-modern.

In Section 3, Chapters 14 and 15 take us away from the house to the garden and pool area. They deal with gazebos. In Chapter 14 we discuss styles and uses, and in Chapter 15 we build a six-sided gazebo on a block foundation. This is a project that really tests your skills. But if we work together as the chapter lays out the work and describes the tasks, we can have a great addition to the livable outdoors. For this project panels replace posts that keep the roof up. We also use the open rafter end design. Solving the peak problem where all hip rafters join is simplified for us.

In Section 4, Chapters 16 and 17 show us where to use a trellis and how to make one. Trellises are fun to make and provide an added dimension, dividing yards or larger property into different functional areas. We generally build trellises from treated lumber. Sometimes we even use oversized timbers, such as 3×10s and 6×8s. Did you know that we can add a floor to a trellis? In Chapter 17 you and I build a floor from pine straw and another one of paver bricks. We add sides by constructing lattice panels, and we use gingerbread in place of common bracing. Finally, we plant shrubs and vines to add style.

In Section 5, Chapters 18 through 20 deal with an often-encountered problem, terracing. In Chapter 18 we work with building a topographical map of the property. We look at the advantage and use of a transit tool. We identify ground clay, sand, and rocks, and how these help and hinder terracing design. One part of the chapter helps us understand the uses of terraces in urban, suburban, and country habitats. Urban backyards are narrow and long, as a rule. Terracing converts these into enjoyable, interesting places to spend many hours. In Chapter 19 we solve terracing problems with single-material techniques. These include wood ties, or brick or stone. There is a project for each one so that we can be sure to understand how to proceed. In the one on brick, six or seven different bricklaying patterns are shown. In the one on stone, two different patterns are shown. The generic project with wood uses wood ties, but we could substitute landscape timbers if the wall were low. Where property has slopes, stairs may be a better solution than sloping walkways. Chapter 20 provides two generic projects. One is for a gentle slope stair design; the other is for a steep slope stair design. You will find both well illustrated and easy to use.

Section 6 deals with fences. In Chapter 21 we discuss fence design and construct one with added features. Figure 21-4 in this chapter illustrates numerous fence designs and styles. In Chapter 22, the final chapter, we replace the wood fence post with a brick one. Details on design and fence attachment techniques are well covered.

HOW TO USE THIS BOOK

As a Textbook

This book is sectioned so that you are able to select the type of applications in which you are most interested to study. Each section stands alone; that is, there is no need to flip pages back and forth from section to section. Within a section there are chapters that further subdivide it. In each chapter the text, charts, figures, and other related information are presented in a building-block format. The subject is treated in a generic way so that a foundation of understanding is achieved through study.

As a Builder's Guide

The following notations are used:

" = inch/inches (in art); in. (in text)
' = foot/feet (in art); ft (in text)
1 × 6 assumes 1″ × 6″ stock lumber
2 1 × 6 assumes 2 boards 1 × 6
2 1 × 6 8 assumes 2 1 × 6 boards 8 feet long (in material lists), 2 1 × 6 8 ft (in text)
Fractional inches to 1/16″

You should use only those sections of each generic project that you need. Adapt your designs to the generic projects. Then follow the design concepts, plan well, and use good workmanship. You will do a fine job. I wish you the best of success on every project you attempt.

Byron W. Maguire

1

The Basic Design and Construction of a Concrete Patio

OBJECTIVES

- Plan for the construction of a ground level concrete slab patio.
- Plan a specifications and materials assessment.
- Establish the ground reference level and height of the finished patio.
- Define the precise parameters and shape of the patio.
- Determine the layout, forming, pouring, and finishing tasks, plus other conditions that you may have to deal with.
- Ascertain the landscaping and cleanup requirements.
- Finalize the materials listing with computations included.

BACKGROUND

Through the study of this chapter, or by the selective use of segments of this chapter, a well-planned, successfully constructed concrete patio can be built at ground level. The ultimate goal is to use this data to build a patio that is sound, decorative, and useful, which meets specifications and has a long, durable life expectancy.

What we are faced with is a project to build a patio from concrete, reinforced properly, which conforms to an area 20 ft by 30 ft. The area must be properly located. For this batter boards and mason line will be employed. The ground must be prepared, leveled, backfilled, and so on, and we will need to establish reference levels for this work. The forms must be built. The reinforcing rebars and wire mesh need to be laid properly. Trenching for perimeter footing needs to be done. The concrete must be ordered, poured, and finished. Some method of control must be used during the initial curing cycle. Form removal, clean-up, and landscaping must follow in logical order. If all of these parts of the project are accomplished with attention to detail, a quality product will result.

Rather than clutter the chapter with many variables such as varying sizes of patios, various thicknesses, a multitude of ground conditions and such, we use a generic approach. This simple, straightforward technique makes it easy to understand the basic elements of each segment of the project. With these as fundamentals, adaptations can easily be made to meet the requirements of a unique situation.

Are there any physical requirements that we need to be concerned about? A project of this type does require one to have certain physical capabilities. Moving dirt, for one thing, is heavy work. Driving stakes into the ground with a 10-lb sledge hammer is hard work. Transporting sand fill in a wheelbarrow is very physical. Cutting $\frac{1}{2}$-in. rebar with bolt cutters or saw is strenuous. Unrolling 6×6 wire mesh is dangerous as well as strenuous; cutting it with bolt cutters is not difficult. Moving a ton or more of concrete is very strenuous. Leveling and screeding the concrete adds muscle, as does troweling the surface. Building and removing forms is moderately strenuous, since some forms may be 16 ft long. Constructing a patio from concrete is strenuous; one needs good health and should have the assistance of a helper.

New Terms

Some terms new to you may be used in this chapter. *Topography,* understanding how to distinguish ground elevations from a drawing, is one. *Batter boards* include stakes and horizontal 1 × 6s set to exact heights. *Rebars* are steel reinforcement. A unique tool, a *line-level,* is used to establish reference points. Terms associated with concrete, such as *curing, screeding,* and others, will be used.

Compared with all the other projects or jobs included in this book, building a ground-level concrete slab is the simplest. On the whole, the project requires the fewest number of decisions, simple design planning, and straightforward application of skills and knowledge. To perform the variety of tasks requires a minimum of hand and power tools.

However, to accomplish this job satisfactorily, considerable skill is required on at least one worker's part. Things can go wrong, and if they do, considerable cost will be incurred. For example, the greatest likelihood for mishap occurs while pouring and finishing the concrete.

Later in the chapter a great deal of data is provided that will aid in estimating materials. Some is listed in the specifications section. More discrete data is found in the materials assessment area. Finally, illustrations provide information. By using the formulas provided, we can develop a material inventory.

Although the specifications section will state a surface design, several alternatives will be discussed. These are all made with masonry tools. No other building or natural materials are included in these styling efforts.

Finally, a job well done will be a satisfying experience. The result will give years of pleasure with few maintenance requirements.

Now let us examine the specifications for the concrete patio.

SPECIFICATIONS

In every project there must be a set of parameters that bound the project and give it structure and form. In the building trade the plans and specifications do this. The plans show where critical measurements and design are included. The specifications show or explain parts of the project which may be sometimes found in plans, but more often than not state considerations or conditions which must be met that are not shown in plans.

Specifications are customarily included on one page of a set of drawings or blueprints. Since this is a textbook, showing a reduced plan with specifications in a figure would make them unreadable. Therefore, specifications for the concrete slab patio (and other projects in this book) are shown as separate tables. For this chapter it is Table 1.1. Each specification table includes two parts. The first is a narrative description of the project. The second is a specific detailed listing of the criteria to be met.

To many, the specifications are easily understood. Several may need to be explained. Sloping the slab so that water slowly sheds off the surface is a good idea. Further, the $\frac{1}{2}$-in. overall slope is not noticeable to the users. Concrete can be premixed with different types of cement and different sizes of aggregate and may contain various amounts of water. For normal climatic conditions, above freezing and below 100°F, no special cement need be used. Concrete has certain curing requirements. Concrete reaches about 90 percent of its total strength in

TABLE 1.1 Specification Listing
PROJECT: *Concrete Patio Slab, Ground Level*   DATE: _____

General Description

Build a 20-ft by 30-ft by 4-in. reinforced concrete ground-level patio slab. This patio shall be constructed with a solid, earth base which extends a minimum 3 ft beyond the outer perimeter of the patio. It will contain perimeter reinforcing rebars, and wire mesh laid throughout the area within the form shall be wired together and wired to the rebars. A self-footing 4 in. deep and 12 in. wide shall be formed around the form. A single pour of ready-pour concrete shall be used. Styling and surface finish shall be as indicated in the list of specifications. Curing shall be maintained for seven days as prescribed by weather conditions. Forms removal, cleanup, and landscaping shall be performed. Topsoil, sod, shrubs, and ground cover shall be used around the perimeter except for walkways. All support materials shall be removed from the job site upon completion of the work.

Specifications

Item	Specs
Dimensions and accuracy	Slab; 20′ wide by 30′ long, min 4″ deep: Footing; 12″ wide by 4″ deep, self forming
Slope and percent of error	$\frac{1}{2}$″ +/− $\frac{1}{4}$″
Surface design	Smooth trowel, scoring 12″ in from all outer edges (see plan)
Concrete mixture	3000 lb/cu yd
Subsurface preparation	All stumps, roots greater than 4″ in diameter shall be removed. Clean fill dirt shall be used to establish a subsurface that extends a minimum 3′ beyond the perimeter of the slab area. Soil compacting with water shall be used to insure a solid subsurface base.
Reinforcements	$2\frac{1}{2}$″ rebar shall be laid into the footing area. 6 × 6 wire mesh shall cover the entire formed area but no closer to the form than 2″. Rebars shall overlap 4″, shall be wired, and shall be wired to the mesh. Overlap of mesh shall be 6, and shall be wired.
Curing requirements	Maintain surface moisture 7 days.
Landscaping	Grassed areas shall be sodded, shrub areas shall be $\frac{1}{3}$ ft, ground shall be covered with bark or mulch.

seven days. To do so, however, it must have moisture present and it must not freeze. The thermal action stops any time the water evaporates too quickly or if it freezes. Subsurface requirements and reinforcing the concrete go hand in hand. Improper subsurface, such as pockets created by rotting tree stumps or made by underground water flow, causes the concrete to stress when its own weight and live loads are sufficient to crack it. Rebars and wire mesh form a steel network that increases the stress capability of the slab. It is not overkill to first ensure a proper subsurface and to reinforce the slab. Remember, there are no expansion joints in a patio slab.

MATERIALS ASSESSMENT

In each job there are three assessments that must be made. The first, direct materials, is a listing of the variety of building materials necessary to complete the project. Without these the project cannot be done. In Table 1.2 the direct mate-

TABLE 1.2 Materials Assessment
PROJECT: *Concrete Patio*   **DATE**: _____

Direct Materials

Type or Description	*Use or Purpose*
Washed sand	Backfill uneven areas under slab
6 × 6-in. wire mesh	Reinforcement for concrete
Concrete	Basic element of the slab

Indirect Materials

Type or Description	*Use or Purpose*
Batter boards and supports	Establishes lines of slab dimensions
Forms (wood or metal)	Shapes the form of the slab
Stakes and braces	Holds forms in position
Nails	
Mason line	Establishes outline of slab

Support Materials

Type or Description	*Use or Purpose*
Masonry hand tools	Construction and finishing
Carpentry tools	Construct batter boards and forms
Rakes, shovels, and hoes	Prepare subsurface as well as distribute wet concrete
Power tools	Aids for building; smoothing concrete

rials needed for the ground-level patio slab are identified; since this is a textbook, the use or purpose for each is provided. The second, indirect materials, is a listing of materials that must be used during the construction effort. Some are consumables, such as stakes and braces, while some are reusable for other purposes, such as forms. These materials are part of the cost of the project and must be recognized as such. Third and last, support materials, is a listing of a wide variety of materials that are necessary to accomplish the tasks associated with completing the project. These include tools and machines. Associated with each is a cost. The cost of a tool must be amortized over its life cycle, so a fractional value must be charged to the project. When rental tools and rented power equipment are used, their entire costs are part of the cost of the project.

If you are interested in determining cost models for projects, you might wish to secure a copy of *Deskbook for the Contractor and Manager,* by Byron Maguire (Englewood Cliffs, N. J.: Prentice-Hall, 1986). This book provides cost analysis, such as fixed and variable operating expenses, profit, and other related data.

A review of Table 1.2 illustrates that a very limited variety of materials is needed to build the ground-level concrete patio. The variety of tools necessary for the job is also limited. For example, useful carpentry tools would include a hammer, a 10-lb sledgehammer, a cross cut saw, framing and combination square, a 50-ft tape measure, a 6-ft folding ruler, a 2-ft level, a line-level, and a crowbar. Even fewer mason tools are needed. These include a float, flat trowel, edge and center groovers, and a darby. Since the planned patio is 600 feet, a power trowel would be very beneficial. A power saw would make wood cutting easier.

GROUND PREPARATION

We know where the slab patio will be located. We know its size and that it needs to slope away from the house by $\frac{1}{2}$ in. We also know that it must be uniformly thick and the self-footing needs to be 8 in. deep and 12 in. wide. What we don't know is the exact topography of the ground.

Topography is the study of the variations in the earth's surface. On a global scale there are mountains and valleys. In the backyard we are considering inches and feet. Figure 1-1 is a topographical representation of our generic project. Let us be sure it communicates and defines the task of ground preparation. There are two views, the elevation view and the topographic view. In the elevation drawing on the right side, the main house footings, foundation, and wall are shown. A reference level-line shows where the top of the patio will be. The sloping line with earth symbols below it shows that the ground slopes away from the house. Since this picture is only a slice, we do not know if it represents the entire backyard or not. Therefore, we need to observe and study the topographic view.

On the right of the view the back wall of the house is shown. A grid with each side equal to four feet has been superimposed so that we can better understand the needs for fill dirt.

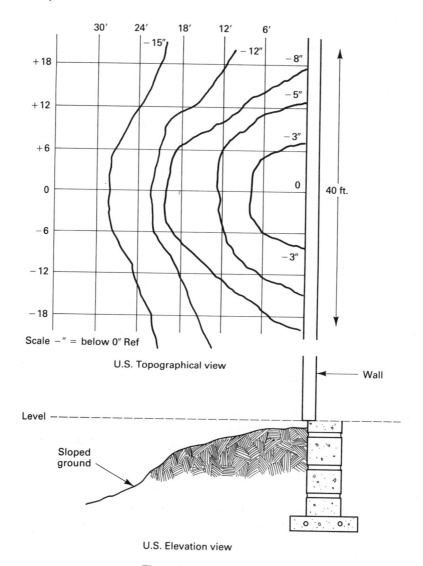

Figure 1-1 Site topography.

The wavy lines illustrate the shape of the ground. Notice that each line has a number assigned.

Since our project is to prepare the subsurface for a slab, we can make the numbers mean something specific. Notice that there is one place near the house with a "0" zero reference. This point is exactly four inches below the finished slab surface. Therefore, we can use this to make all other notations. By using a mason line and line-level we can actually plot the variation in ground levels at four-foot increments. Then these points can be indicated on a graph. The points with the same measurement from ground to line are then connected with the wavy line. These measurements may be either negative or positive. A negative number represents an area below our necessary level. A positive number represents a high spot that would need to be lowered to the reference.

In our generic project, we see that quite a bit of fill dirt is required. The ground slopes down 15 inches at about 24 feet. Since, according to the specifications, we must provide a minimum 4-ft flat surface beyond the 20-ft slab on each end of its 30-ft length, this area will use a considerable amount. Not nearly so much is needed on the ends, since the slope is less, only about -6 in.

Next, an inspection of the ground must be made to ensure that no stumps have been left to rot. If a stump rots slowly, eventually a hollow depression results. The concrete over this area would be subject to cracking and sinking. Therefore, stumps need to be removed, and the hole created must be backfilled and compacted.

Fill dirt for our generic project must be bought and dumped. It should *not* contain any vegetation. It should be a mixture of sand, clay, small stones, or rocks. As it is moved around and leveled to the appropriate reference, it should be compacted. Compacting can be done with a truck, or water from a hose can be used to eliminate the air and cause the dirt to settle. Sand is an excellent final top fill to use. It can be moved easily, fills low spots readily, and simplifies the leveling task.

Before dispensing with the tools and trucks used in preparing the surface for the slab, consider using them to do several other important tasks. One important task is to make the area safe to work. Remove old trees, shrubs and boulders, sheds, and the like from the work area. Eight- to 10-ft clearance is not too much. Another important point is to make sure that there is a way for the concrete ready-mix truck to pull up or back up to the formed area. Some fill may be required. If a wheelbarrow must be used to transport the concrete, a path may have to be constructed. A tool called a darby will be used to float the fresh concrete. Because this tool has a long pole attached, the worker will need ample room to work with it. In other words, plan for a safe work site and consider all the needs for other tasks.

LAYOUT

One nice thing about a textbook, compared with a job site, is that we can see a pictorial representation of the project. Figure 1-2 shows us the finished form, fully braced on one side. It also shows the position of one set of batter boards, and it clearly shows that the patio butts up to the house. The partial perspective drawing shows the one side of the form and provides a better relationship of batter board height.

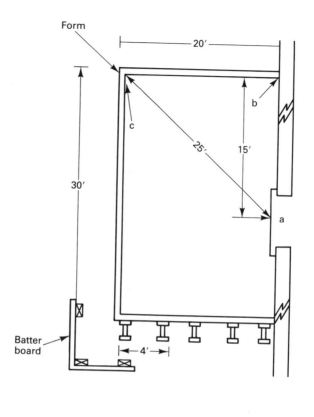

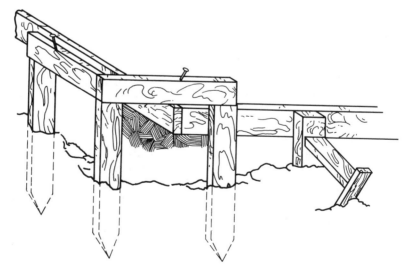

Figure 1-2 Forms and bracing.

The following task list/checklist shows us the layout work that must be done.

Task No.	Task	Done
	Task list/checklist	
1	Locate the perimeter points against the house.	————
2	Locate the two outside corners of the patio.	————
3	Install batter boards and patio lines.	————

For this patio project, we assume that the patio will extend 15 ft on either side from the center of the sliding glass patio door. So we need to mark a point on the wall accordingly. Step one is easy, and is very easy if a 50-ft tape measure is used. At each location drive a nail into the siding or block.

Next, cut two 2 × 2 stakes several feet long. Each one will be used to represent the location of an outside corner of the patio. Using the tape, extend it out from the house 20 ft and approximately perpendicular to the side of the house. Tentatively drive the stake into the ground. Now use the Pythagorean theorem for right angles to finally locate the stake. Or we can use a variation of the 3-4-5 right triangle. (Refer to Figure 1-2 for points: a = 15 ft, b = 20 ft, and c = 25 ft.)

where we multiply each value by five.

$$3 = 15 \text{ ft} \qquad 4 = 20 \text{ ft} \qquad 5 = 25 \text{ ft}$$

Therefore: a. The center of the patio door is point a and from a to b is 15 ft.
b. The 20-ft side of the patio is 20 ft. long.
c. The hypotenuse is 25 ft long from the stake back to the 15-ft mark.

While one person holds the tape at the 15-ft point, the other one maintains a 20-ft distance and adjusts the position of the stake parallel to the wall until the tape is tight and the distance is equal to 25 ft. At this point drive the stake into the ground.

Using a second stake, measure out 20 ft from the opposite end of the patio position along the wall. Then, maintaining that distance, measure 30 ft from the first stake. Drive the stake into the ground. Step 2 is done.

Next, cut the batter boards from 1 × 4 or 1 × 6. Six stakes of 2 × 4 about four feet long will support the batter boards. The stakes need to be installed about 2 ft outside of the patio corner stakes. Drive three into the ground as shown in Figure 1-2.

Before the batter boards can be nailed to the stakes, a reference height must be set. For this project assume that the patio surface will be 6 in. below the threshold of the sliding patio door. To permit proper working room for installing forms, we should keep mason lines about 12 in. above the form. So mark a point plumb (up) above the desired top of the patio's finished surface at each end of the patio. Drive a nail into the siding (if possible). Tie one end of the mason line to the nail, install a *line-level* about 10 ft away from the wall, and while one person reads the level the other marks the center (corner) 2×4 batter board stake. Alongside the pencil mark, write "+12-in. level." Then repeat the process on the other corner stake for the batter boards.

According to the specifications, the patio must slope away from the house $\frac{1}{4}$ in. in 10 ft for a total $\frac{1}{2}$ in. Mark another line on the batter board stake $\frac{1}{2}$ in. below the first one, and label it "$-\frac{1}{2}$-in. slope."

Nail the batter boards to the stakes, using the $-\frac{1}{2}$-in. mark and a 2-ft spirit level to ensure that they are level.

Now the final and precise layout of the patio perimeter must be done. It is almost a repeat of the early work done to locate the stakes. One method is as follows.

1. Using a tape, a nail, and a hammer, locate the precise point on the top of the patio corner stake. First, remeasure to locate this point, using 20 ft from the house to the stake, then measure 15 ft, along the wall from the intersect of house and patio line (Figure 1-2, point b to point a). Finally stretch the tape from point a (Figure 1-2) to the 20 ft mark on the top of the stake. Where the 20 ft and 25 ft lines intersect is the precise right angle point of the patio side.

2. Fasten one end of the mason line to the nail in the wall 12 in. above the patio surface. Stretch the line to the batter board.

3. Either hold a 2-ft level in plumb fashion against the nail in the corner stake, or tie a short line and plumb bob so that it hangs over the nail.

4. When the tight mason line is positioned, drive two nails into the batter board. One nail must touch the line; place the other 6 in. away.

5. Wrap the tight line around the first nail and tie it off around the second one with several half-hitches.

6. Repeat the process at the other end.

Now we need to install the third mason line. It goes parallel to the house wall, 20 ft out.

1. Using either the plumb bob in place or the level placed over the nail in the stake, measure from this point to the batter board. Transfer this tentative mark to the batter board perpendicular to the house wall. Repeat the process at the other end.

2. Stretch a mason line between the batter boards, using the tentative locations and wrapping the line around the 1×4 or 1×6.

3. Use the plumb bob or level to locate the line exactly. This may require several adjustments on each end.

4. Drive nails into the exact locations on each batter board, wrap the line around each, and tie off each end.

We now have accomplished one very difficult part of the project. But the work has provided several very important features. Our parameters are precisely located. The slope of the patio is established, and the patio is a perfect rectangle.

One last concern. A line stretched 30 ft will sag. Therefore, a single batter board installed 15 ft along the 30-ft side should be so placed just to take out the slack and sag.

FORMING

Figure 1-3 shows the layout of the forms and how to install them. Since the length and width of the patio slab are longer than a form member, they must be spliced. What we usually do is install one piece at a time.

From the material assessment listing we can recall that stakes and braces are necessary to hold and secure the form in place. So the first task is to cut and shape the stakes and braces. There should be two stakes and one brace for each four feet of form.

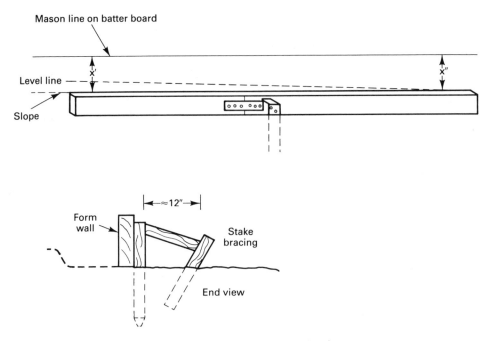

Figure 1-3 Installing forms and bracing.

Therefore: 20 ft + 30 ft + 20 ft = 70 ft of form

Divided by: 4 ft per pair of stakes and brace

Result in: 18 pair of stakes = 36 stakes, and 18 braces

Each form is $7\frac{1}{2}$ (2 × 8) in. high, and a stake should be into the ground about 12 to 15 in. This means we need to cut the stakes about 20 to 23 in. long.

Each brace should be 18 in. long.

In summary, we need 36 2 × 2 23-in. stakes and 18 2 × 2 18-in. braces, plus 6d and 10d common nails.

With form members, stakes cut and pointed, braces, nails, a 24-in. level, hammer, ruler, saw, and shovel, we are ready to install the form. The tasks are repetitive and follow this order:

1. Place the form member under the mason line.
2. Use a ruler to aid in setting its rough height.
3. Position the member to the outside of the mason line and drive one stake near each end.
4. Raise the form to its final height (in this project 12 inches below the mason line).
5. Secure the form to the stake and install braces and second stakes.
6. Add required additional sets of stakes and braces.

The key to this effort is to ensure that the inside of the form (slab side) is plumb with the mason line and exactly 12 in. below it. The simplest, most efficient way to do this is by using dirt, bricks, scraps of wood, and the like to set the form on to establish its almost final height. Once this is done at both ends, the form can then be slid back or forth for exact alignment. Once aligned, a stake must be driven into the ground against the outside of the form across from where the level was used.

Once the stake is driven into the ground and its top is just *below* the top of the form, raise the form to exactly 12 in. below the mason line and nail the stake to the form. Repeat the process at the other end of the form member.

The other stakes and braces are done at the other end and along the member in the same manner. Where the form members join, a splice of 1 × 6 must be made to ensure that the concrete will not move either member's end.

A few cautions must be observed when you install the braces. Use the picture to generally understand how to do the task. But be sure that when you toenail the brace to the stake the form is not moved. A recheck with the level is necessary. After experience is gained, form movement will be minimal. Several tricks you can use are (1) Drive nails above the brace into the stake holding the form erect. In this way the brace is wedged between the stakes and nails. (2) Drive a 10d nail through the outer stake into the brace and then toenail the brace into the other stake.

Remember, place stakes about four to five feet apart, and brace each one.

POURING AND FINISHING

Preparation

Overall, the pouring and finishing phase of the job includes several subtasks as well. These include final subgrade corrections, installing wire and rebars, and reinspecting the forms. Certain tools must be available at this time, as well, to move the concrete and smooth it. Finally, making the pattern in the top will be done as part of the smoothing operation.

The 6 × 6-in. wire mesh is sold in 6-ft wide rolls. It is unrolled at the job site and cut with bolt cutters. It is generally overlapped one 6-in. width; on better-quality jobs, bailing wire ties are used to tie the overlaps together. In our generic patio project we need 600 square ft, or 6 × 100 ft.

Our specifications call for rebars in the self-(earth)-formed footing. Rebars are sold in different diameters; one size is $\frac{1}{2}$ in. They are easily bent around corners with a pipe-bending tool or a makeshift wooden bender. They are cut for length with bolt cutters. Small stakes made from short pieces of rebar and tie wires are used to support the rebar in the footing area. Overlaps of rebars are tied together. On the best jobs the wire mesh is tied to the rebar. Since 100 ft of footing (20, 30, 20, 30) and two rebars are needed, we will need about 210 ft (or 19 12-ft pieces).

Before the wire and rebars are installed, the final subsurface adjustments are usually made. This is where washed sand is put to good use. Mason line is strung from form to form across the patio, and several short 1 × 1 stakes driven into the ground under the line quickly establish the desired level reference. Then rakes and shovels can move the ground flush with the top of the stakes.

Pouring the Concrete

Now we are ready for the concrete. Concrete is ordered from the plant. It may be ordered with varying amounts of water per yard of concrete. If minimal water is added to the aggregates and cement, it is stiff and difficult to work with. If more water is added, it is easier to work with. If too much water is added, it is structurally weak and will crack and otherwise decay rapidly. We are ordering a 3000-lb-per-cubic-yard mixture.

The concrete truck will chute the wet mixture into the form; usually from the farther form or house side to the near side of the form. The chute is moved left and right to spread the concrete. Rakes are used to spread it against the forms and generally level it.

Grade stakes are frequently used in the center area of the slab to aid in ensuring that the concrete is about the right height before moving to fill another area. These stakes are removed later and concrete by the shovel is used to fill in the holes left, if necessary.

Once the concrete is in the form and tamped with the rakes, the concrete around the form must be worked with. To avoid the development of large air pockets and the appearance of gravel on the surface, use a 1 × 4 or a spade-type shovel alongside the form in an up–down movement. This action brings the cement and sand in the concrete to the form, removes the air pockets, and drives the large aggregate back into the concrete.

Finally, a darby is used to level the concrete. The darby is about four feet wide and has a long pole attached. It is placed on top of the concrete and pushed and/or pulled across the surface. As it moves, it levels the concrete some more and causes the concrete and sand in the mixture to rise to the surface. When finished, the surface should have a generally flat appearance and no large aggregate should show.

Now we wait for the concrete to set and become dull. Once this action occurs, we will use the electric- or gas-powered rental float. First test the concrete to see if it can be walked on without causing footprints. If yes, float and trowel the surface. It should be smooth and level. The corners may need to be floated and troweled by hand if the power trowel does not reach.

The final operation is the scoring of surface designs. Figure 1-4 shows the design for the generic patio. Two mason tools are used. One is used to round the edge along the forms. The other is used to make a groove through the concrete

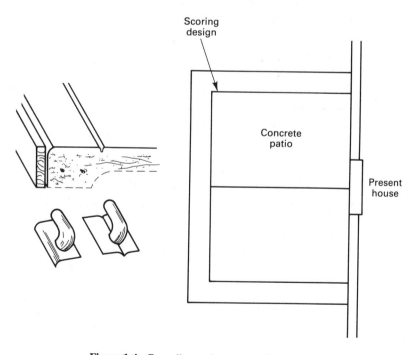

Scoring design

Concrete patio

Present house

Figure 1-4 Rounding and grooving the concrete.

similar to an expansion joint. Using a chalk line, snap the lines where the style grooves are to be placed. Using a 1 × 4 about 8 ft long, make the grooves and with a flat trowel smooth any concrete that was disturbed.

LANDSCAPING AND CLEANUP

The title probably should be cleanup and landscaping, since the order of work follows that sequence. But cleanup is an element in the larger effort, which is to landscape the ground around the new patio.

The forms should be left in place for a few days. This will allow the concrete to reach 70 to 85 percent of its full strength. After this time, the forms, batter boards, and all stakes can be removed. During the removal process, clean all materials of nails and concrete.

Next, remove all spilled and hardened concrete, wire, and rebar scraps from the job site.

Follow up the cleanup with adding top soil in such a way that it remains several inches below the surface of the patio. Level or slope the soil with rakes.

The final phase of landscaping is then done. In this project, a shrubbery garden is planned for each corner of the patio. A crepe myrtle tree is the central theme, and six boxwood plants border the patio. Ground is covered with mulch. All other areas are sodded.

The actual work for the project is complete.

MATERIALS INVOICE

Throughout this project we have been using a variety of materials. Early on we made a *materials assessment*. Now the job is to make a listing of materials that is more precise. In this listing there are two parts: one, all materials used, and two, all rental tools needed. We also give a formula for computing the concrete required.

The method of computing concrete requirement is not difficult. Concrete is sold by the cubic yard. (3 ft × 3 ft × 3 ft = 27 ft). When the thickness of a concrete pour is less than 36 in. deep, more square feet of coverage can be expected. Further, most needs are easily computed in square feet and then factored with the thickness to obtain cubic feet. From this point simple division using 27 as a divisor results in cubic yards. Let's use the patio as an example:

1. Footing needs: 12 in. wide × 4 in. deep × 100 ft long

$$\text{sq ft} = 12 \text{ in. wide} = 1 \text{ ft} \times 100 \text{ ft long} = 100 \text{ sq ft}$$

$$\text{cu ft} = \tfrac{4}{12} \times 100 \text{ sq ft} = 33.3 \text{ cu ft}$$

$$\text{cu yd} = \frac{33.3 \text{ cu ft}}{27 \text{ cu ft}} = 1.23 \text{ cu yd}$$

2. Slab needs: 30 ft × 20 ft × 4 in. thick

$$\text{sq ft} = 30 \times 20 = 600 \text{ sq ft}$$

$$\text{cu ft} = \tfrac{4}{12} \times 600 \text{ sq ft} = 200 \text{ cu ft}$$

$$\text{cu yd} = \frac{200 \text{ cu ft}}{27 \text{ cu ft}} = 7.4 \text{ cu yd}$$

$$
\begin{array}{lll}
\text{total:} & \text{footing} & 1.23 \\
& \text{slab} & \underline{7.40} \\
& \text{total} & 8.63 \text{ cu yd}
\end{array}
$$

Formula

$$\text{cu yd concrete} = \frac{(\text{width in ft}) \ (\text{length in ft}) \ (\text{thickness in ft})}{27 \text{ cu ft}} \qquad (1.1)$$

You'll notice that the list in Table 1.3 includes all consumables necessary for the project. You will also notice that two items are not shown. First, pricing data

TABLE 1.3 Materials Invoice
PROJECT: *Patio Slab*

DATE _____

Quantity	Type	Total
6	2 × 8 – 10 ft, forms	60 lin ft
1	2 × 8 – 12 ft, forms	12 lin ft
6	2 × 2 – 12 ft, stakes	72 lin ft
2	2 × 4 – 12 ft, batter board stakes	24 lin ft
1	1 × 4 – 14 ft, batter board	14 lin ft
10	½″ × 12 ft, rebar	120 lin ft
100	6″ × 6″ × 6 ft, wire mesh	600 sq ft
1 roll	Bailing wire	50 ft
7 cu yd	Concrete	7 cu yd
1 cu yd	Washed sand	1 cu yd
5 cu yd	Fill dirt	5 cu yd
1 pallet	Sod	1 pallet
2	Crepe myrtle trees—6 ft tall	2 ea
12	Boxwoods 18″ tall (3–4 yr old)	12 ea
8 bags	Mulch	8 bags

Rental Equipment

Item		Duration of rental
Darby		4 hr
Power trowel		4 hr
Bolt cutters		1 day

are not shown. This information is to be determined during the planning and estimating phase. Second, no hand tools are listed. Hand tools are usable for many years and are considered to be required to do the work.

This project is interesting to do. It is a lot of hard work. It requires quite a bit of attention to detail as well as accuracy. However, the finished product is useful and one that provides pleasure for many.

2

Modifications and Enhancements to the Concrete Slab Patio

OBJECTIVES

- Plan for the use of other materials to be included in the slab patio.
- Identify how to anchor redwood or treated lumber, brick, tile, and slate into the slab.
- Identify exposed aggregate, rock salt, and coloring exposures that can be obtained.
- Identify how to create patterns with trowel and broom.

USING LUMBER IN THE SLAB

A common practice in constructing a concrete slab patio is to include a design using wood. Including wood does several things. First, it breaks up large expanses of concrete. Next, it creates specific patterns which should complement the adjoining house and surrounding grounds. It partitions the concrete, thus creating unique applications. One of these would be the natural pathway from the house to the pool or garden area. Another would identify the area for lounging or eating and cooking.

Figure 2-1 shows two examples. In both examples 2-in. materials such as redwood, cypress, or treated pine are used around the perimeter and elsewhere. Notice that geometric shapes are used. These are simpler to construct than ones with curves and arcs, since wood does not easily bend.

In Figure 2-1a we have created partitioning using 90-deg angles. We also have left a section across the slab untouched, thus creating (1) a walkway from door to garden, (2) two seating areas, one on each side of the walkway.

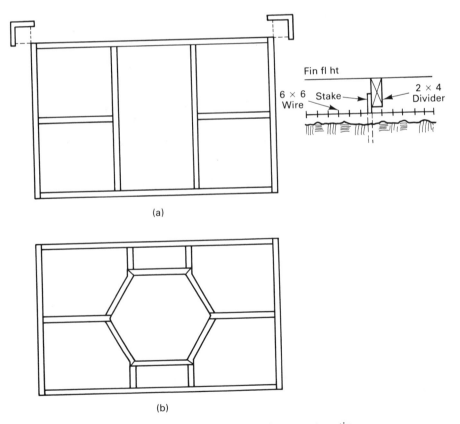

(a)

(b)

Figure 2-1 Wood dividers in the concrete patio.

In contrast, Figure 2-1b has a central theme of a hexagon. The angle cuts are not 90 deg. This design requires greater understanding of joinery than the other one. Later in this section we detail making the various joints.

When using lumber to enhance the patio, we make certain assumptions, and we use certain principles. First, the assumptions: The basic form must be constructed as was detailed in Chapter 1. All of the preparations for the subsurface must also be done as was illustrated in Chapter 1. Next, we assume that the 2-in. members will *not* extend the full thickness of the concrete within the formed area. In other words, the concrete will flow under each piece. Finally, the rebars and wire mesh must be laid in place before the wood members are added.

The principles to employ are simple. The lumber (2 × 3s) must be installed at *finished floor height*. This can be done with either a level and straightedge, or with a mason line. Stakes cut and fastened well below the top of the member will hold each piece in place. Next, the angles used in making the joints must be accurately fit and cut. For this task use a combination or bevel square. Finally, place the members in such a pattern that produces the fewest number of joints and avoids splices.

The members around the perimeter of the patio should be nailed flush with the top of the form, through the form into the member with double-headed 12d nails. Just prior to form removal, these nails can be withdrawn. The remaining member will show no nails.

To ensure that the divider members and perimeter members stay in place, drive galvanized nails into each as shown in Figure 2-2. Make sure that all mem-

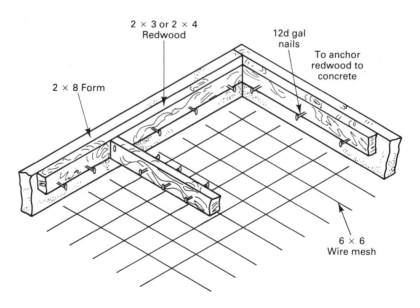

Figure 2-2 Forming the wood dividers and installing the anchoring nails, partial view.

bers are securely nailed to each other and are still in alignment after the anchor nails are driven in place.

Just before pouring the concrete, use 1½-in. tape to cover the tops of all members. This reduces the effects of the concrete and cement staining the wood. After the concrete sets and forms are removed, the tape should be removed. If any staining has occurred, it can be removed with a muratic acid solution. The task is done.

Before leaving this task several additional facts are provided for your use. The data may be useful where a variety of geometric shapes are to be employed. Figure 2-3 contains a chart and a series of illustrations. Following these examples and then using the data from the chart should solve any problem.

Four-, five-, six-, and eight-sided geometric shapes are usually used as patterns. In each illustration two references are always used. Reference 1 indicates the position of wood member 1. Reference 2 is perpendicular and always 90

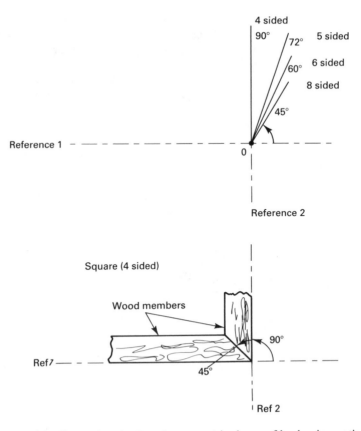

Figure 2-3 Cuts and angles for other geometric shapes of lumber in a patio.

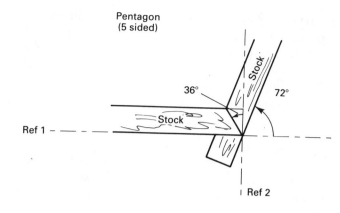

Pentagon
(5 sided)

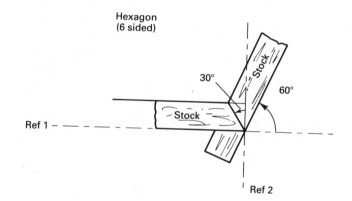

Hexagon
(6 sided)

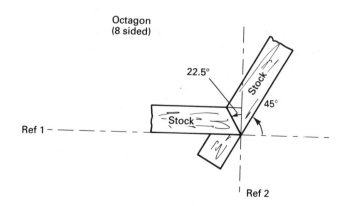

Octagon
(8 sided)

Figure 2-3 (continued)

degrees from reference 1. As is shown, all multisided forms use angles greater than 90 degrees except the square. Therefore, the bevel or miter cut on each member will be 45 degrees for the square and less than that for all other polygons.

USING BRICK IN THE SLAB

In this section on using brick in a slab patio as a decorative feature, quite a bit of technical know-how is required. We shall examine the concepts and practical applications of using brick around the border and then partitioning or segmenting the slab with brick. Finally, the method of cleaning brick coated with cement will be discussed.

In Figure 2-4 you see all the detail information necessary to plan and construct a patio with border brick. Let's begin with Figure 2-4a. When the brick is mortared in place, the surface of each brick must be flush with the concrete slab surface. The mortar joints must be uniform in thickness and struck with a curved striking tool. The corner needs to be mitered as shown in Figure 2-4d. This is the most pleasing design as well as the most professional. Bricks can be cut with a power saw using a masonry blade.

Let's make several assumptions. The basic form has already been constructed according to the specifications. The subsurface soil is level and compacted. The rebars are in place, and the wire mesh is cut to fit, in place, and tie-wired.

The tasks remaining are

1. Determining the offset needed in the form to make the recess for brick and mortar.
2. Installing the inner form.
3. Laying the brick.

Observing Figure 2-4a, we note that the dimensions x and y are variables. These variables would normally be known when purchasing the brick, since different styles of brick are sized differently. For this generic project our bricks are $7\frac{5}{8}$ in. long $\times$ $3\frac{5}{8}$ in. wide $\times$ $2\frac{1}{2}$ in. thick.

The x and y dimensions are

$$x = 7\tfrac{5}{8} \text{ in.} + \tfrac{3}{8} \text{ in. mortar} = 8 \text{ in.}$$

$$y = 3\tfrac{5}{8} \text{ in.} + \tfrac{3}{8} \text{ in. mortar} = 4 \text{ in.}$$

Locate *form b* in Figure 2-4b and c. For our generic project this form member must be cut 4 in. wide from 1 × 6s or 2 × 6s. Its top edge must be level with the outer form. Its bottom edge is the finished height of the offset. The inside

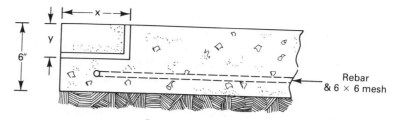

Cross section

x = Brick length or width & mortar joint
y = Brick thickness & mortar base

(a)

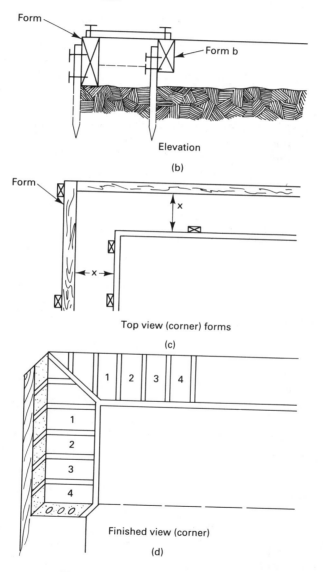

Elevation

(b)

Top view (corner) forms

(c)

Finished view (corner)

(d)

Figure 2-4 Brick border in a concrete patio.

surface (concrete side) of form b must be set to equal x, or 8 in., held in place with stakes and spreaders. Notice that the stakes are placed between forms a and b.

During the pouring operations excess concrete must be removed from the recess with a trowel. Remember to make sure that no excess concrete is left in this area to avoid extra work during bricklaying operations.

Bricklaying follows form removal. The corners are the most critical areas, and all corners should match. Therefore, the bricks 1, 2, 3, and so on (see Figure 2-4d) should be laid at each corner before the corner bricks are laid.

This enhancement project is difficult but readily achievable. The results are very pleasing.

Sectionalizing the Patio Slab with Brick

When the sectionalizing of a patio includes brick as illustrated in Figure 2-5, there are a number of problems to solve. The bricks must be laid in place before the concrete is poured. Essentially, there are two different concrete pours. The first is for the footing for the brick. The second is for the slab.

Let's use Figure 2-5 throughout this discussion. Several assumptions must be stated. The batter boards and lines have already been installed. The forms have not been installed. The surface grading is not yet complete. Wire mesh and rebars are not yet installed.

The tasks remaining are the following:

1. Establish a subsurface grade level 4 in. below finished floor height (one brick + mortar joint) and grade the soil to this level.
2. Excavate the soil where footings for the brick will go. If possible, retain side walls perpendicular and maintain 16 in. width for intermediate areas and about the same width for perimeter bricks.
3. Install 2 × 4 forms with tops at "finish floor level minus brick and mortar bed thickness (4 in.)." Refer to Figure 2-5 for details. If the earth form walls are not accurate, then all footings need forms on both sides; 1 × 4s or 2 × 4s are acceptable. Stakes are sufficient to hold them in place. No braces are needed.
4. Install $\frac{1}{2}$-in. rebar in each footing and suspend it or them midway.
5. Pour footings and screed. Do not trowel smooth.
6. Mortar brick according to the floor plan.
7. Remove forms and reestablish the subsurface level of earth. Compact with water and tamping.
8. Cut wire mesh to fit into each section.
9. Pour concrete slab. Float, trowel, and let cure.
10. Clean brick with an acid solution.
11. Seal patio floor.

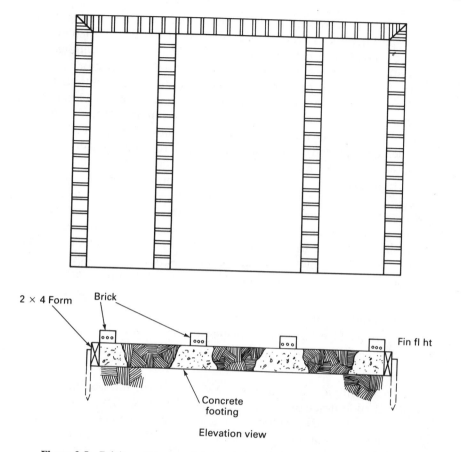

2 × 4 Form   Brick

Fin fl ht

Concrete
footing

Elevation view

Figure 2-5 Brick partitioning of the patio slab, including elevation drawing.

Now let's go over some of the more difficult tasks and make sure that the fundamentals are clearly understood.

The first task of establishing the surface level of the soil needs to be taken from the lines installed on the batter boards. Small stakes about $\frac{3}{4}$ in. square by about a foot or less should be used strategically as reference points. A ruler held alongside the line, resting on top of the stake, is the easiest way to determine the height the stake should be. As a real example, let's assume that the lines are set at 12 in. above finished floor height. We know that our brick is $3\frac{5}{8}$ in. thick, and a mortar bed under it should be $\frac{3}{8}$ in. thick. Therefore, the reading on the ruler needed to establish the subsurface level is 12 in. + $3\frac{5}{8}$ in. + $\frac{3}{8}$ in., for a total of 16 in.

After the stakes are in place (approximately one per four or five square feet), any adjustments to the subsurface should be made until the soil everywhere within the confine of the project area is the same and compacted.

The next most difficult problem is locating and forming the footing areas for the perimeter and section bricks. Most of the time trenching for footings looks pretty good. But careful examination always reveals wide variations in footing width. In my lifetime experience, I saw only one person (in his late 50s at the time) who could perform this task accurately. In addition, trying to use earth sidewalls for forms is made more difficult when exact parameters are required, which ultimately causes two specific situations. One, the amount of concrete used for filling the footings frequently reaches excesses of 50 percent (half again as much as is needed). Two, accuracy standards that precisely place footings at their optimal position with sides that are vertical surfaces can not be achieved with earth forms. Consequently, the best solution and least costly in terms of material costs is to form each footing area with forms on both sides.

Let's jump ahead and assume that the trenches have been located and dug to the correct depth and are wide enough to accommodate the forms. What height should all forms be set too? The answer: 16 in. from the batter board lines. Besides height, their physical position beneath the boundary lines must be precise. This means that the forms must be installed in a certain sequence.

1. Outer perimeter forms first.
2. Inner form members adjacent to outer forms—separated 12 in.
3. Sectional forms + and −8 inches from the center line of the section.

Bracing of these forms is not necessary, since a simple backfill of earth is sufficient to brace them. Staking should be done, however, at 4-ft to 5-ft intervals.

Laying bricks on top of the footings can commence one day after pouring the footings. This task should start at the corners as we explained in detail in Chapter 1. All bricks must be installed and the joints struck with a curved striking tool. Then the bricks and mortar joints can be coated with protective sealers, if desired, to inhibit wholesale contamination by cement during the slab pouring and finishing tasks.

The level of the concrete is established by the brick. This makes the job somewhat easier than pouring a large slab, as we studied in Chapter 1. The darby will again be a useful tool in leveling the concrete and bringing cement to the surface. Electric or gas troweling follows the use of the darby; the final surface pattern of smooth trowel or broomed finish is done at this time as well.

About four days to a week after pouring the slab sections, the brick must be cleaned. A muriatic acid and water solution is brushed onto the brick to remove the spillover of cement from the concrete. Since the acid acts quickly when applied to fresh concrete, little or no acid solution should spill onto the concrete. One technique that seems to work well is to scrub one to two dozen bricks and then to wash thoroughly with clean water from a hose. Then repeat the technique until all the bricks are cleaned.

USING TILE IN THE SLAB

Ceramic and clay tiles are used to enhance concrete patio slabs. They may be employed to create a border or to create various patterns. They, like brick, are mortared in place, which permits us to conclude that the process used with brick enhancement works equally well with tile enhancement.

Let's begin with several assumptions. The layout for the patio has been done and the batter boards and lines are in place. The subsurface ground has been prepared. All vegetation has been removed, new clean fill dirt has been added where necessary, and the dirt has been leveled and packed at a depth of 4 in. below finished floor height.

For a border of tile to be used to enhance the patio, a recess must be made into the slab. As Figure 2-6 shows, the width and depth of the recess must be determined by the dimensions of the tile. Let's use a square generic tile whose dimensions are $7\frac{3}{4}$ in. $\times \frac{1}{2}$ in. thick. Let's further define a specification of a $\frac{1}{4}$-in. mortar bed and joint for each tile. This means that the recess must be 8 in. wide by $\frac{3}{4}$ in. deep.

Because the offset is only $\frac{3}{4}$ in. deep, a solution different from the one used in brick border enhancement can be used. A single form set at finished floor height

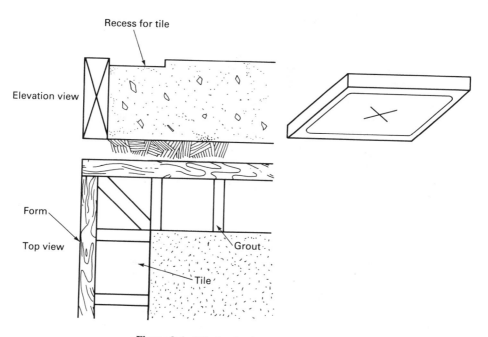

Figure 2-6 Tile border in a concrete patio.

should be built and braced. Then a 1 × 10 trimmed to exactly 8 in. wide should be cut for use in making the recess. The concrete must be removed where the 1 × 8 is to be placed. The concrete under the 1 × 8 must be solidly in contact with the board.

The discussion just concluded identifies the special considerations necessary for the job. Now here is the task list.

1. Establish the footing area.
2. Grade the patio area.
3. Install the rebars and wire mesh, as well as reference stakes for screeding.
4. Pour the concrete and screed.
5. Remove enough concrete around the border to permit laying the 1 × 8 boards in place flush with the top of the form and against it.
6. Use an edger tool to round the concrete alongside the 1 × 8.
7. Let the concrete set.
8. Trowel the entire surface and finish with a trowel or broom as per the specifications.
9. Let concrete cure and then remove the forms.
10. Mortar the tiles in place and strike the joints.
11. Clean up the site.
12. Seal the patio surface.

If a design pattern is more extensive than just a border, the same techniques can be used. A board can be used to create the recess at each line or area to have tile. A piece of plywood would be used if squares of tile were the design scheme, that is, four or 16 tiles per square.

In every attempt the critical element is to make the edge of the concrete a perfect 90-deg corner or to round it with an edger. Under no circumstance should the concrete be left ragged. A ragged edge requires patching with mortar, and mortar does not provide the same surface finish as the concrete.

USING SLATE IN THE SLAB

I have seen entire patios covered with slate, and I have seen slate embedded into a slab for decorative effect. In this section we shall plan to install slate into the concrete in a random pattern for decorative effect.

Before we discuss the mechanics of the task, some fundamentals about slate must be understood. Slate is a stone that is found naturally and is layered. This means that it is really layers of stone whose structure is flat and elongated, similar to the edge grain of a straight piece of wood.

A quantity of slate may be many feet thick and can cover a fairly wide area. But what makes it desirable is the ease with which it can be split along its natural grain. When splitting tools are inserted into the ends of the slate, a splitting action results along the grain. Although the split piece looks to be relatively uniform in thickness, there are variations.

Besides variations in thickness, natural slate's sides are irregular in shape horizontally and vertically throughout the piece. Cutting machines are frequently used to trim the sides to rectangular patterns.

When natural broken pieces of slate are used to enhance a patio, the technique of embedding them is different from those used with tile and brick. Fundamentally, concrete must be removed, the slate is embedded, and the floating and troweling activities are resumed. Let's examine how to do this. Let's assume that all the steps up to pouring the concrete into the form have been done.

Tasks remaining to do:

1. Decide on the number and placement of the slate.
2. Pour the concrete and screed it.
3. When firm enough to stand on, remove concrete in each area where a piece of slate will be installed.
4. Set the slate in place and flush with the concrete.
5. Fill in the perimeter of the slate with concrete.
6. Float the slab and trowel to a finish.
7. Protect for curing.
8. Clean slate and seal patio.

Not all tasks need discussion, but several do. In considering task 1, a model on bond paper could be made for the placement of the slate. Or the pieces could be laid on the ground as they would be placed in the concrete later.

Figure 2-7 shows the idea for tasks 3 and 4. The central idea is to place the slate into the concrete so that it bonds to the concrete. Remove enough concrete while it is still workable to make room for a piece of slate. Set the piece in place in the hole and use a straightedge to check the evenness of the slate with the concrete. Screed concrete around the slate with backfill concrete previously removed. When all pieces are in place, begin the floating operation.

The technique just illustrated is used to create a natural bond between the edges of the slate and the concrete. The cement and sand will fill small voids around the slate. The cement will bond to the bottom as well as sides of the slate.

Cleaning the slate is a task that is unavoidable. During the floating operation, cement will surely cover the surface of the slate. However, it is easily removed with an acid solution or other cleaner. Brush on small quantities of the solution. Then wipe clean with coarse rags until the slate is its natural color and surface. Avoid using excess solution, and avoid having the solution spill onto the concrete. The effects on the concrete at this stage of curing could be very bad.

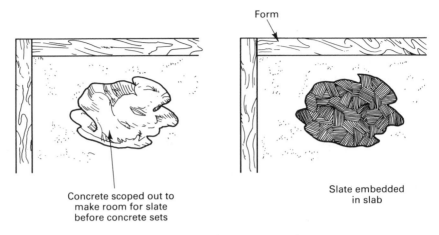

Figure 2-7   Slate in a concrete patio.

While you are performing task 3, it might be wise to place the removed concrete onto a piece of plywood to preclude interfering with the screeded concrete. Once the slate is in place, this excess concrete can easily be slid or lifted off the patio surface.

Before setting each piece of slate in the concrete, all foreign materials must be removed from the slate with high-pressure water and a wire brush. Cement will not bond to vegetation or dirt.

The remainder of the tasks should be familiar, since they have been discussed before. The enhancement technique is not difficult. It does require some care, some physical effort, and a sense of design.

USING EXPOSED AGGREGATE AS THE TOP SURFACE

The technique of exposing aggregate for a patio surface is not used frequently for several reasons. The aggregate creates an uneven surface, since aggregate is not exactly all the same size and shape. Furniture can not sit exactly flat on the surface. It is sometimes uncomfortable to walk on. It can be difficult to keep clean of food unless the surface is protected well. If pea gravel or washed river stone is used, it must be small. If blue stone or other quarry-type crushed stone is used it will be very attractive, but will be very irregular. Yet there are some who will desire to have this surface.

The usual method of creating a patio with exposed aggregate is to apply the aggregate onto the newly poured and screeded slab. With a shovel or rake a uniform coat of aggregate must be applied. Then the aggregate is tamped into the concrete. Figure 2-8 shows some of the actions. An alternative method is to order concrete with aggregate the size needed for the exposed aggregate finish. Then a water spray is used to flush away some of the cement and sand, which then exposes the aggregate.

In terms of tasks to perform, the following list will do. The assumption is made that all forming is complete and reinforcing materials are in place:

1. Pour and screed the concrete.
2. Ensure that the broadcasted aggregate pea gravel or crushed stone is washed thoroughly and is *saturated*.
3. Spread the aggregate evenly over the concrete and tamp into the surface cement.
4. Spray with water very lightly to remove cement and sand that has covered the surface aggregate.
5. Allow time for curing to take place.
6. Apply sealers to preserve the surface.

The tasks are simple to understand, although they require considerable physical effort. For a large patio several yards of aggregate could be hand moved onto the surface.

One thing that may be new and needs to be discussed is step 2. The preparation of the aggregate is indicated and a comment is made about saturation. As hard as aggregates may be, they are all capable of holding moisture. For use in concrete, aggregate must be fully saturated. It must have within it the most mois-

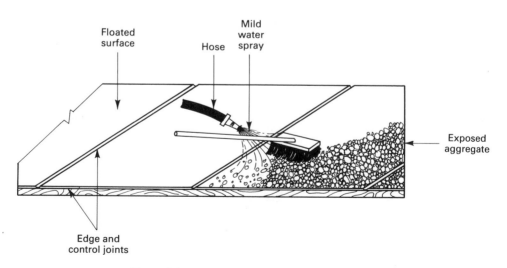

Figure 2-8 Exposed aggregate surface on the patio.

ture it is capable of holding. Here's why! Water is the item in concrete that causes the thermal hydraulic action that makes cement harden. Water must be present throughout the setting process, which lasts up to six months.

Stone that is saturated does not absorb moisture from the concrete mixture. When needed, the moisture in the saturated aggregate, if necessary, provides additional liquid to aid in the setting process and curing. If, on the other hand, unsaturated stone is used, the stone will draw moisture from the concrete mixture. This will decrease or stop the setting and curing actions (thermal setting action).

Where exposed aggregate is concerned, stopping the hydraulic action means that the exposed aggregate will not have a solid bond, and some will likely be swept away or will be easily dislodged. To avoid this, aggregate needs to be soaked for several days or purchased saturated and kept covered until used. Then a light spray of water should be applied daily for 7 days.

USING ROCK SALT TO CREATE A FINISH FOR THE SLAB

Rock salt is, as its name implies, large pieces of salt, some as large as an inch in diameter. The effect created in the top of the patio when rock salt is used is really a "pocked surface" (Figure 2-9). In practical terms rock salt is spread over the screeded surface of the concrete and trowelled into the concrete. Later, water is used to dissolve the salt and create holes in the concrete.

The technique in using rock salt versus exposed aggregate differs. Where it was imperative to completely cover the slab with aggregate, the entire surface should not be entirely covered with salt. Most of the finished surface needs to be troweled and smooth. The pock marks add character. If 100 percent of the surface were covered with salt and later it was washed away, the result would be a totally unusable floor. So sparsely cover the surface with rock salt so that about

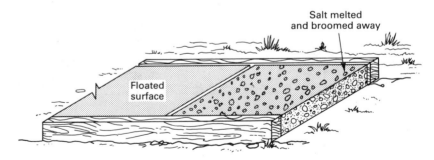

Figure 2-9 Concrete patio finished with rock salt enhancement.

10 to 15 percent of its surface will show pock marks and the remainder will be flat and smooth.

On a final note, before we list the tasks, the salt should be flush with the surface. This will facilitate washing it away. The washing action should be gentle and should be done after the concrete has set sufficiently so that water does not disturb the concrete and the finish.

Tasks to be done after the concrete is poured and screeded are

1. Perform a coarse troweling action.
2. Apply the rock salt by broadcasting it.
3. Continue the troweling activities.
4. Let the concrete set.
5. Dissolve the rock salt with water, thoroughly rinsing the slab.
6. Allow time for curing.
7. Seal the floor while avoiding filling the pock marks.

USING COLORING AGENTS IN THE CONCRETE FOR THE SLAB

Coloring agents may be natural, such as aggregates of quartz, marble, granite, or ceramic, or they may be pigments, such as pure mineral oxides that are ground finer than cement, with colors ranging from white through the color spectrum to black. The predominant ones are white, black, red, green, and various buff colors. All are prepared and sold in powder form, thus making them easy to acquire, measure, and use.

When coloring agents are used in a slab, the usual gray cement employed in concrete affects the final color. Therefore, concrete should be made with white cement. This will probably add to the overall cost of the product, but the final color will be more true and more intense.

There are two processes to select from when using coloring agents. In one process the agent is added to the plastic concrete at the time it is mixed. In the other method the agent is broadcast over the screeded concrete.

In the first method measured quantities of powder are spilled into the mixture either at the concrete plant or at the job site just before the pour. This technique produces a uniformly colored concrete. No matter what type of final surface finish is used, the color remains the same. If designs are made with grooving tools or edgers, the color is the same. When forms are removed, the color on the exposed edges is the same. No special emphasis or skill is required, since the concrete may be considered normal.

In contrast, the surface-applied coloring agent does not penetrate the concrete to any significant depth even when masons work hard with floats and trowels. When grooves are made for design, for example, additional coloring agent must be added to these. Then after the forms are removed, the edges will need to be plastered with a colored mortar.

These added activities add cost, so a careful cost assessment must be made. All contractors must employ an economic analysis to determine the most efficient process to use.

All coloring agents are subject to ultraviolet rays. This means that fading is predictable. The life of the color can be prolonged if protective coatings are applied as soon as the situation permits.

Colored concrete is also susceptible to weathering, like any other concrete. Where the powder was surface-applied, the natural color of the concrete, either gray or white, will begin to show through and will become more pronounced as the aging process continues. However, where the powder was mixed through the concrete, the colors remain uniform regardless of the weathering. What will alter the color of the slab as weathering continues is the natural color of the large aggregate. Again, protective sealants delay the normal weathering actions.

USING TROWEL AND BROOM
TO CREATE SURFACE PATTERNS

The simplest finish of all concrete finishes is the broom finish. Usually, a large, stiff-bristle, corn push broom is used. Its stiff bristles actually cut into the soft concrete surface, making depressions. The forward or pushing motion creates the greatest force and the deepest markings. The backward or pulling motion makes finer markings because the bristles glide along the surface of the concrete. For patios the pulling motion is more desirable than the pushing motion. If brooming is used, the final troweling operation need not be done. Rounding edges and making design grooves in the surface should be done first.

The trowel is another tool that can create a pattern, although generally the trowel is used to eliminate marks from the concrete. If the trowel is used to make a design, the design is usually swirls or semi-arcs. The mason will actually cause a slight depression in the concrete with either the heel or leading edge of the trowel.

3

Concrete Patio on Top of a Foundation

OBJECTIVES

- Plan the footings and foundation that will support the concrete patio floor.
- Establish elevation requirements and the need to be below the frost line with the footings.
- Establish the height of the footings from the batter boards and from the elevation drawing.
- Identify how cement blocks must be placed exactly correct for maintenance of height and spacing to create proper alignment of blocks.
- Identify mortar mixture information and formulas for making and using mortar.
- Identify striking joint techniques.
- Describe the backfill requirements after the foundation is cured.
- Identify filling the foundation techniques.
- Identify the techniques for forming and finishing the slab flush with blocks and alternately with a $1\frac{1}{2}$-in. overhang.
- Describe forms removal and floating the exposed edges of the patio floor.
- Briefly list the cleanup requirements via a checklist.
- Describe the possible use of sealers to protect the floor.

BACKGROUND

The job to be done is a complex one. We need to build a slab above ground level, but to do so, a foundation must be built from cement blocks. Then the area inside the blocks needs to be filled with dirt and compacted. To make the final level of the dirt flush with the top course of block, sand is used, and this is wet with water. Next the slab form is built; before the concrete is poured, the reinforcement materials are placed in the formed area. After the pour, finishing its surface and later finishing the edges of the exposed concrete are to be done. Finally, the outside area around the foundation must be backfilled and cleaned up.

The project in this chapter is generic, but everything that is described is applicable and transferable to a specific project that you might build. However, the project is not easily done even when skills are already known. There may be a need to learn to use new tools and techniques, especially in block laying.

Since the materials themselves are quite bulky, they are heavy. Moving concrete is also a strenuous task, as is mixing mortar. The tasks are all physical. In some cases it is desirable to have assistance.

There are some familiar terms such as *footings, batter boards, finished floor height*, and others. There are also new terms associated with block laying, unique tools to use, and others.

As we shall see, it is more difficult to estimate costs, because a wider variety of materials may be employed. Further, style changes can affect the cost figures.

Even though the project is complex and physical, there is a great deal of satisfaction in a job well done. Now let's begin the study of the generic concrete slab above ground.

SPECIFICATIONS

The types of specifications needed for a project of this type include footing requirements, block wall needs, techniques used to strike joints, types of forms to contain the concrete, mortaring requirements, concrete finishing tasks and designs, safety concerns, reinforcements, and surface preparations. The specifics are listed in Table 3.1.

A close look at the specifications reveals no issues that need clarification. Most of the issues have been studied in Chapters 1 and 2. We shall examine the block laying more closely later.

MATERIALS ASSESSMENT

The materials necessary to complete the project are quite varied. The complete listing is provided in Table 3.2. The lists place the materials identified in the specifications in their proper classification.

TABLE 3.1 Specification Listing
PROJECT: *Concrete Patio on Top of a Foundation*   **DATE:** _____

General Description

Build a concrete slab patio above ground level and 8 in. below the house finished floor height. Build the patio 12 ft by 20 ft long with a 4-in.-thick slab. Pour the footings below frost line and then lay blocks to 4 in. below finished slab height. Strike all mortar joints. Form the slab area after backfilling inside the foundation is completed and packed. Install rebars around the perimeter and wire mesh across the formed area. Finish the concrete with a smooth trowel. Make patterns with a grooving tool, and round the outer edges with the edging tool. Backfill around the foundation and clean up. Add shrubs and mulch. Protect the slab surface with a protection agent/coating.

Specifications

Item	Specs
Dimensions	12′ × 20′, 8″ below house fin fl ht slab 4″ thick
Slope	$\frac{3}{8}$″ per 12′
Surface design	Smooth trowel, round edge
Mortar mixture	Standard mortar mix and sand
Type of block	Cement, 8 × 8 × 16
Concrete mixture	3000 lb/cu yd
Subsurface preparation	Backfill inside of foundation with clean dirt, compact with water spray; final leveling done with washed sand
Reinforcements	$2\frac{1}{2}$″ rebars in the footing, spaced evenly, one rebar around the perimeter of the formed slab. 6 × 6 wire mesh cut to fit in the formed area but no closer to the form than 2″. Wire tie mesh pieces that overlap. Wire tie mesh to rebars.
Footings	16″ × 6″ continuous pour concrete, reinforced with 2 rebars. Natural earth side forms permitted. Footings positioned to permit 4″ exposure each side of block.
Shrubs	3-yr-old boxwood plants spaced 3 ft

CONSTRUCTION

Several fundamentals must be performed in completing the tasks of installing or setting batter boards, trenching for footings, laying out footings, and pouring the concrete. Let's begin with the batter boards.

Batter Boards

For a project that requires trenching to construct below-ground-level footings and then the erection of foundation walls that are partly below ground level, adequate

TABLE 3.2 Materials Assessment
PROJECT: *Concrete Patio*   **DATE**: _____

Direct Materials

Type or Description	*Use or Purpose*
Washed sand	Backfill uneven areas under slab
6 × 6-in. wire mesh	Reinforcement for concrete
Concrete	Basic element of the slab

Indirect Materials

Type or Description	*Use or Purpose*
Batter boards and supports	Establishes lines of slab dimensions
Forms (wood or metal)	Shapes the form of the slab
Stakes and braces	Holds forms in position
Nails	Fasteners
Mason line	Establishes outline of slab

Support Materials

Type or Description	*Use or Purpose*
Masonry hand tools	Construction and finishing
Carpentry tools	Construct batter boards and forms
Rakes, shovels, and hoes	Prepare subsurface as well as distribute wet concrete
Power tools	Aids for building; smoothing concrete

work space is required. So it is best to keep the batter boards about four feet outside the corners of the foundation. This means that the batter boards should be about five to six feet long. The added length makes establishing the wall and footing lines simpler. Since the patio floor will slope away from the house $\frac{3}{8}$ in., the top of the batter boards should be set to account for the slope. In that way, footing, foundation walls, and slab will all use standard measurements and will not require adjustments. (See Figure 3-1 for illustrated details.)

Tasks for batter board installation:

1. Locate the exact outer corners of the foundation with the floor plan, tape measure, and stakes. (Refer to Chapter 1 for more details if necessary.)
2. Set 2 × 4 batter board stakes 4 ft outside the corner stakes.
3. Establish the finished floor height of the slab as 8 in. below the main floor of the house.

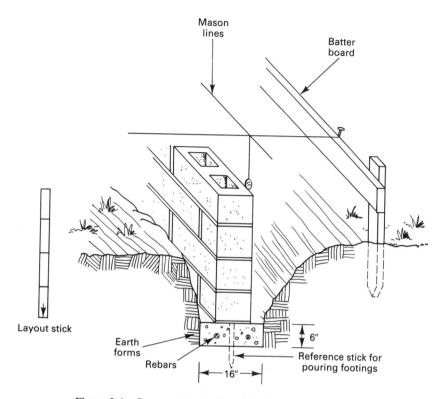

Figure 3-1 Cross-sectional view of the foundation and details.

4. Use a line-level or a 16-ft 2 × 4 to define the top edge position of the batter boards on the 2 × 4 stakes parallel to the house. Mark a pencil line there.
5. With a ruler, make a second mark $\frac{3}{8}$ in. below the first mark. This is the one to use when nailing the batter boards to the stakes.
6. Nail the boards in place and be sure that they are level.
7. Using a plumb bob and mason line, establish the outside foundation corner on all four batter boards by ensuring that the plumb bob is steady over the corner stakes previously set.
8. Mark the footing line 4 in. outside the foundation line on each of the four batter boards. Mark this "footing line."
9. From the footing mark, measure 16 in. toward the inside of the foundation and make a second mark. This indicates the opposite footing. Label this one "footing line."
10. Stretch mason line on all footing marks in preparation for the trenching.

Trenching and Layout for Footings

The trenching work should start wider than the 16-in. footing width. As the final level is reached, the plumb bob should be hung from the footing lines to constantly verify that the natural earth forms are accurately cut. A ruler or 1 × 2 cut to length from the line to the bottom of footing trench should be used repeatedly to ensure that the final depth is accurate.

Although it is common to throw the dirt from the trench to both sides, in this project more of the dirt should be thrown into the foundation area to reduce the fill requirements.

Tasks for trenching and footing layout:

1. Dig the trench to form the walls of the footings.
2. Drive 1 × 1 stakes into the center of the trench about 5 ft apart to use as reference for the pour.
3. Check and recheck all measurements and parameters.

Reinforcement and Pouring Concrete

Several steps need to be done before the concrete is directed into the footing area. First the rebars must be cut and installed. As we learned earlier, rebars are more easily installed if they are bent around the corner. They must be overlapped about 6 in. and wire-tied. Then the rebars must be held above ground level in the footing area so that they will be inside the concrete and not underneath it.

The tasks include:

1. Lay a rebar in the trench and mark the point for the bend with chalk.
2. Bend the bar and place it 4 in. away from the outer edge of the earth form.
3. Overlap the second bar by 6 in., and if no bending is required, wire-tie the two together.
4. Lay the third piece in place or measure to the next bend and bend the rebar.
5. Cut the final piece and complete the wire ties.
6. Repeat tasks 1 through 4 for the second rebar, but place this one 4 in. in from the opposite earth form wall.
7. Elevate the bars about two to three inches by placing stone or broken brick, and the like under them. Keep them separated with 8-in. wood spreaders, which are held in place with tie wire that is wrapped around the both bars. The wood can be removed while the pouring is done.
8. Chute the concrete into the trench very carefully to avoid disturbing the trench side walls, to avoid contaminating the concrete, and to avoid moving the rebars. Use caution while filling footing forms.

9. Use the rake and hoe to level the concrete to the previously installed grade-level stakes.
10. Float the footing concrete, but do not make it very smooth.
11. Remove the grade stakes during the floating operation.
12. Allow for a minimum of one day setup and curing.

Let's calculate the rebar and concrete requirements for the footing in this project.

Requirements

$$\text{Rebars} = 12 \text{ ft} + 20 \text{ ft} + 12 \text{ ft} + 1 \text{ ft overlap} \times 2$$

$$= 90 \text{ lin ft}$$

$$\text{Concrete} = 10 \text{ ft } 8 \text{ in.} + 20 \text{ ft} + 10 \text{ ft } 8 \text{ in.}$$

$$= 41.3 \text{ lin ft (length)} \times 1.3 \text{ ft (width)} \times \tfrac{6}{12} \text{ ft (thickness)}$$

$$= \frac{26.84 \text{ cu ft}}{27.00 \text{ cu ft}}$$

$$= 0.99 \text{ cu yd or } 1 \text{ yd of concrete}$$

Note: Allowance was made to avoid double-counting the corner concrete—10 ft 8 in. vs 12 ft.

Block Laying

A quick look at Figure 3-2 tells us a lot about the task of block laying. As you see, each block has a number. The number represents the order in which the blocks are mortared in place. We'll refer to this figure again, but first several fundamentals must be discussed.

Mortar is a mixture of washed, saturated sand and a combination of cement and lime. Mortar mix that has proper proportions of cement and lime is sold premixed. To create workable mortar means mixing mortar mix with sand and water in proper proportions. These are usually printed on the bag.

Mortar of proper consistency should be somewhat stiff, rather than loose and juicy. It should hold its shape when placed on the block. This ensures that the mortar joint thickness will remain constant as more layers of block are added.

The tools needed to lay block are few. They include an 8-in. pointed trowel, a striking tool, a level (2 or 4 ft), mason line, layout stick, and either a wide coal chisel or power saw with mason blade installed. What is a layout stick? Look at Figure 3-2 again; the stick of 1 × 2 has equal gradations marks of eight inches. This stick aids in establishing and maintaining course integrity and is used while laying each course and each corner.

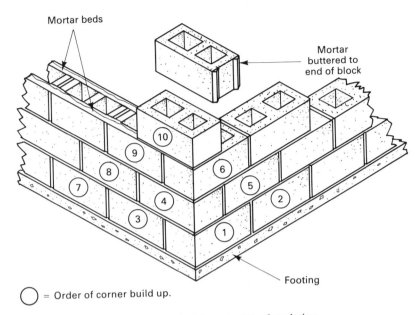

Figure 3-2 Block layout of the foundation.

Now let's decide how to proceed with block laying. A block measuring 8 × 8 × 16 is really 8 in. wide by $7\frac{5}{8}$ in high by $17\frac{5}{8}$ in. long. The $\frac{3}{8}$-in. mortar joint completes the dimension for height and length. Using even inch increments aids in determining how to lay out the blocks. In our generic project we have two 12-ft walls and one 20-ft wall. By using simple division, there will be exactly 15 blocks on one course of the 20-ft wall and 14 blocks on the alternate course of the same wall. There will be exactly nine blocks in each 12-ft wall. But because of the overlap at the corners, half blocks will be needed on alternate courses. Since there are four courses in the project, the rough count for blocks will be 58 for the 20-ft wall and 35 blocks in each 12-ft wall for a rough total of 128 blocks.

Tasks needed to lay blocks:

1. Ensure that the footings are free of dirt; if not, wash with water.
2. Make a layout stick with 8-in. graduations.
3. Lay up the outside corners.
4. String a mason line flush with the top of the first course at the corners and lay the rest of the first course of blocks. Maintain $\frac{3}{8}$-in. joints.
5. Move the line up a course and lay those blocks.
6. Repeat tasks 4 and 5 until all blocks are laid.
7. Strike all joints.

We have discussed task 2 and part of task 3. When laying up the corners, make sure to use the level outside the blocks vertically, and across the top to ensure plumb and level courses.

Using a pointed trowel, apply a bed of mortar to the blocks, in a line about 1 in. high by 1 in. wide and shape it like a pyramid. Apply this to both outer edges of the blocks already mortared in place. Then apply the same technique to the end of the next block to be set in place. Grip the block along the top with both hands and set it in place. Make sure that the joint is $\frac{3}{8}$ in. and that the block aligns with the mason line. Sometimes it requires a tap with the handle of the trowel to make fine adjustments to the positioning. Then use the trowel with forward and upward sweeping motion to remove excess mortar from the joint. Apply this excess further down the line or on the end of the next block.

Within an hour after laying blocks the joints should be struck. The tool described in Figure 3-3 is the one to use. Striking joints means, laying the curved edge of the tool into the joint mortar and, using forward and backward movements, compressing the mortar.

Backfilling Inside and Outside the Foundation

Freshly laid blocks appear to have sound, firm mortar joints after they have been struck. But this is not true. The mortar must set and cure to obtain strength. Therefore, we must wait a day or more before backfilling against the walls.

Let's assume that several days have passed and we are ready to backfill the trench and fill in the foundation area. The outside of the wall must be done first for safety reasons. The work remaining includes transporting fill, compacting it,

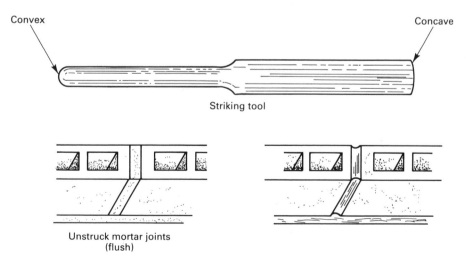

Convex

Concave

Striking tool

Unstruck mortar joints
(flush)

Figure 3-3 Striking mortar joints.

building forms, pouring and finishing concrete, and removing forms. It is much safer to do these tasks when working on level ground.

Only clean fill must be used inside the foundation. "Clean" means free of vegetation, trash, biodegradable materials, and clay. It may contain stone, rocks, broken masonry, building materials, and the like. As the fill is loaded into the area, it must be periodically tamped and sprayed with water to force the air pockets from the dirt.

There is no need to fill the holes in the blocks. So screen wire pieces or old newspapers can be used. Strips of screen wire can be laid over the top course of block, which will prevent dirt and later concrete from filling the block holes. If newspaper is used, wads are stuffed into each hole. In either case, it does not matter what happens to these materials once the concrete slab is in place.

The fill should be flush with the top course of block when the job is done. To achieve this level, washed sand may have to be used.

Preparation of the Form for the Concrete Slab

The specifications call for a 1½-in. overhang of the concrete slab, and we will discuss the forming process for this. As an added feature, we shall also discuss a variation where no overhang is planned.

Overhang 1½-in. form.   Figure 3-4, a cross-sectional drawing, shows us the essential elements and points to the job to do. We see that materials needed

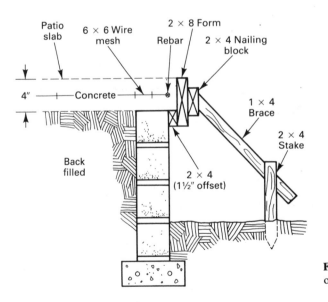

Figure 3-4 Forming the slab with 1½-in. overhang.

include 2 × 4s for the offset form, blocks, and stakes, 2 × 8s for forms, and 1 × 4s for the braces, plus some nails.

The 2 × 4 offset form pieces are used to establish the 1½-in. overhang of the slab. These pieces can be nailed either flush with the top of the block or held ½ in. below to ensure that no gap will exist between block and concrete. The 2 × 8 forms are fastened to the 2 × 4s so that their top surface is at finished floor height. Blocks of 2 × 4 at corners and spaced at about 4-ft intervals are nailed to the 2 × 8. Then stakes and braces are installed to ensure that the form is secure and plumb. So the tasks are

1. Cut and nail 2 × 4 offset pieces to the block wall.
2. Cut and nail 2 × 8 pieces to the 2 × 4 offset at finished floor height.
3. Add bracing and ensure a plumb form.

Flush form. A modification to the idea shown in Figure 3-4 is the one shown in Figure 3-5. The flush form differs in that no 2 × 4 offset pieces are used. One way of making work easier is to nail the 2 × 4 blocks onto the form before nailing the form in place on the block wall.

Comment about bracing. If for some reason nailing the forms to the block wall is unsuccessful or undesirable, additional bracing not shown in Figure 3-5 can be used. A scrap piece of 2 × 4 18 in. long or so would be laid on the ground. Another 2 × 4 would be cut to fit on top of this 2 × 4 base and fit snugly under the form. Both ends could be toenailed. These braces retain the form height while the others retain its position and prevent the form from moving away from the blocks.

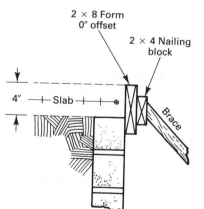

Figure 3-5 Forming the slab flush with the foundation walls.

Pouring the Concrete

Actually there are several tasks to deal with. These are

1. Cutting, bending, tying together, and positioning the $\frac{1}{2}$-in. rebar inside and around the perimeter of the form.
2. Cutting, laying, and wire-tying the 6 × 6 wire mesh.
3. Estimating the concrete.
4. Pouring the concrete.
5. Finishing the concrete surface and edges, and adding design features.
6. Protecting the slab during curing.

Tasks 1 and 2 need no further discussion, since we have done this in both Chapters 1 and 2. Task 3 is a good one to discuss here. We know that there are 27 cu ft in one cu yd. So let's use formula (1.1) again.

$$\text{Cubic feet} = (\text{length in ft})(\text{width in ft})(\text{thickness in feet})$$

$$\text{Cubic yards} = \frac{x \text{ cu ft}}{27 \text{ cu ft}}$$

$$\text{Solution:} \quad = (20 \text{ ft long})(12 \text{ feet wide})(\tfrac{4}{12} \text{ ft thick})$$

$$= 20 \times 12 \times \tfrac{4}{12}$$

$$= \frac{80 \text{ cu ft}}{27 \text{ cu ft}}$$

$$= 3 \text{ cu yd (rounded up)}$$

Pouring concrete should be done with care. This means chuting the concrete mixture into the area but away from the forms. Drag the concrete to the forms with rakes and hoes. This greatly reduces the force on the forms and pressure placed on the braces and nails. Use a 1 × 4 by 4 ft scrap of wood or spade to tamp the concrete against the form. This forces cement and sand against the wood and moves the large aggregate away. Do this all around the form. Screed the surface, let set, and then trowel to a smooth finish. Then add design with a dividing tool and round the edges with an edger. For your selection four designs are shown in Figure 3-6. In each case snap chalklines and use the grooving tool to make the sections. In the case of the free-flowing design, make the repeat patterns very similar, or better yet cut a pattern of the curve from cardboard.

Removing the Forms and Floating the Slab Edges

A critical part of removing the forms is the avoidance of breaking corners and edges of the concrete and chipping the blocks where nails were used. If the forms

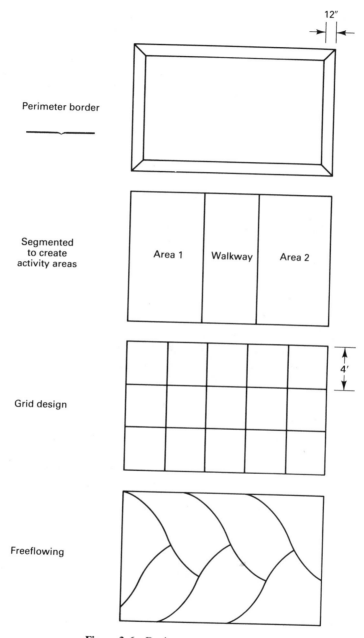

12″

Perimeter border

Segmented
to create
activity areas

Area 1 | Walkway | Area 2

Grid design

4′

Freeflowing

Figure 3-6 Design patterns for the slab.

are left in place for 7 days the concrete is good and hard, and the chance of damage is greatly reduced. First, remove the braces by withdrawing the nails. In this way little stress is placed on the concrete. Then remove the nails holding the forms to each other. Finally, remove the pieces nailed to the cement blocks.

If the edges are not as nice as the top, and there is a real likelihood that they won't be, make a small amount of mortar. Use a float and apply a coat of mortar to all the edges. If desired, use a smooth surface trowel as a final step.

CLEANUP

There are several tasks associated with cleanup:

1. Remove all nails from forms, braces, and stakes.
2. Clean cement and concrete from the forms and other pieces.
3. Store these pieces away from the job site.
4. Remove the batter boards, clean nails from the pieces, and store them with the forms.
5. Put spilled and hardened concrete into a wheelbarrow and move it to a safe refuse area for later disposal.
6. Rake the ground to pick up all nails and small scraps of materials, such as ends of rebars and 6 × 6-in. wire mesh.
7. Remove sawhorses and workbench, if one was used.
8. Pick up and store electrical drop lines.
9. Take an inventory of all tools.
10. Clean and lightly oil all masonry tools.

These are routine tasks, but they must be done to preserve the support materials and indirect materials. Further, they must be done to prepare the grounds around the patio for planting and landscaping.

LANDSCAPING

For our generic above-ground patio we are using a preformed set of concrete steps. These need to be set in place against the block foundation. Once these are in place, the remainder of landscaping can be done.

The specifications call for 3-year-old boxwood plants spaced every 3 ft around the foundation. This translates to four on each end and six across the 20-ft length. The specifications also call for a mulch bed around the foundation 4 ft out. The mulch is to be held in place with border. The landscaping seems simple enough for most to do, although several problems may be present that will result in loss of plants. The contaminants from the concrete, leaching into the soil during the pouring and finishing operations, can inhibit growth of plants and shrubs. Further, fill dirt may be heavily acidic or may contain other elements and minerals that will render the dirt unsuitable for plants. The only sure way to proceed successfully is to have soil samples evaluated by the local extension service. The results will include fact sheets that specify what types of chemicals and fertilizers are necessary for the boxwoods and other plants you might select.

Another problem to resolve is weeds. If time permits chemicals can be applied to the ground and covered. This treatment kills the seeds and seedlings, thus eliminating the problem of weeds, at least for the time being.

MATERIALS LISTING

The materials listing is a summary of materials actually used in the construction of the above-ground patio, plus rental equipment. An invoice is shown in Table 3.3.

TABLE 3.3 Materials Invoice
PROJECT: *Above-Ground Concrete Patio*   **DATE:** _____

Quantity	Type	Total
128	8 × 8 × 16 cement blocks	128 ea.
4 cu yd	Concrete, footing and slab	4 cu yd
13	$\frac{1}{2}''$ × 12' rebars	156 lin ft
5	2 × 4 12' forms	60 lin ft
5	2 × 4 10' stakes	50 lin ft
2	1 × 4 10' batter boards	20 lin ft
7	1 × 4 8' braces	56 lin ft
240 sq ft	6 × 6'' wire mesh	240 sq ft
1 roll	General-purpose tie wire	50'
3 lb	8d comm nails	3 lb
3 lb	12d double-headed nails	3 lb
1 yd	Washed sand	1 yd
2 bags	Mortar mix	2 bags
13	3- to 4-year-old boxwoods	13 ea
10 bags	Bark—mulch	10 ea
50 lin ft	Plastic garden border	50 lin ft
17 yd	Fill dirt	17 yd

Rental Equipment		*Duration of Rental*
Darby		4 hr
Power trowel		4 hr
Bolt cutters		1 day

Figure 3-7a Concrete protector. (Courtesy of Thompson's, Memphis, Tennessee.)

Figure 3-7b Applying concrete protector. (Courtesy of Thompson's, Memphis, Tennessee.)

PROTECTIVE COATING TECHNIQUES
FOR CONCRETE SURFACES

Concrete protective coatings are chemically prepared by several companies, including Thompson's. Thompson's Water Seal® Concrete Protector is prepared in a dispensing container as shown in Figure 3-7a. Figure 3-7b shows how easy it is to apply. When applied as directed, this product is effective against the effects of rain, snow, ice, and deicing salts. The company recommends that it be applied before freezing weather sets in. The container shown in the figure provides enough to cover about 700 square feet. For the generic projects in these first three chapters, one container would meet the needs. Although it specifically states concrete protector, the information sheets indicate that it is also effective on brick and other masonry surfaces. (See reference list for name and address.)

4

Resurfacing an Old Concrete Slab Patio

OBJECTIVES

- Refinish an old and worn patio/slab, using one of several techniques.
- Tiling over an old but sound concrete slab.
- Overbricking an old but sound concrete slab.
- Calculate the materials needed to restore a concrete slab.

GRINDING THE SURFACE OF THE SLAB AND SEALING IT

The object in using this technique to recapture an otherwise sound concrete slab is to remove contaminants from the surface that cannot be removed by an acid solution. A certain amount of the concrete must be taken off the surface, and machines must be used. The machine resembles a sanding machine. However, the grinding wheels or pads are made from abrasive materials that are capable of grinding away the concrete surface.

Before undertaking such a job a careful examination of the concrete must be made to determine if the technique is suitable. Let's make a list of the possible conditions that may render this technique not suitable.

1. *The patio has at least one severe crack.* A patio with a severe crack (one that is several feet long and extends most of the way through the patio) can not be repaired by this technique; the grinding will not remove the crack.

2. *Broken corners and edges.* Before any resurfacing can be done, the broken areas must be repaired. It is very likely that the repair materials will create a color different from the original weathered surface. The mismatch creates an unsolvable problem, so the grinding technique is unsuitable.

3. *The patio has a high degree of spalling and splitting.* Spalling caused by weather, salts and other chemicals plus any splitting may be so deep that the best solution is to resurface the entire patio with a cement mortar. In this event the grinding technique is not a proper one to use.

4. *The patio should not show any significant percentage of aggregate.* Whenever the grinding technique is used, some aggregate will show. If it already shows, the technique will reveal more.

In summary, the technique is suitable in a very limited way. It should be used only if the patio surface is sound, is free from cracks, broken edges, and corners, does not require repairs that add new materials, and if the final result is acceptable if the large aggregate is on the surface. Spalling must be limited in depth for the technique to be effective.

Physical protection is a very important aspect of the technique. While the machine is in operation, protective clothing, goggles, gloves, and sturdy work shoes must be worn. We have no idea what reaction the grinding wheel will produce when it comes in contact with the different surfaces. Split slivers of cement or some stones may be dislodged and fly. A significant amount of dust can be generated; it should not be inhaled. So a mask should be worn. The heavy work shoes protect feet and ankles from flying debris and harm if the machine gets out of control for some reason.

Table 4.1 outlines the various materials necessary for the job. Just as in other chapters, there are some direct, indirect, and support materials needed.

TABLE 4.1 Materials Assessment
PROJECT: *Grinding and Sealing Patio Slab Surface*   **DATE**: _____

Direct Materials

Type or Description	*Use or Purpose*
Concrete sealer	Seal newly surfaced concrete

Indirect Materials

Type or Description	*Use or Purpose*
Grinding wheels/pads	Expendable part of machine

Support Materials

Type or Description	*Use or Purpose*
Gas or electric grinder	Grind the surface of concrete free from decay
Gas or electric vacuum, blower	Cleanup operations
Brooms	Cleanup operations
Garden hose	Used to apply sealer coat

The actual movement of the machine depends on the type rented. However, for the first-time user, it is best to remove small amounts of materials at a time rather than try to grind away, say, more than ⅛ in. This conservative approach is safer, prevents inadvertent further damage, and permits the option of maintaining a specific pattern of removal. Periodically, use the electric or gas blower to remove dust and debris from the work area to make inspections of work accomplished. Include in the inspection judgments about the even pattern that is occurring. It needs to be even, no gouges or grooves.

After the grinding activity is complete and the slab is free of debris and dust, the sealer should be applied as per the manufacturer's directions. This is the most opportune time to accomplish the task, especially because the surface is free of contaminants.

ACID CLEANING OF THE SLAB'S SURFACE AND SEALING IT

In accomplishing this project of using an acid solution to rid the slab of decayed cement and other contaminants, a certain amount of physical precautions must be employed. Although the acid is diluted when used, it is purchased in full strength. Generally, the acid solution is applied with a mop, or sometimes is

TABLE 4.2 Materials assessment
PROJECT: *Acid cleaning of a sound concrete patio*   **DATE:** _____

Direct Materials

Type or Description	Use or Purpose
Muriatic acid	Cleans and etches the concrete
Detergent	Used to wash the slab before applying the acid solution
Water	Mixed with the acid
Concrete sealer or paint (optional)	Recommended for protection

Indirect Materials

Type or Description	Use or Purpose
Stiff bristle corn broom	Spreads and works the acid solution into the slab surface

Support Materials

Type or Description	Use or Purpose
Mop and bucket	Scrub the floor
Garden hose	Wash acid from the floor

broadcast onto the slab. Then it is worked into the surface, permitted to set there for a short time, and finally is washed away with water. Before doing this work, there are several considerations that should be attended to. These will be identified. Finally, a sealing agent should be applied. This can be a type of paint suitable for concrete or a clear solution such as Thompson's Water Seal™ Concrete Protector.

Table 4.2 provides a listing of all the materials required to perform and complete the job. The only dangerous product listed is the muriatic acid. Most items listed should be fairly well-known, so no further discussion is needed about them.

Table 4.3 provides a model that can be used if the manufacturer's container of muriatic acid does not provide the data.

Procedure

After we list the tasks, the discussion will follow:

1. Wash the slab surface with detergent and rinse thoroughly.
2. Don the protective clothing.

TABLE 4.3 Estimating Muriatic Acid Requirements

	Standard Solution (light cleaning required)		
Square feet	*Amount of acid*	*Amount of water*	*Ratio acid/water*
100	2.25 gal	2.25 gal	1/9
250	0.5 gal	4.5 gal	1/9
500	1 gal	9.0 gal	1/9
	Heavy Solution (moderate to heavy cleaning)		
Square feet	*Amount of acid*	*Amount of water*	*Ratio acid/water*
100	0.5 gal	2.5 gal	1/5
200	1 gal	5.0 gal	1/5
500	2.5 gal	12.5 gal	1/5

3. Prepare the acid and water solution by measuring the water into a nonmetallic container and then pouring the measured amount of acid into the water. **Caution:** Do not add the water to the acid.
4. Apply the solution to the concrete with a mop and then use a stiff-bristle corn broom to vigorously rub the mixture into the concrete.
5. Keep the solution from drying on the floor.
6. Wash thoroughly with water from a hose to neutralize the acid.
7. Let dry and inspect.
8. Repeat with a second application to those areas that need it.
9. Apply sealer.

We know most of what to do from the task list. Here are the items that make up the protective clothing list: protective eye goggles, long gloves that overlap the shirt sleeves, long-sleeved shirt buttoned at the sleeves and at the collar, a hat, and rubber boots or rubberized work shoes. Since the patio is outside, no respirator is necessary. If the work were done in a place with restricted ventilation, a respirator would be required.

TILING AN OLD BUT SOUND PATIO SLAB

The object of this section is to provide detail on the job of applying ceramic or clay tile over a sound concrete slab patio. In general, we will need to clean the old slab surface to ensure a good bond between the mortar and concrete. After this a mortar with a bonding additive is applied over which evenly spaced tiles are pressed into the mortar as shown in Figure 4-1. Then grout is forced into the

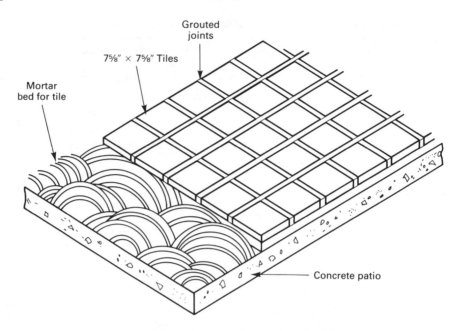

Figure 4-1 Tiling a sound concrete patio slab.

spaces between the tiles and the excess is cleaned off. Sometimes a sealer is applied over the tile to add protection.

Materials Assessment

Table 4.4 provides the assessment of materials necessary to do the job of tiling the old patio floor. In the list of indirect materials burlap is listed. This is used to rub the excess grout from the tiles.

Procedure

The tasks in this job will include:

1. Clean the slab surface to free it of contaminants and salts.
2. Fill in areas of spalling and cracks in the patio with mortar.
3. Plan the layout of the tiles.
4. Estimate the number of tiles and other materials needed.
5. Prepare the mortar and apply it to about 4 square feet.
6. Snap a line for the first row of tile.
7. Lay the tiles and impress them into the mortar—maintain $\frac{1}{4}$ in. separation.
8. Apply the mortar to another 4 sq ft and continue to lay tiles.
9. Prepare grout according to instruction on the bag.

10. Apply grout and force it into the spaces between tiles.
11. Wipe the tiles with burlap to remove excess grout.
12. Clean up tools.

Task 1 is the procedure that was described in the previous section, so no further discussion is needed. Tasks 2 and 3 are related and can be discussed together. For the generic project, let's say that the patio is 12 ft by 20 ft and the tiles are $7\frac{3}{4}$ in. square. To satisfy task 2 we would snap chalklines every 8 inches. This permits a $\frac{1}{4}$ in. spacing for grout. But where will the first row of tiles begin on the side and outer or inner edge of the patio?

Since there are 144 in. in the width of the patio, at 8 in. per tile we need exactly 18 per row. Since there are 240 in. in the length of the patio, at 8 in. per tile we need exactly 30 per row. The total quantity is 540 tiles ($18 \times 30 = 540$).

TABLE 4.4   Materials Assessment
PROJECT: *Tiling the Surface of a Concrete Patio Slab*   DATE: _____

Direct Materials

Type or Description	Use or Purpose
Tile 8 × 8 or equivalent	New surface for the patio
Mortar mix for tile	Cement tile to concrete slab
Grout	Fill between tiles
Sand	Included in the mortar

Indirect Materials

Type or Description	Use or Purpose
Muriatic acid	Cleans and etches the concrete
Water	Wash surface
Burlap bags	Cleans tiles free of grout
Detergent	Wash concrete surface

Support Materials

Type or Description	Use or Purpose
Mortar box	Prepare mortar mixture and grout
Rags	Clean tiles
Mason tools, including serrated trowel	Lay mortar bed
Chalkline	Establish references for tile alignment
Broom	Sweep surfaces
Wheelbarrow	Transport materials
Shovel and hoe	Mix mortar and grout

Through this estimating we gained one valuable piece of information. We now know that there will be no requirement to cut any of the tiles. The final $\frac{1}{4}$-in. joint/space can be made up by adding a bit of space to the last several rows.

Refer again to Figure 4-1. Applying mortar in this case is a slight bit different from the general applications. A serrated trowel is used to apply the specialized mortar such that its depth is equal to the serrations. This amount is all that is needed for proper bonding. To avoid allowing the setting action to extend too long, only 4 sq ft of mixture should be laid at a time. This minimal amount of mortar makes it easy to have all tiles even.

If rectangular tiles or other shapes are used, determining the pattern layout is more difficult. For our generic project we do not have this problem.

Let the tiles set for a day or more before applying the grout. After working the grout into the spaces with a trowel or scrap of wood, use a piece of burlap to even it and wipe excess from the surfaces. Let this set for a day or more. Finally, wash the tile floor with detergent; when it is dry and all tiles are free of grout, apply a sealer if necessary. Spills of grout or residue of cement powder may have to be removed with a rag and very mild acid/water solution. Before doing this, check to see what the reaction will be by using the solution on a spare tile or in an out-of-the-way corner.

Make sure that all safety procedures are used when working with acids.

Materials Listing

We began with a materials assessment to gain a general understanding of the requirements for the project. Now the accrual materials necessary for the project are shown in Table 4.5.

TABLE 4.5 Materials Invoice
PROJECT: *Tiling the Surface of a Concrete Patio Slab* **DATE**: _____

Quantity	Type	Total
540	$7\frac{3}{4}'' \times 7\frac{3}{4}'' \times \frac{1}{2}''$ ceramic tiles	540 ea
5 bags	Tile-bonding mortar mix	5 bags
2 bags	Grout, buff	2 bags
3 yd	Burlap cloth	3 yd
1 gal	Muriatic acid	1 gal
$\frac{1}{2}$ yd	Sand	$\frac{1}{2}$ yd
1 box	Detergent	32 oz
Tools		
1	Serrated trowel	
1	Mortar box	
1	Mop	

OVERBRICKING A CONCRETE SLAB PATIO

Figure 4-2 shows us the project of applying brick pavers to the surface of an old, otherwise sound, concrete patio. The pattern of brick shown in the figure is a soldier course laid flat as a border and a basket weave for the rest. The laying of the brick explained in the generic project differs from the laying of tile discussed before; we wish to show you an alternative technique. It is possible to use the tile application procedure for the overbrick but a problem arises with squeezing the mortar into the spaces between the brick. An experienced bricklayer would find that technique very time-consumming and unsatisfactory. One not so experienced might find the technique simpler than trying to keep bricks in perfect alignment with their side and end butted.

Materials Assessment

As with every project, we should always make a materials assessment. As shown in Table 4.6, more materials are needed for the project than were used in tiling and some are not necessary. Quite a lot of mortar will need to be mixed. Therefore, an order of washed sand should be ordered. When it arrives, make sure that it stays saturated and covered. It might even be a good idea to rent a mixer.

Procedures

There are only five tasks associated with this project. They include:

1. Cleaning the old surface and making any patches if needed.
2. Mixing mortar.

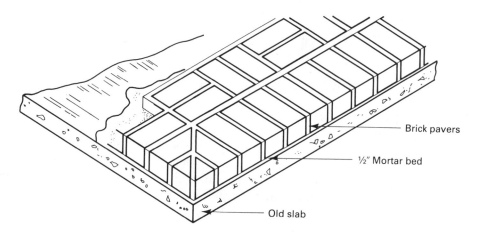

Figure 4-2 Over-bricking a sound concrete patio slab.

TABLE 4.6 Materials Assessment
PROJECT: *Overbricking the Surface of a Concrete Patio Slab*   **DATE:** _____

Direct Materials

Type or Description	Use or Purpose
Paver bricks	New surface for the patio
Mortar mix and sand	Cement bricks in place

Indirect Materials

Type or Description	Use or Purpose
Muriatic acid and water	Etching and cleaning concrete
Rags and brooms	Apply acid
Mortar board	Hold working mortar

Support Materials

Type or Description	Use or Purpose
Mortar box	Mix mortar
Mason tools (trowels, pointing tool, striking tool, etc.)	Apply mortar to brick and slab, strike joints
Wheelbarrow	Transport mortar
Broom	Cleanup
Shovel and hoe	Mix mortar
Chalkline	Establish references for brick alignment
Cement mixer (optional)	Eases the work of mixing mortar

3. Bricklaying technique and pattern layout.
4. Striking the joints.
5. Cleaning the surfaces of cement residue.

Of the five tasks listed, the one requiring added information is number 3. The others have been covered before. (1 and 5, for example, probably require muriatic acid. Mixing mortar is easy to accomplish by following the directions on the bag.)

Two parts of the task must be done at about the same time. In fact, if they are both understood they will mesh. The first is the layout and installation of the border bricks. The second is the order and installation of the basket weave brick pattern. Let's assume that the patio is 12 ft wide by 20 ft long. Let's further assume that the paver bricks are $3\frac{5}{8}$ in. wide by $7\frac{5}{8}$ in. long by $2\frac{1}{2}$ in. thick. The mathematics involved in planning the order of bricklaying is as follows:

Step 1. Estimate the number of bricks by determining the square surface of one brick and two mortar joints. Then divide this result into the total area of the patio.

$$(3\tfrac{5}{8} + \tfrac{3}{8}) \times (7\tfrac{5}{8} + \tfrac{3}{8}) = 32 \text{ sq in. per brick}$$

Total square inches in the patio = $144 \times 240 = 34{,}560$ sq in.

$34{,}560$ divided by $32 = 1080$ bricks

Step 2. Make an allowance for breakage and waste at 5 percent.

$$0.05 \times 1080 = 54$$

Total needed = 1134

Comment: We will stay with this model, but in real terms a larger paver would be better suited. Here's why: Bricks are sold in lots of 500 per pallet. The need for 134 bricks from the third pallet is added cost, since the other 366 bricks would be excess to the job.

Border pavers. The first order of business is to begin laying the bricks away from the corner so that the mitered corner pieces can be laid against the two full bricks. Lay in a bed of mortar slightly more than $\frac{1}{2}$ in. thick. Place a brick onto the bed aligned with the edge of the slab and 8 in. in from the corner. Butter the next brick along its long side and place it next to the first one. Make sure the joint is $\frac{3}{8}$ in. thick. Repeat the process until the row is finished and then do the other two rows/edges. Use a power saw to cut the 45-deg angles on bricks that complete the corners.

Basket weave pavers. Each two bricks and mortar joints equal 8 in. and their lengths plus a mortar joint equal 8 in., so a square is formed. Due to the length of the patio, and the length of the bricks plus mortar joints, 30 equal and even increments of 8 in. exist. This means that when we subtract the two rows of border bricks there will be 28 basket weave squares per course. In the 12-ft dimension there will be 17 basket weave squares. With proper installation and strict adherence to $\frac{3}{8}$-in. joints the job will turn out perfectly.

Striking joints. Strike the joints to compress the mortar to seal it. Do not make the depressions too deep.

Safety. Always use caution when working with acid. Wear proper protective clothing. Add the acid to the water, not the other way around. Use care when mixing mortar; it is a very strenuous job.

Materials Listing

Once again, the materials listing is a reflection of the expense items associated with the project. Even though prices are not provided, a casual review of the invoice in Table 4.7 shows us that this project can be expensive.

Other Brick Patterns

Along with the basket weave pattern, seven more are shown in Figure 4-3. Notice the subtle difference in the patterns b, c, d, and g. Also notice that the offsets from row to row in e and f are different. Where those in f are at the midpoint, the ones in e are at the $\frac{1}{4}$ point. Finally, h shows a stacked pattern.

Closing Comments

This project makes a very pretty patio floor. It is well worth the expense and effort. But before attempting a project like this, make sure that a detailed plan of organization for pavers is made on paper. Calculate all measurements and double check their accuracy several times before starting the work. Where possible, use chalklines to maintain accuracy while laying the bricks.

TABLE 4.7 Materials Invoice
PROJECT: *Overbricking the Surface of a Concrete Patio Slab*   **DATE:** _____

Quantity	Type	Total
1134	$3\frac{5}{8}'' \times 7\frac{5}{8}'' \times 2\frac{1}{2}''$ brick pavers	1134 ea
34 bags	Mortar mix	34 bags
1 yd	Washed sand	1 yd
1 gal	Muriatic acid	1 gal
1 box	Detergent	32 oz
Tools		
1	Rental—cement mixer	
1	Mortar box	
1	Mop	

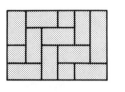

(a)

(b)

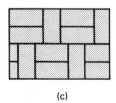

(c)

(d)

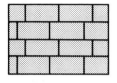

(e)

(f)

(g)

(h)

Figure 4-3 Brick patterns for patios.

5

The Wood Deck Patio—
Basic Design and Construction

OBJECTIVES

- Plan for the construction of a wood deck above ground and attached to a house.
- Plan the specifications and materials assessment.
- Establish the elevations for freeze line, footings, and finished floor line, using the elevation drawing.
- Define parameters of the deck footings and piers.
- Determine the layout of the footings and piers, and the sequence of forming and block laying.
- Define termite shielding requirements.
- Determine the joist and frame construction to support specific design live and dead loads.
- Identify the decking and installation method.
- Finalize the materials listing.

BACKGROUND

The job is to build a wood patio deck onto the main house. The finished floor height must be 8 in. below the main house floor. Since the deck will be elevated, three piers will be used along the 20-ft length to support the frame and decking.

For the study, a generic 14 ft by 20 ft deck has been selected. The specifications call for a dead and live load of 40 psf. This means that certain grades of lumber will permit these heavy loads and others will not. The use of the L-sill configuration makes it easy to anchor the framing to the piers. Masonry anchors or expansion bolts should be used to fasten the header along the main house foundation.

Several parts of the job will require considerable effort and strength. These include digging the areas for the footings, mixing the footing concrete with hoe and shovel, lifting and placing the headers and joists, and driving nails and installing anchor bolts.

There may be several new terms introduced in this chapter. Several that already have been mentioned include *headers, joists, masonry anchors, J-bolts bridging*, and *termite shields. Headers* are wood members that create a method of supporting the ends of the joists. *Joists* are the basic members that make up the frame for the decking. *Bridging* is used to stiffen the joist frame, thereby taking the sway out of the frame.

This job is a complex one. Batter boards are necessary because of the several references needed; footings, block piers, and framing all have different ones. Make the deck square is also a problem that must be solved. Setting the footing to the right depth is also vital so that even courses of block can be used. Proper anchoring of headers, sills, and joists are a must. Decking must be installed with offset joints for both added strength and improved appearance.

A beautiful deck can be built if the procedures listed and explained in this chapter are employed in an actual project. The specifications should be followed. The materials assessment provides an overview of the variety and purpose of these items, and at the end of the chapter a materials listing (invoice) lists the actual materials used in the generic patio. Now let's begin with the specifications.

SPECIFICATIONS

Table 5.1 lists the specifications for the generic wood deck patio. We shall use these throughout the chapter as the different tasks and phases of the job are discussed. Take a few minutes to study these specs.

TABLE 5.1 Specification Listing
PROJECT: *The Wood Deck Patio*   **DATE**: _____

General Description

A wood deck patio, 14 ft × 20 ft, is to be constructed on the rear of a home. The finished floor height is 8 in. below finished floor height of the main dwelling. The deck will be supported by three piers made of cement blocks, which will rest on a footing that is below freeze level. The dead and live load capacity will be 40 psf. All wood materials will be treated lumber capable of meeting load requirements.

Specifications

Item	*Specs*
Dimensions	14′ × 20′, with $\frac{5}{4}''$ decking
Decking	Joints must be offset min. 2 joists and two rows. Two nails per joist, 4 nails per joint
Headers	2 × 10 treated southern pine No. 2
Joists	2 × 8 treated southern pine No. 2
Sills	2 × 6 treated southern pine No. 2
Termite shields	Aluminum—1 per pier
J-bolts	$10'' \times \frac{9}{16}''$ dia
Piers: cement blocks	8 × 8 × 16″
Piers: concrete footings	16″ × 24″ × 6″ thick
Mortar	M-type mortar mix and sand
Nails	16d, 12d, 8d, 4d gal common
Joist hangers	Support 2 × 8 joists
Wood protector	Clear commercial wood protector, 1 coat
Masonry expansion bolts	$\frac{5}{16}'' \times 5''$

MATERIALS ASSESSMENT

The three parts of Table 5.2 show us the materials necessary for the generic patio project. Most of the items listed should now be familiar, but let's discuss the saw horses. The purpose of using sawhorses is to make work easier and safer. A pair of them should be spaced about 10 feet apart; several joists placed on top can be used as the bench. Some carpenters prepare a 2 × 12 as a tool that simplifies the work of cutting joists, headers, and bridging. They nail a 2 × 3 along one or both sides and make a guide frame for the portable power saw to slide back and forth during cutting operations. The masonry tools needed include a pointed trowel, 2- or 4-ft spirit level, and striking tool. The carpentry tools include the framing square, combination square, level, 8-point crosscut saw, hammers, adjustable

TABLE 5.2 Materials Assessment
PROJECT: *The Wood Deck Patio*   DATE: _____

Direct Materials

Type or Description	Use or Purpose
Concrete	Footings
Cement Blocks	Piers
Mortar mix and sand	Cement blocks in place
Termite shields	To block termites
Framing	L-sills and joists
Bridging	Stiffens joists
Decking lumber	Provides walking surface
Nails (assorted)	Fastens wood members
J-bolts	Anchors sills to piers

Indirect Materials

Type or Description	Use or Purpose
Batter boards and posts	Establishes references
Mason line	Specifically defines footings, piers, and perimeters

Support Materials

Type or Description	Use or Purpose
Sawhorses	Provides safety and convenience
Mortar box	Mix mortar and concrete
Electrical extension cords	Portability of machines
Shovel and hoe rake	Mix mortar and concrete, level ground, dig footings
Carpentry tools	Build batter boards porch
Masonry tools	Set blocks and smooth footing
Power saw	Cut wood and block more easily

wrench, electric drill and bits (including masonry bits), and electric power saw and blades.

GROUND PREPARATION AND MASONRY TASKS

Figure 5-1 provides many of the factors we must consider and do something about when building the piers. Note the topography of the ground where the patio will be built. Notice that the freeze line is a little more than a foot below the ground. We will place the footing about two feet below this line. More important, the top

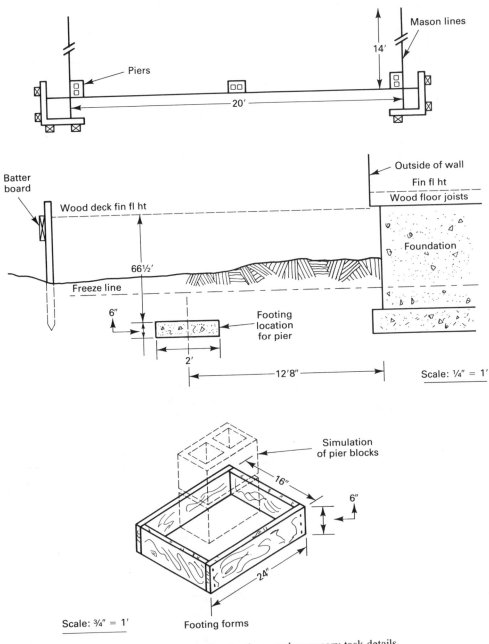

Figure 5-1 Topography, footings, and masonary task details.

of the footing must be $66\frac{1}{2}$ in. below the finished floor height. This distance represents the following:

Decking	$1\frac{1}{4}$ in.
Deck framing	$9\frac{1}{4}$ in.
7 course of blocks	56 in.
Total	$66\frac{1}{2}$ in.

The tasks in this phase include the following:

1. Clear the land around the patio.
2. Install the batter boards about 17 ft away from the house and about 3 ft on each side of the 20-ft dimension of the patio's length.
3. Pinpoint the position of the three piers on mason lines.
4. Dig the area for each pier.
5. Prepare three forms for the pier footings.
6. Install pier footings.
7. Mix concrete from premixed bags and pour into established forms.
8. Lay pier cement blocks.
9. Cement J-bolts into the top course of each pier.
10. Cut, fit, and install the termite shield.

Again we use Figure 5-1 for more details about this project. At the top of the figure, locate the floor plan view that shows the positions of the piers, footings, and batter boards. Notice that the middle pier is turned so that the 16-in. face is outward. This provides more resting surface for the sills, which should be joined over the top course of block. One of the two holes in the top course needs to have a J-bolt embedded in mortar. The batter boards could be marked with four indicators; footing line, pier line, frame line, and finished floor overhang line. The last one is not really necessary. Obtaining the overhang is done simply during the laying of the deck.

Note: If you need a refresher on locating the center of the piers, squaring the framing positions, and locating the footing forms, refer back to Chapter 1.

Let's review! The first task is to clear the land of vegetation and unwanted obstacles. Then lay out the positions of the three piers with stakes. Next drive 2×4 stakes for the batter boards. Dig the holes for the forms. The forms should be made from 1×6 or 2×6 materials, as shown in the lower corner of Figure 5-1.

With the hole dug, the position of the form can most easily be defined with the use of a plumb bob. Since the form is 4 in. wider on all sides than the block, you could use the pier lines to locate the precise position of the form. This technique would further reduce the number of reference lines to two. With the corner of the form located, the other ends going left and right can be verified and positioned by sliding the plumb bob along the line. While the position is correct, drive stakes outside the form. Now remove the plumb bob and make the final adjustment to form height, which in the generic project is 66½ in. down from the finished floor height. Nail the stakes to the form and backfill with dirt against the form. You are ready to make the concrete and fill the form.

For this project the cheapest way to prepare the concrete is to buy ready-mix bags that make ½ cubic foot of concrete per bag. Since our forms are 16 × 24 × 6 in., there are 1.33 cu ft per form times 3 forms = 3.99 or 4 cu ft. Therefore, eight bags are needed. Mix the concrete, fill the forms, and screed the surface flush.

Block laying is next (see Figure 5-2). Make a layout stick with seven equal 8-in. marks, one for each course. Mix the mortar and set the blocks. Continue to use the level to make sure that each column is plumb. After installing the sixth course, either stuff the course with paper or place a small square of screen wire

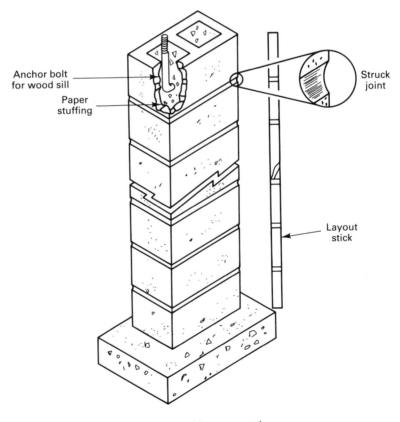

Anchor bolt for wood sill

Paper stuffing

Struck joint

Layout stick

Figure 5-2   Pier construction.

over the holes to prevent mortar from falling into the lower courses when the J-bolt is installed. After the last course is in place, fill the outer hole with mortar and bury the J-bolt into the mortar, leaving 3 in. sticking out ($1\frac{1}{2}$ in. for the 2 × 6 sill and $1\frac{1}{2}$ in. for installing the nut and washer). Before the mortar hardens, strike the joints to improve their weathering capacity and looks.

BUILDING THE FRAME FOR THE DECK

What are we faced with when building the frame work for the deck? Let's do this with a task list:

1. Fasten a header against the house foundation.
2. Install the three termite shields over the piers.
3. Install the sill pieces across the three piers.
4. Install the remaining headers.
5. Layout the position of the joists at 16 in. o. c. (o. c. means *on center* spacing).
6. Cut the 14-ft joists to exact length.
7. Install the joist hangers onto the header against the foundation.
8. Install the joists.
9. Cut and install the bridging if wood is used. Install metal bridging, if used.

Figure 5-3 provides all the detail we need for this phase of the project. In Figure 5-3a we see how to install the 2 × 6 sills. These are located flush with the outside of the pier blocks and flush with the ends of the two end piers. Make the joint over the middle pier.

Look at the rest of the figure and see that the header is bolted onto the foundation wall. This is done by drilling holes into the foundation and matching holes in the header. The exact position of the 2 × 8 header is $\frac{5}{4}$ in. below the finished floor height, the thickness of the decking.

I would complete the L-sill by installing the 2 × 10s on the 20-ft side first, since these pieces can be held even with the bottom of the sill and nailed to it. Then the end pieces can be cut and nailed into place. If you do the end pieces first as shown, the 2 × 10 would be nailed onto the 2 × 10 header and into the end of the sill, even with the bottom of the sill.

Use your framing square to step off the position of each joist for 16 in. o. c. If you start 16 in. from the outside of the header and mark all Xs away from the mark, the layout will be proper even though the spacing of the last joist will slightly exceed 16 in. o. c.

Nail the 2 × 8 joist hangers in place. Since the area behind the header is cement, use 6d common nails for the job.

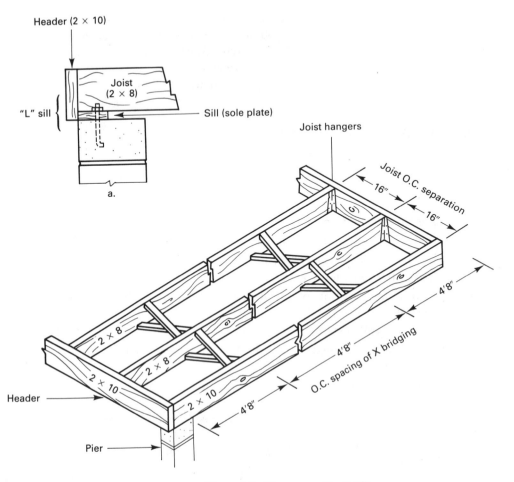

Figure 5-3   Floor assembly details.

Measure the length of the joist. It should be around 14 ft less 1½ in. Cut several at a time and install them with the *crown up*.

The final task is the installation of the bridging. Bridging is both materials and a technique. As a technique it removes sway from the joist assembly. It further eliminates the deflection that a single joist has when it is walked upon. Several materials may be used. Metal x bridging for 16 in. o. c. may be purchased from a building supply store. Wood bridging made from 1 × 3 spruce stock is cut on site. Sometimes solid blocks of 2 × 8 are used as bridging. For our project we will need 15 pairs of bridging pieces per row. For a 14-ft joist assembly we need two rows. Total: 30 pairs or 60 each.

Two chalklines must be snapped as Figure 5-3 shows for the positions of the bridging. Then one piece of bridging is nailed each side of the line. As a rule the tops of the bridging are nailed first. Then the bottoms are nailed from underneath.

This instruction set concludes the framing phase of the project. All that remains is the installation of the decking.

DECKING THE WOOD DECK

There are several selections of materials that can be used for decking. We know that the specifications call for $\frac{5}{4} \times 6$ in. treated material. But many decks are planked with 2 × 4, 2 × 6, or 2 × 8 stock. In some situations 1 × 3 or 1 × 4 tongue and groove is used. Where the deck is fully exposed to weather, the best solution is to use thicker materials and plan spacing between the pieces. Another characteristic to consider is the quality of the materials. Only good to best quality must be selected. Using materials of lower quality would mean the chance of a rupture and very probably personal injury.

Now for our project. (See Figure 5-4.) The boards may be laid from the house outward or from the outer edge backward toward the house. Meeting the offset requirements for joints in the decking solves several problems and produces a desirable finished product. The fewer joints possible, the better. Since the cost of 22-ft decking is very expensive, several different lengths are employed to ensure that the joints are scattered throughout the deck. The wider the scatter pattern, the more pleasing the overall effect. This is the plus. Each joint must rest on half the thickness of the joist. Then when the ends are nailed with 12d common nails, a slight toenailing should be used.

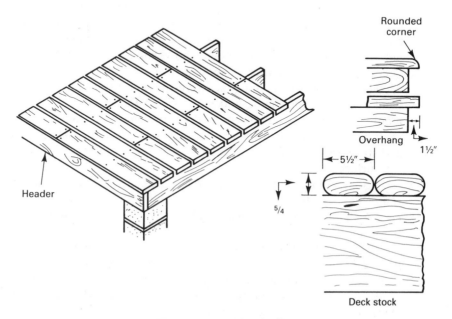

Figure 5-4 Decking details.

There remains the question of the amount of decking required. Calculating the quantity is relatively straightforward.

1. Determine the number of boards (rows) needed.
2. Multiply the number of boards by 21 ft.
3. Add 5 percent for waste.
4. Divide the total by 10, 12, 14, or 16 ft or a combination of these.

Solutions

1. The width of the deck is 14 ft 3 in. (which includes a 1½-in. overhang). The number of boards at 5½ in. per board is 31 (171 in. divided by 5.5 in.)
2. The number of lineal feet required is 651 lin ft (21 ft times 31 rows)
3. Waste is 65 lin ft (5 percent of 651)
4. Options:
    · 71 10-ft lengths
    · 60 12-ft lengths
    · 51 14-ft lengths
    · 45 16-ft lengths

The nailing sequence for each board should be two 12d galvanized common nails per joist. The nails should be about ¾ in. in from each outer edge of the board. There is always the chance of missing the nail and making a hammer mark, but the best-looking jobs do not show hammer marks around the nail head. Second, the best jobs always show a recessed nail head. Both standards can be accomplished easily as follows: Drive the nail into the wood until the blow that would send the nail home and stop. Use either a large nail set or (more commonly) use another nail as the nail set by using its head. Simply hold onto the shaft parallel to the board, place the head on the nail partially driven into the deck and strike the side of the nail head several times until the nail is about ⅛ in. below the surface.

Some refinement can be made to the deck. Two are shown in Figure 5-4. A router and quarter round bit can make the pattern shown with the rounded corner. A slight bevel can be made with the block plane, as shown in the finish below the rounded corner.

Before this finishing can be done, however, the edges must be trimmed to 1½-in. overhang. The last piece against the house must be trimmed to exactly 1½-in. overhang. A power saw cannot go closer than the next to last piece. A chalkline snapped at the 1½-in. overhang position establishes the cutting line. Simply cut along the line and the task is done.

Applying the Protective Coating Material

Several weeks after the patio has been constructed, the wood will have leached some of the excess moisture customarily found in treated lumber. This is the time to apply the protective coating materials, which will protect the wood against weathering. The job will take about 2 gallons for one coat. The simplest method of application is with a $3\frac{1}{2}$-in. to 4-in. paint brush.

FINALIZE THE MATERIALS LISTING

We have discussed all the aspects concerning this project. All materials for the generic project were identified. All that remains is to put them into a form or invoice, as Table 5.3 shows.

TABLE 5.3 Materials Invoice
PROJECT: *The Wood Deck Patio*   **DATE:** _____

Quantity	Type	Total
21	$8 \times 8 \times 16$ cement blocks	21 ea
8 bags	Concrete, footing	4 ea
1 bag	M-type mortar mix	1 ea
100 lb	Sand	100 lb
3	$10'' \times \frac{9}{16}''$ J-bolts	3 ea
6	$\frac{5}{16}'' \times 5''$ expansion bolts	5 ea
21 lin ft	1×6 footing forms	21 lin ft
2	2×6 10' sills, southern pine No. 2 treated	20 lin ft
2	2×10 14' headers, southern pine No. 2 treated	28 lin ft
2	2×10 10' headers, southern pine No. 2 treated	20 lin ft
1	2×10 22' header, southern pine No. 2 treated	22 lin ft
2	1×4 10' batter boards	20 lin ft
2	2×4 16' batter board stakes	32 lin ft
15	2×8 14' joists southern pine No. 2 treated	15 ea
3 lb	8d common nails	3 lb
3 lb	4d common galvanized nails	3 lb
10 lb	12d common galvanized nails	10 lb
2 lb	16d common galvanized nails	2 lb
15	2×8 joist hangers	15 ea
30	1×3 2' bridging	60 lin ft
60	$\frac{5}{4} \times 6$ 12' treated decking	720 lin ft
3	Termite shields for $8 \times 8 \times 16$ blocks	3 ea
2 gal	Wood protector coating—clear	2 ea

SUMMARY OF THE PROJECT

There were two phases to this project. In the first one we built and installed footings and in the second we constructed the framework and decking. Rather than using earth forms, we used simple wooden footing forms. We also learned how to install J-bolts into blocks so that sills could be anchored. In the framing phase we learned about the L-sill and boxed in the joists with headers. Joist hangers were used and bridging stiffened the joist assembly. Finally, the jointing scheme used while installing the decking was deliberate and necessary for the appearance of the finished product.

For projects of this kind several types of drawing are always needed. A floor plan is required, and an elevation plan provides a great deal of information. The figures for the block piers, footing form, joist assembly, and decking are not necessary. These ideas must be memorized.

6

Railings, Steps, and Perimeter Seating

OBJECTIVES

- Define the construction techniques applicable to building wood deck railings, steps, and perimeter seating.
- Prepare a materials assessment for the type of enhancement selected for the wood deck.

METHOD OF CONSTRUCTION
OF WOOD DECK RAILINGS
AND MATERIALS ASSESSMENT

We assume that the wood deck is already built to the approximate dimensions studied in Chapter 5. Recall that the patio was built on cement block piers and was decked with $\frac{5}{4} \times 6$ in. treated lumber. For this generic project we shall assume that the patio is 14 ft wide and 20 ft long. Further, the posts must be installed flush with the headers of the frame or held back from the edge $1\frac{1}{2}$ in. Look at Figure 6-1 and grasp an overview of the project. Find the following; railings everywhere except at the exit, where steps will be built, equally spaced sections on both 14-ft sides, two sections on one side of the opening and one on the other side. All posts and newels are 4×4 treated lumber (see detail corner post and railing). A 2×6 cap is beveled and installed on top of each post. Rail sections are made from 2×4s, and the balusters are 2×2 with simple shaping made on a bandsaw.

One problem that must be solved in every installation is the one about fastening the posts to the deck or frame below the deck. For the generic project we shall opt for the surface mounting of posts on the top of the decking. Three post anchoring techniques are shown in Figure 6-1. The one on the left requires an electric drill and $2\frac{1}{2}$-in. screws installed on both insides of each 4×4 post. (Note: Wherever you see the word *screws,* always assume *screws for drywall.*) The center one employs an angle iron coated heavily with zinc (galvanized). Screws or lag bolts hold the metal to post and floor. The one on the right employs a U-plate specially bent for 4×4. This one requires a wood chisel to make a groove in each side to receive the U-plate; alternatively a router can be used to make most of the groove; then a chisel is used to clean out the corners. In addition, a 1-in. hole needs to be made into the bottom of each post to make room for the lag screw head. The U-plate is lag-screwed to the floor first, and then the post is placed over it and held in place with screws. In terms of greatest strength to least strength, the U-plate is best and the screw nail technique is poorest.

Materials Assessment

Table 6.1 provides a materials assessment for this generic project. A scan of the list should reveal no surprises. There may be a question about the indirect material—layout 1×2. If the sections are equal in length as shown in the figure, the layout stick should aid in maintaining the exact spacing of the balusters—2×2 uprights.

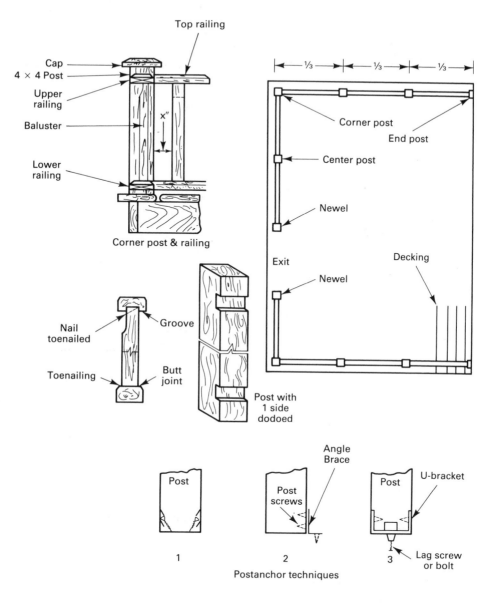

Figure 6-1 Railing design and details for wood decks.

TABLE 6.1 Materials Assessment
PROJECT: *Installing Railings on a Wood Deck*   **DATE:** _____

Direct Materials

Type or Description	*Use or Purpose*
2 × 4 railings	Sets perimeter of deck
2 × 2 molded uprights (balusters)	Part of railing assembly
4 × 4 posts	Supports for the rail assemblies
Anchor plates	Provides sound post support
Nails, screws (for drywall), bolts	Anchoring devices
2 × 6 post caps	Decorative touch to posts

Indirect Materials

Type or Description	*Use or Purpose*
Layout 1 × 2 stick	Spacing 2 × 2s in rail assemblies

Support Materials

Type or Description	*Use or Purpose*
Carpentry tools	Preparation and installation of railings
Power saw	Ripping 2 × 2s, cross-cutting posts, rail pieces
Router	Shapes edges and grooves rail
Drill bits (including a plug maker bit)	Drive screws and bore holes for bolts
Bandsaw or saber or jigsaw	Shape the upper curve in 2 × 2s
Sawhorses and planks	Workbench

Construction Techniques

There will be some need to use a router, power saw, bandsaw or saber or vibrator saw, and drill plus several different bits. But let's start the usual way by listing the tasks to be accomplished:

1. Lay out the positions of each post and newel.
2. Measure the 4 × 4 and cut all posts 30 in. long.
3. Dado each post side that will receive a railing.
4. Prepare a post cap from 2 × 6 materials.
5. Install the posts, using an anchoring technique and brace plumb.
6. Cut all upper and lower rails to length and mark each 1, 2, 3, and so on.
7. Turn the upper rails upside down and make a 1-in.-wide dado about $\frac{3}{16}$ in. deep with router.

8. Style the upper rail with bevels and slightly bevel the lower ones.
9. Install the rails, using toenailing.
10. Lay out the baluster positions, using the layout stick.
11. Cut the correct number of balusters and shape the top end as shown.
12. Nail the 2 × 2 balusters in place with toenailing; set nails.
13. Add trim cap to each post.
14. Clean up.

Now let's discuss some of the tasks beginning with step 2. The 30-in. height specified actually makes the post and cap 31½ in. high. But the top rail is 28½ in. high (3 in. lower). If you desire a different height, make the adjustment to meet the need.

Dadoing in the posts may be a problem for you. It can be done with a portable saw and chisel or router in a guide. The dado needs to be only ¼ in. deep but it makes the entire project more professional-looking and a great deal stronger. With the rails inserted into the dadoes there is no chance of the railing collapsing from force. For task 7, a dado should be made 3 in. in from each end of the post. On the corner posts make them on sides that touch. On center posts make them on opposite sides.

Making the dado on the under side of the top rail is important; it should be done with a ¾-in. dado bit in the router. Then two passes with the router, one from each side, makes the 1 in. by $\frac{3}{16}$ in. deep groove. Installing the 2 × 2 uprights is infinitely easier and the possibility of rot is removed. For task 8, the top of each rail piece should be rounded or beveled as shown in Figure 6-1.

The alternative to step 9 is to assemble each section on the bench. If this technique is used, the bottom of each 2 × 2 can be nailed through the lower 2 × 4. Two nails are a must. Toenailing is superior, even though the nail head holes will need filling. As each section is completed, it can be slid into the dadoes on the posts and toenailed in place.

With regard to task 11, the French curve made into the top of each 2 × 2 upright should extend down from the top about 5 to 6 in. Once cut, each should be sanded smooth. Also dress the sawn side of the 2 × 2, since it was ripped from a 2 × 4. (It is rare to find treated 2 × 2s.)

The portable saw, a bandsaw, or the router may be used to bevel the 2 × 6 post caps once they are cut for size. First, make a cap for each post that is square (2 × 6 square). Then make a bevel on all four top sides with either a bandsaw or a portable power saw set to a bevel. These cuts are most easily made on a table saw. If a router is used, a ½-in. ¼ round bit should be used; but the design will be different.

Refinements.   Several refinements should be made. One is to use a block plane or router and slightly round the four corners of each post. The same technique should be used on each 2 × 2 baluster. The anchoring of each post can be improved. If anchor scheme 1 is used, predrilling each screw hole with a pilot screw drill bit ensures that a ledge exists inside the hole. This makes the anchor more secure. If scheme 2 is selected for anchoring posts, lag bolts/screws should be used in the post. The lag screw used in the floor should be longer so that it penetrates the flooring and is deeply embedded into the header. If scheme 3 is used, the lag bolt/screw must also penetrate the flooring and be deeply embedded into the headers. Finally, the cap pieces should be predrilled with a $\frac{3}{8}$-in. seat where wood plugs can be glued in place after the screws are installed.

Concluding Comments

The entire project is one that requires considerable skill. Every piece must be measured and cut exactly right. Every post must be exactly the same length, and it must stand exactly plumb. This means that even pressure must exist everywhere. If one piece is too long or too short, the total job looks bad. Each 2×2 baluster must be exactly spaced and when installed it must be exactly plumb. The rails must be made from lumber that is free of defects and knots. This work is the most visible of any concerning the deck. No top nailing must be done in the top rails. Do a really good job. Throw away materials that are defective, twisted, or split and ones that contain knots.

METHOD FOR CONSTRUCTION OF WOOD DECK STEPS AND MATERIALS ASSESSMENT

For this project we use Figure 6-2 to obtain illustrations of the most difficult aspects. There are many new terms associated with building stairs; these are all found in the figure. Locate the *treads, stringers, block pier,* and *angle iron bracket.* Not shown are the newel post, which is fastened to the stringer through the lower stair tread, the railings, and the 2×2 balusters which are cut with angles to permit plumb installation.

We have several problems to solve in this generic project to ensure that sound construction results. First, there must be a sound footing for the stringers to rest on. Next, the stringers must be laid out for equal rises and runs. Next, the stringers must be securely anchored to both the footing and the deck framing. Finally, after the treads have been installed, the railings must be stable and sound.

The opening on the deck railing from Figure 6-1 was about 5 ft wide. The stairs for the generic project will need to be 6 in. wider on each side than the opening. This translates to a 6-ft wide stair. The outside stringer must be centered on each deck newel for maximum strength of the rail assembly.

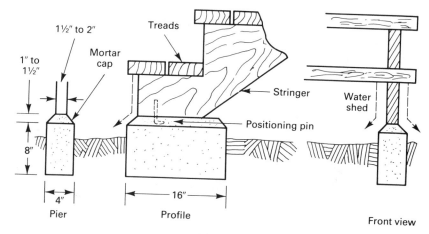

(a)

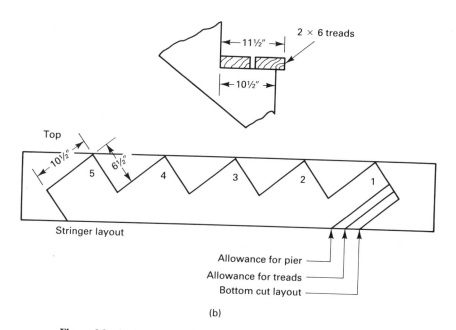

(b)

Figure 6-2 Stair design and detail for above-the-ground wood deck.

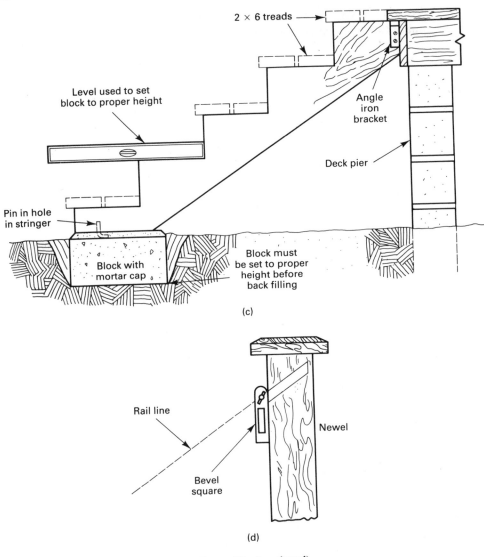

(c)

(d)

Figure 6-2 (continued)

Materials Assessment

Table 6.2 provides an assessment of the materials necessary for this generic project. Even though the power saw is listed and used, the final cutout of each run and rise on the stringer must be made with the hand saw. In no way can the cut be deeper than the cutting lines indicate. Structural failure will surely happen if the electric saw is used to make the full cut.

TABLE 6.2 Materials Assessment
PROJECT: *Wood Deck Steps and Railings*   **DATE:** _____

Direct Materials

Type or Description	Use or Purpose
Stringers	Main supports of stairs
Treads	Step surfaces
Footings, block and mortar	Anchor base of stringers
Bolts, J-bolts, nails, screws (for drywall)	Anchors, fasteners
Mortar mix and sand	For runoff and J-bolt anchor
Railing assemblies and newel posts	Safety and convenience

Indirect Materials

Type or Description	Use or Purpose
Backfill dirt	Establish the height of footings
1×2	Spacer stick for 2×2s and bracing newel during assembly

Support Materials

Type or Description	Use or Purpose
Carpentry tools	Construct stairs
Mason tools	Install blocks, footings
Mortar box	Mix mortar in
Shovel and hoe	Mix mortar
Power saw and drill with bits	Aids in construction
Sawhorses and planks	Work surface

Construction Techniques

There is much to learn and do to build the stairs. Let's begin with making several assumptions. Let's assume that the finished floor height to ground is as shown in Figure 6-2c. Further, we want each step to fall within the "rule of 17." This means that the combination of rise and run of each step sum to about 17 in. The treads will be made from two 2×6s spaced $\frac{1}{2}$ in. As shown in the Figure 6-2b detail, the stringer *run* cut is $10\frac{1}{2}$ in. The *rise* for our generic project is $6\frac{1}{2}$ in. This design will produce a very comfortable and gentle stair.

The tasks are as follows:

1. Lay out and cut three stringers as shown in Figure 6-2b.
2. Cut 10 treads 6 ft long and bevel the edges with a block plane.
3. Cut three pieces of 2-in. angle iron, 6 in. long; drill holes for screws.
4. Position each pier block.

5. Cap each pier block with a mortar bed and J-bolt embedded.
6. Drill a pilot hole into the bottom of the stringer after trimming it.
7. Bolt the three stringers in place.
8. Install the treads.
9. Build the railing assemblies.

Task 1 is somewhat difficult to accomplish, but it is mostly easily done with the framing square. Since the given specifications are 10½ in. by 6½ in., use one measurement on the blade and the other on the tongue. Step off the five steps needed. At the top mark 10½ in. back from the outer point and then make a 90-deg turn back. This will be the mounting surface for the angle bracket. Reserve the trimming of the bottom of the stringer until the block piers are in place. Should there be any variation in their height, each stringer can be custom cut to fit where the run part will be absolutely level (see Figure 6-2c).

In each application the rule of 17 should be maintained as closely as possible when standard stairs are to be built. The way to determine the number of runs is to divide the expected height of the stairs from ground to the porch or deck floor by numbers ranging from 6 to 8 in. The object is to find an equal number of risers. For example,

A 35-in. difference equates to 5 7-in. risers.
A 40-in. difference equates to 5 8-in. risers.
A 44-in. difference equates to 6 7⅜ in. risers.

Tasks 2 and 3 should need no explanation, but task 4 does. The positioning of the piers requires use of several techniques and principles. First the position of each is required. If the stringers were cut first, as I suggest, they can simplify the location and height of the piers. Simply placing the stringer against the header on the deck, tacking it, and then squaring it with the framing square from deck header to stringer identifies its ground position exactly. Once it is located, a rough mark on the ground will show where to dig the hole. While the stringer is positioned, it can be raised and lowered to level the tread run. This information translates into how deep to set the block into the ground. One easy way to maintain the height information is to drive a small stake into the ground near each hole area. Minor adjustments can be made during the installation of the pier. Backfill is tamped around the pier. Then the J-bolt and mortar cap are added. The exact height of the mortar should be about 1 in.

Installing the railing assemblies follows the rules we studied in the previous section. If you are using path B, refer there for specifics. For the differences we are faced with here, the problem is with the angle cuts on the rails and the 2 × 2 balusters. Here is where the bevel square comes in handy. First install the bottom newel posts centered over the outer stringers. Use the same anchoring techniques as was used on the posts of the railings.

Transfer the position of the rails on the upper newel posts to the lower ones. Then use a piece of railing materials slightly longer than necessary to reach between posts and mark the angle on the newels. Set the bevel square to align alongside the post and line, as shown in Figure 6-2d. Then you have the angle for all pieces. The wood part of the bevel square represents the angle of the railing pieces, and the blade represents the angle of the tops and bottoms of each 2 × 2 baluster. Be sure to plumb and temporarily brace each newel before making any measurements. Once in position, hand-fit each piece. Be sure to groove the bottom of the rail and chamfer the top edges before installing them.

Try to maintain the same spacing on the 2 × 2s that was used on the deck railings to continue symmetry. The top bevel must be cut first in order to maintain the dimensions of the curve in each 2 × 2. Then the level should be used alongside the 2 × 2 to ascertain the exact length of the piece. With one cut exactly right, it can and should be used as the pattern for the remaining pieces.

The railings and 2 × 2s are all held in place with toenails. The nail holes should be filled to prevent staining, which usually happens with weathering.

Remember, no nails must be driven through the top railings into the 2 × 2s.

METHODS FOR CONSTRUCTION OF WOOD DECK PERIMETER SEATING AND MATERIALS ASSESSMENT

Some people prefer to have perimeter seating around a deck instead of railings. It really is a matter of the functional uses one intends to make of the deck. In this section we shall learn about making a seating arrangement from 2-in. materials that is very attractive, sound, and functional. Take a look at Figures 6-3 and 6-4 to obtain an overall concept of the work that needs to be done. There are, as you can see, no large members that extend down over the headers. Rather, there are frames made from treated 2 × 3s. The idea is to make enough of these frames to space one about every four feet as well as additional ones near the corners. The frames are fastened to the flooring, and then the seat and back materials are screwed to them.

Let's identify the various pieces we will need to prepare. In each frame there is a long back piece (back leg) that also acts as one of the two legs. The shorter front leg supports the seat support or brace. Two 2 × 6s and one 2 × 4 make up the seating material. Depending on how high one wants the back, three or four 2 × 6s make up the back. Finally, one 2 × 4 or 2 × 6 is used as the cap. Aside from screws and several blocks of wood, which are used in the corners, no other direct materials are needed.

What we must be concerned with is building strength in the frames. We shall spend some time later with the details. But, as an overview, certain joinery techniques and skills must be used. The principal joint is the *ship-lap*. In itself the

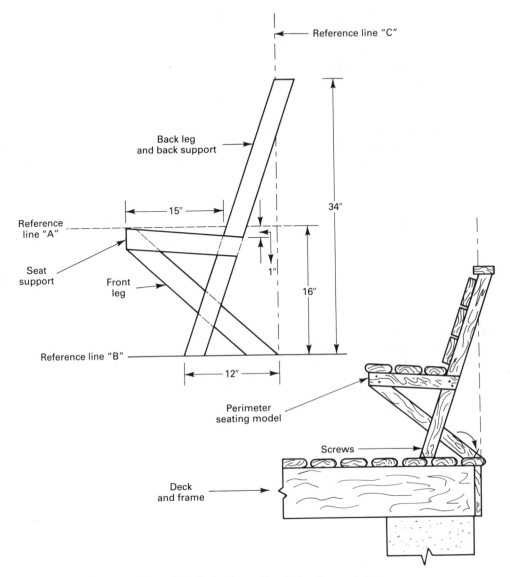

Figure 6-3 Perimeter seating design for wood deck.

joint is not that difficult to make, but the angles required for the task are considerably more difficult to make. Therefore, patterns must be made.

Let's assume that the deck we are to install the perimeter seating around is the same one shown in Figure 6-1. It is 14 ft by 20 ft. It has a 5-ft opening for the exit to the stairs. This means that we will have 14 ft of seating on each end, 5 ft on one side of the opening and 10 ft on the other side. These lengths do not require splicing for the seating, backing and cap.

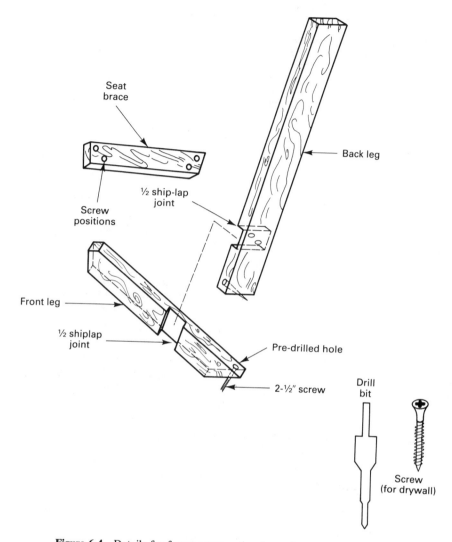

Figure 6-4 Details for frame construction for perimeter wood deck seating.

Materials Assessment

Although we have discussed the variety of materials needed for the project, it is a good idea to make an assessment, as shown in Table 6.3. The best type of power saw for this work is the table saw. Ripping 2 × 6 pieces into 2 × 3s is easier. Making the ship-lap joints with compound miters is very easy once the fence is set. If a portable power saw is used, a jig must be constructed to ensure the accuracy needed for the joints and other angles.

TABLE 6.3 Materials Assessment
PROJECT: *Wood Deck Perimeter Seating*   DATE: _____

Direct Materials

Type or Description	*Use or Purpose*
2 × 3s	Seat frame pieces
2 × 4s and 2 × 6s	Seats and backs
2 × 4s	Seat back caps
Screws (for drywall)	Secures frames together, secures frames to deck, and secures 2-in. materials to frames
On-site-made wood hole plugs	Fill holes where screws are installed and would be visible

Indirect Materials

Type or Description	*Use or Purpose*
Pattern of seat frame pieces	Reusable pattern
1 × 2 and 1 × 4	Maintains seat frame alignment while seats and backs are installed

Support Materials

Type or Description	*Use or Purpose*
Power saw and drill with bits	Prepare and assemble frames; also secures seats and backs
Carpentry tools	Construction
Router (optional)	Molding the edge of the seats and back cap

Construction Techniques and Tasks

In agreement with the organization of the book, let's first itemize the tasks that must be done:

1. Rip 2 × 6 material into 2 × 3s unless 2 × 3s are available for the frames.
2. Dress the sawn edge with a plane; chamfer the edges with a block plane.
3. Prepare a pattern by using the data in Figure 6-3. Observe Figure 6-4 to understand the relationships of each piece.
4. Cut all like pieces at one time. Cut several extra in case one or more crack or split.
5. Predrill holes for each screw, as shown in Figure 6-4.
6. Assemble all the frames.
7. Locate the position of each frame on the deck.

8. Install each frame as illustrated on the drawing, with the back of the leg even with the line of the header.
9. Install a 1 × 2 temporarily across the top of each frame to establish vertical alignment.
10. Cut and install the seating material.
11. Cut and install the back material.
12. Cut and install the cap.
13. Fill and seal the screw holes.

Preparing the Frames.   (Refer to Figure 6-3.) We need five frames for each 14-ft end, three for the 10-ft length, and two for the 5-ft section for a total of 15. Rough-cut 17 pieces of 2 × 3 38 in. long, 17 more 28 in., and 17 more 18 in. This gives us an idea of how much we need to prepare for tasks 1, 2, and 3. Now let's make the pattern.

We will use the shop method to describe and make all measurements rather than deal with a wide variety of angles. Once the angles are indicated on the pattern, the bevel square can be used to set the guide on the table saw.

Find a piece of plywood about 2 ft by 4 ft (hardboard or a workshop bench top may also be used). Draw reference lines *a, b,* and *c* as shown in Figure 6-3. Next take the frame back piece and lay it flat, in position, as shown in Figure 6-3. Mark the position along both sides. While it is in place, make a line on the bottom even with reference *b.* Make another 90 degrees from reference line *c,* near the top of the back piece. Remove the piece and cut both angles. (*Note:* Both angles are the same angle.) Next take the front leg piece and position it as shown. Make sure that at least 1 in. of it extends above reference line *a* and is no shorter than 23 in. from reference line *c.* Mark the position on the plywood or other work surface. While it is in position, mark the base angle and the two angles at the top of the leg. Cut the angles.

Now for the difficult part—laying out and cutting the ship-lap joints. By describing the one for the front leg, we shall understand the process for layout of the other. Begin by laying the front leg exactly over the pencil lines drawn earlier. Set the combination square equal to the thickness of the 2 × 3. Then draw four lines—one at each point where the back leg lines intersect with the front leg. Next use the adjustable bevel square and set it to connect each pair of lines in the direction of the back leg. Next, set the combination square for exactly half the thickness of the 2 × 3. Draw a line as shown in Figure 6-4 midway between the vertical lines on each side of the 2 × 3. Put an "X" on the top to signify that this is the wood to remove in making the joint. The piece is ready to cut.

When repeating the process for the back leg, connect the four lines on the *bottom* and mark the "X" there, since that is the material to cut away.

Make the two halves of the ship-lap joint and test for precision and accuracy. The joint is correct if:

1. The surfaces are flush when joints are together.
2. The two pieces slip firmly, not sloppily or so tight that they must be driven together with severe hammer blows.

Next predrill two holes with a head recess of $\frac{1}{8}$ in. in one of the outer surfaces of the joint as shown in Figure 6-4. Use two $1\frac{1}{4}$-in. screws (for drywall) and fasten the pieces together.

Then, lay the seat brace 2 × 3 in the following position. The front of it must be flush with the front leg and the rear must be even with reference *a*. When it is in position, predrill four holes (see Figure 6-4). The screw head should be $\frac{1}{8}$ to $\frac{1}{4}$ in. below the surface. The bit must penetrate the entire thickness of the 2 × 3 and part way into the front and back legs.

Screw the 2 × 3 to the legs. Then take the frame to the deck and position it. While someone holds it, observe its position and imagine the finished seat. If all looks well, take all the screws out and use the three pieces as the pattern. Make all the frames.

Tasks 7, 8, and 9 involve installing the frames. Each leg is screwed to the deck with $2\frac{1}{2}$-in. screws (for drywall) in a toenailing or bevel fashion. The frame will stand by itself when fastened. Task 9 would have you use a 1 × 2 to tack nail each frame in a plumb (vertical) alignment. The best way to start is with the 14-ft 1 × 2 butted against the wall of the house. Then one by one, use a spirit level and align each frame. When plumb, drive a 6d fin nail part way into the back leg through the 1 × 2.

Since the closest a frame will be set to the outside corner is about 22 in., let the 1 × 2 overhang a couple of feet. Either clamp the two 1 × 2s together on the corner, or tack nail the two together. This sets the reference again and eliminates the need for constant rechecking for plumb on the front or leading edge of the deck.

Tasks 10, 11, and 12 can now be done. Begin with the outer 2 × 6 seat pieces. Make them extend out about $\frac{3}{4}$ in. beyond the front leg. Bevel both leading and back edges of every 2 × 6 and 2 × 4 in the seat.

Fitting the corners requires a compound miter cut. Set the portable saw for an undercut of no more than 5 deg. Then use the combination square to mark the 45-deg lines for cutting. This compound miter will take into account the slight backward tilt of the seat.

After all seat pieces are in place, a 2 × 6 block must be cut and installed *under* each corner so that half of the 2 × 6 supports the ends coming from one direction and the other half supports the other ones. Use the same screwing techniques to fasten the seat pieces to the block.

Next, cut and install the back pieces, beginning either at the top or at the seat, your choice. The important thing is to lay out the space for equal separation. When making the outside corner let each piece overhang as needed, then mark and make the compound miter. After the piece making up a corner are fit, install screws (for drywall) from the outside of the deck area when joining the seat ends together.

Finally, cut the pieces for the cap and install them. The outer edge of each piece should be flush with the outside of the frame back leg. Plug holes with wood plugs and trim these with either a portable sander or chisel.

Conclusion

The three enhancements to the above-ground deck are really necessary, although either a railing or seating arrangement must be selected. More important than anything else is the need for excellent craftsmanship. Joinery is used in these projects, and all joints must fit accurately. Sloppy joint making will result in a bad job. If necessary, practice making the joints until you are successful.

7

Finishing Techniques for Wood Decks

OBJECTIVES

- Identify the techniques used to preserve wood.
- For each condition that can destroy the wood in a deck, identify the proper materials that will prevent its happening.
- Identify the various finishes that can be used for finishing the wood surface of the wood deck.

PROTECTION TECHNIQUES AND MATERIALS
FOR THE WOOD DECK

After spending several hundred, or more, dollars to build a wood deck, many choose to allow it to weather naturally. Depending on the species of wood used, most turn gray, but some turn black. Still other woods immediately begin decaying, knots fall out when the wood binding them decays, and the sun twists and turns the pieces, splitting and warping them.

Even treated wood, where the treatment permeates throughout the thickness, has weathering problems. Some of these problems can be attributed to the effects of sun. Most, however, are caused by improper application of chemicals in mass production operations.

In this chapter we look at some preservation techniques that extend the life of the wood in a deck, and we also examine other problems caused by insects and fungus. We reverse the usual method of listing the tasks first. Here we describe the problems and solutions, and then list the tasks.

Mechanical Protection Methods

In Figure 7-1 you see several different applications of mechanical deterrents to ground-type insects. The device is called a *termite shield*. We used one in the project of building a wood deck above ground. A termite shield is made from

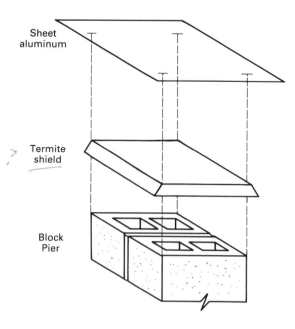

Figure 7-1 Termite shields.

aluminum or copper or sometimes galvanized sheet metal. It is used to prevent wood borers, including termites, from attacking the wood. Note that the shield is made to fit over the pier and extend about 1 in. greater on all sides. Note also that the overhang is sloping down about $\frac{3}{4}$ in. to 1 in. Borers are attracted to the wood and actually climb or crawl up the cement pier to the wood. Because of the downward slope of the termite shield they cannot crawl on the surface, and thus cannot reach their goal. Termite shields of this type are used along foundations as well when necessary.

In most new construction termite shields are not used around the foundation, because ordinances require the entire ground under and around the house to be treated for termites before the house foundation is constructed or the slab is poured. But when enhancements are made after several years, the termite shield is necessary.

The tasks are

1. Determine where the termite shields are to be used.
2. Measure the amounts of material needed.
3. Purchase the aluminum in a standard width most suitable to the termite shield size needed.
4. Cut, bend, and install the shields at the proper time.

Wood Preservatives

For a single product to be effective in protecting wood it must contain several ingredients: a sunscreen to reduce the effects of the sun's drawing power, a waterproof agent that causes the water to shed instead of penetrating, and a fungicide that prevents or retards the accumulation of fungus and mildew spores, and a chemical that retards or prevents wood borers. The other property a wood protector must have is the consistency to penetrate deeply into the wood.

There are several chemicals listed in Table 7.1 which can be used singularly to protect wood from one or more of the problems stated above. As indicated, they may be brushed on, sprayed, or dipped. These chemicals can also be applied commercially under high pressure or by immersion under pressure.

TABLE 7.1 Preservatives and Application Methods

Types of Preservatives	Method of Application
Water-borne salt solutions	Pressure
Creosote and creosote coal tar solution	Brush, pressure
Pentachlorophenol	Pressure
Copper naphthenate	Brush, Dipping
Thompson's Wood Protector[1]	Brush, roller, spray, dipping

[1] Wood Protector is a trademark product of Thompson & Formby, Inc., Memphis, Tennessee.

The salt preservatives leave the wood comparatively clean, comparatively easy to paint, and free from odor. Creosote, on the other hand, blackens the wood and after many years bleaches to a dark brown. It cannot be painted over, and it retains a strong odor for many years. Copper naphthenate turns the wood green; when air-dried, the treated wood may be painted and will take stain. Penta-chlorophenol is an effective agent against fungus and other spores and leaves the treated wood green when dry. The wood after treatment may be painted or coated with semitransparent or heavy-bodied stains.

Protection Schemes

There are several protection schemes that produce different effects as well as meet different goals. We shall briefly discuss some of these. They all include using one or more products which are applied to the lumber or require specific conditions to be met.

Protecting the wood, but retaining the natural color and texture. Varnish, polyurethane, and other products such as Thompson's Wood Protector and Thompson's Water Seal[1] have properties to penetrate the wood surface to varying degrees and seal the cells against water. Varnish was for many years the only solution to wood protection. Later polyurethane was widely accepted. Both of these products are tough, but cannot withstand the ultraviolet rays and break-down in the form of cracking and peeling. Once the moisture gets behind the outer coating, the product fails much more quickly. Therefore, resurfacing must be done every several years.

According to Thompson's information, Thompson's Water Seal contains water sealing agents that penetrate rather than just top cover the wood. The Thompson's Wood Protector protects against water damage as well as biological and weather damage.[2]

Application Techniques. In every case the wood surface to be coated needs to air-dry several weeks to a month. If pressure-treated lumber is used, the 30-day time frame is desirable. If untreated lumber is used, two weeks is appropriate. There is a need for the lumber to air-dry because the usual stacking methods in lumber yards do not permit drying to take place. More frequently than not moisture is trapped between boards, and this must escape if a good seal is expected.

After several weeks of good weather, following the instructions provided by the manufacturer of the product should result in a satisfactory job. For example, Thompson's Wood Protector and Thompson's Water Seal should be applied in

---

[1] Thompson's products are registered trademarks. Information about them can be obtained from Thompson's, 825 Crossover Lane, Memphis, Tennessee, 38117.

[2] Thompson's Wood Protector, Product Information Sheet.

thin even coats. Usually, one coat is enough for these products, and they *do not recommend applying a very heavy coat* (see Figures 7-2 and 7-3).

This is good advice. In fact, a test can be made to see if a second coat is really needed. Wet the surface that was coated with water. If there is no darkening, coverage is complete. If blotches or dark patches appear after several minutes, reapplication is indicated.

The tasks are

1. Allow the appropriate time for natural air-drying.
2. Fill nail or screw holes with a wood filler or carpenter's putty.
3. Clean the surfaces to be coated with a mixture of detergent and bleach mixed with water; wash with water and let dry several days.
4. Following the instructions on the product, apply one or more coats.
5. Clean up tools, brushes, sprayer, and so on.

Protecting the wood and staining it as well.   This is frequently a two-step operation, but some companies make a stain that contains a sealer as well. If a product contains the stain and surface protector in one can, a simpler application is possible.

Figure 7-2 Thompson's Water Seal being applied. (Courtesy of Thompson's, Memphis, Tennessee.)

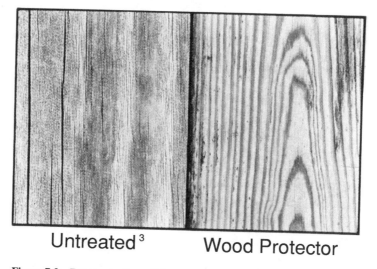

Untreated [3]   Wood Protector

Figure 7-3   Demonstration of Thompson's Wood Protector. (Courtesy of Thompson's, Memphis, Tennessee.)

Exterior stains come in two different types and a variety of colors. One type is the *semitransparent* variety. A light stain, it is usually oil-based. It is applied in the usual ways with brush or sprayed. It penetrates very well. It is subject to fading, but all of the grain of the wood shows. The other type is the *heavy-bodied* or *solid* variety. These stains are more often made with an acrylic-based formula. Once applied, in the same method as semitransparent ones, they tend to disguise the grain to a large extent. Some manufacturers combine both oil and acrylic in the same mixture and also add sealers and other chemicals to improve the lasting and protection capabilities.

If stain does not have the sealer added, a top clear seal coat is necessary. The tasks are

1. Allow the appropriate time for natural air-drying.
2. Fill nail or screw holes with a wood filler or carpenter's putty.
3. Clean the surfaces to be coated with a mixture of detergent and bleach mixed with water; wash with water and let dry several days.
4. Following the instructions on the product, apply one or more coats of stain and let dry.
5. Apply one or more top coat sealers if the stain is not a combination product.
6. Clean up tools and equipment.

Protecting the wood with paint.   The preliminary conditions with regard to allowing the wood to air dry several weeks to a month also apply to finishing the exposed wood with paint. Once this time has passed, primer and a top or final coat of paint must be applied in that order. Again, the best recommendation to follow is the one provided by the manufacturer.

The tasks are

1. Allow the appropriate time for natural air-drying.
2. Fill nail or screw holes with a wood filler or carpenter's putty.
3. Clean the surfaces to be coated with a mixture of detergent and bleach mixed with water; wash with water and let dry several days.
4. Following the instructions on the product, apply the primer and let dry.
5. Apply the top or final coat of paint.
6. Clean up tools and equipment.

Preventing decay on materials by natural means.   Materials exposed to the elements can last a long time if proper air circulation and drainage around them is planned, rather than left to chance. First, the slope of the soil around the wood post, tread, or any vertical or horizontal member should be uniform at sufficient angle to afford complete drainage. When pools of water are not permitted to remain, the development of fungi and rot are significantly reduced. Also reduced is the opportunity for ground bugs normally found in wet soil to eat their way into the damp wood. When air flow is encouraged as well, even greater life expectancy of wood is achieved.

The tasks are

1. Preplan for 100 percent natural air flow around all wood materials.
2. Preplan for natural drainage of water and moisture where wood products are in touch with the ground or are close to the earth.
3. Execute the preplanned actions.

For the wood deck above ground, air circulation is, for the most part, inherent in the structure. But where the steps lead to the ground, a preplan must be developed and used. If you studied the last chapter, you may remember that the stringers were set above ground level at least 1 in.

The technique that solves the problem of moisture run-off and maximum air circulation is to elevate the wood above the ground and slope the ground in the direction of the rainfall. As shown in Figure 7-4, setting the wooden stringer on a cement block whose edges are tapered with mortar enables the rain to run off the wood and the top of the block as well. Tapering or sloping the ground in the direction of the rainfall prevents water from becoming stagnant and thus eliminates the moisture necessary for growth of fungi and the harboring of insects and termites.

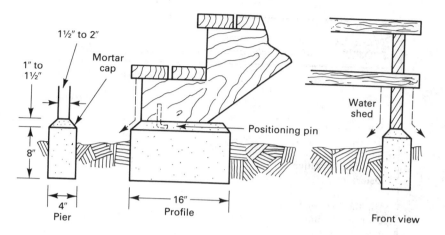

Figure 7-4 Preventing decay and rot with 100 percent air flow and planned drainage.

MATERIALS ASSESSMENT

According to conditions, one gallon of wood protection material, stain, or paint covers from 100 sq ft to 300 sq ft. That is why most manufacturers provide a range of coverage on each can. Therefore, when we make the materials assessment for these kinds of products, we must consider the conditions. Table 7.2 takes several of these considerations into account.

When a stain, paint, or other coating contains petroleum distillates, you will need mineral spirits to clean brushes, spray gun, and other equipment used in the operation. Those products that are thinned with water usually specify cleanup with warm soapy water and rinsing with water.

To ensure that the water sheds properly, use a spirit 2- or 4-ft level or a mason line and line-level to determine the amount of slope. Also identify where any high spots are that may cause puddling. The ground should slope evenly at about a minimum of $\frac{1}{2}$ in. per ten feet of run. Patio stones or slabs laid at the base of the steps must be recessed into the ground to avoid water puddling behind them.

To further enhance air flow avoid placing shrubs against the stringers of the steps. Most foliage on plants is quite dense, thus air flow is restricted. Also, foliage harbors moisture which can promote fungi and thus affect the wood in the stringers and the under sides of the treads. Plants placed a foot or more away from the steps should not affect the air flow and are far enough away to prevent moisture buildup around the stairs.

TABLE 7.2 Materials Assessment
PROJECT: *Finishing Techniques for Wood Decks*   **DATE:** _____

Direct Materials

Type or Description	*Use or Purpose*
Water sealer	Retards the penetration of water into the wood
Stains	Colors the wood
Wood preservative	Inhibits fungi and or insects
Detergent	Cleans the wood before application of finishes
Paint (primer and top coat)	Colors and protects wood
Carpenter's putty or wood filler	Seals nailhead holes

Indirect Materials

Type or Description	*Use or Purpose*
Spray gun and compressor	Apply finishing materials
Brushes	Alternative to spraying
Rollers	Alternative to brushes and sprayer
Mineral spirits	Cleaning agent for finishing materials containing petroleum distillates
Rags	Miscellaneous uses

Support Materials

Type or Description	*Use or Purpose*
Garden hose and container	Apply some products
Pail	Clean brushes, rollers, and spray outfit
Electric extension cord	Power spray outfit
Nail set and putty knife	Apply putty or wood filler
Other carpentry tools	As required

8

Repairing and Refurbishing Old Decks

OBJECTIVES

- Determine the technique best suited to removal and replacement of decayed or broken wood deck pieces.
- Define the sequence of steps needed to repair a wood deck with a defect.
- Use a checklist to make the examination for detecting and another for correcting the defect.

EXAMINING DECKS FOR DEFECTS

Examinations made on a wood deck include both visual inspection and probing under the surface for hidden damage. The examinations must involve all parts of the deck, including its framing, decking, steps, and perimeter seating or railings as applicable. There are three tasks related to inspection. They are

1. Inspection for visible signs of damage and decay.
2. Inspection for nonvisible damage by probing.
3. Making a listing of the damage for later use.

Even though the same types of defects may be present on different parts of the deck, we shall study the possibilities on a section-by-section basis, beginning with the framing.

Visual and Nonvisual Inspection of the Framing

Recall that the framing of the wood deck is made from 2-in. framing members called *sills, headers, joist,* and *bridging.* Each of these parts has a likelihood of sustaining damage and decay.

Sills.   Rot, sometimes called *dry-rot,* frequently occurs in sills. These members, as you will recall, lie flat on the piers and form one of the surfaces upon which the joist ends rest. What to look for are darkly stained spots that have small depressions. A real clue to look for is a ring of stain that resulted from the chemical concentration left when water evaporated. If this condition is seen, an awl can be used to probe center of the stained area to define the extent of the damage. Begin a notebook with the findings. List the exact location and the severity of the damaged wood. For example, as Figure 8-1 shows, the damaged sill is midway between piers 1 and 2. The note in the figure suggests that the rotten spot extends 3 in. under and out the other side of the joist. This may account for the squeak in the deck when family and friends walk there.

The second inspection of the sill is made around the blocks where the termite shields should have been installed. Small piles of sawdust powder are a sign of termite or other borer bugs. Probing is necessary to ascertain the extent of damage as well as to find out if they are still around. Another sign that indicates the presence of termites is scales or shell carcasses of the insects. Also make inspection around the J-bolt and washer. Look for rotted, blackened wood. This indicator could mean rot around the bolt. In terms of the stability of the deck's framing, there is little to be concerned about. The weight of the framing, decking, and railings will keep it still. But the fact that rot is visible may indicate more extensive and widespread damage and that the surface bearing on the pier may be suspect. Replacement of the rotted member may be necessary.

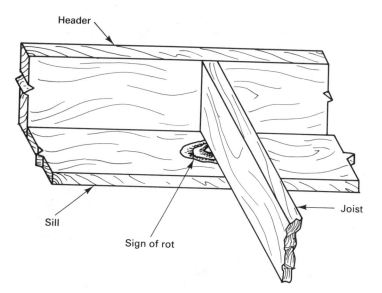

Figure 8-1 Dry rot in a sill.

Framing joists and headers. Joists and headers stand on edge, which, one would assume, makes damage less likely. Not so. Biological rot, wood borers, and physical damage do cause problems. In the situation of the deck where the decking pieces are spaced apart, water is permitted to stagnate on the tops of headers and joists and on flat surfaces of bridging. If air is restricted, rotting begins. The nature of the grain of wood contributes to decay. As wood fibers expand and contract due to water, moisture, and temperature, layers frequently become separated along the sides of the header and joist. This area traps moisture and fungi grows, further rotting the wood. This shows up as darkened wood, which usually can be probed and found to extend quite a way along the grain. If the wood was painted, peeling, discoloration, or bubbling occurs. The final suspect area for rot and insect damage is in the end of each header and joist. Once again, notes should be made when such evidence is present.

Wood borers are not concerned with the direction in which wood is positioned. They will readily eat in any direction.

Headers and joists may also be damaged in such a way from external force that there are resulting splits. Split headers or joists cannot bear the designed live and dead load. They must be repaired or replaced. If for some reason a severe load was placed on a section of the deck and later removed, resulting in overstressed joists, the modulus of elasticity was exceeded, and the joist cannot recover. A common example is an old barn, in which the beams sag after many years of supporting the roof rafters. This happens on decks too. Visual inspections may clearly show the sagged members. Another way of seeing the evidence

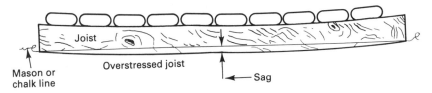

Figure 8-2 Permanently stressed joist.

is shown in Figure 8-2. The decking boards become loose, in that their nails are either pulled out a bit or the wood around the nails is worn away. When deck pieces are walked on, they give evidence of this condition. One sure way to verify that the situation exists and to determine how bad or extensive it is is to use a chalk line from end to end of each suspected joist and header. If the member sags below the line (see Figure 8-2), the member has a permanent defect.

Bridging.   Bridging made from spruce is very soft and can rot or be eaten away, but rarely does either. There is seldom a problem with this part of the framing.

In summary, look for dried water residue rings and probe for rot. Look for pockets of decay in the grain of joists and headers. Examine wood for sawdust collection as evidence of termites and other wood borers. Finally, look for split, sagging, and otherwise damaged members. As you inspect, make a list of these indicators, where they are, and how extensive the damage is.

Visual and Nonvisual Inspection of the Decking

The inspection of the decking is in some ways easier to do than the framing. All three types of problems identified earlier can exist in the decking members, and the rules for making visual and probing examinations apply here too. In addition, one or two other problems usually can be seen. The first of these is *wear* and *abrasion*. The pathways most frequently used, over time, will show wear and abrasion. The most likely spot for this is where the opening to the stairs is located. The continuing travel, as well as dragging furniture, bikes, sleds, and whatever each contribute to this problem. The other problem is *weathering*. Unless the decking is protected continuously, weathering will be significant in time. The first real evidence will show up at the exposed ends of each decking member. As time goes on, the weathering decayed wood will extend into the nailed area. When this happens, decking pieces become loose, and personal injury is possible. If we carry this idea to the extreme, ten years or more, the end can lose its strength, and someone walking on the $\frac{5}{4} \times 6$ in. board could fall through as it gives way under his or her weight. Weathering looks similar to that shown in Figure 8-3.

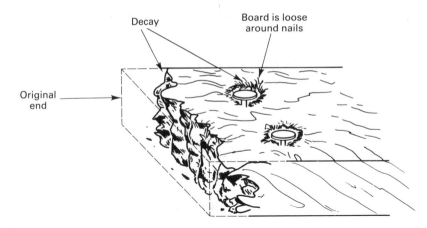

Figure 8-3 Weathered and rotted end of a deck member.

Visual and Nonvisual Inspections of Add-On Features

We could have either railings or perimeter seating, and stairs. The first problem (and probably the easiest one to spot) is a section of railing that gives way when force is applied. If it shakes, it needs fixing. If nails, bolts, or screws are loose, they need replacing; maybe the lumber is defective and needs replacing. If fasteners show rust or rust stains are extensive, decay is evident. They probably do not hold and the railing can be easily rocked. Examine the materials for biological damage, weathering, wear, and fungus growth, and probe for termite and other wood borer infestation. Add all indications to the list of damaged materials.

In the case of the perimeter seating, people will readily tell you when the benches feel unsafe to sit on. It may be any of the causes previously mentioned. Or it may be that physical damage has taken place due to an external force striking a part of the seats or their frames. Look for frames that have been broken loose from the decking, cracked frames especially around the lap-joint, and at joint areas where the caps join and where corners were fastened with the corner block. Newel posts are usually suspect, since these take much of the brunt of force. Check the bolts and angle iron materials for sound wood under washers.

When we talk of checking the stairs for defects, sagging is the first visual indicator. If the footer block has settled, for example, the stairs are uneven. Rot is very likely if dirt has been permitted to build up around the stringers. Physical damage to the stringers can be seen as split or cracked pieces. Stair treads that are not soundly attached to the stringers with nails indicate split or rotted stringer material under the treads.

A sample checklist that one could easily make is shown below:

Checklist to Record Defective Materials

Item	Condition and Location	Degree of damage
Joist Headers Decking etc.	Dry rot from end 2 ft	Extensive

DETERMINING THE EXTENT OF REPAIR

There are three parts to this job. They are

1. Estimating the materials and other supplies needed.
2. Defining the approximate sequence of repair tasks.
3. Applying the checklist to the job.

Let us begin this study with some rules that are essential in estimating the materials and other supplies needed to restore the deck to its former quality and looks.

Rule 1. Splicing alongside a defective member is a solution only if
    a. the splicing is not visible, or
    b. the cause of the original damage will not be carried over to the splice, or
    c. the splice can carry the design load.
Rule 2. Partial replacement is a solution if there is a sound anchoring for both ends of the piece being installed.
Rule 3. Full replacement is a solution where
    a. integrity is to be maintained, or
    b. the appearance is critical and no repairs may be evident.
Rule 4. Solution to the problem permits reuse of original materials.

With these rules we can make a qualified estimate of the extent of the repair job. Let's use several examples as references.

Example 1

A joist is cracked about 8 ft from one end. The floor squeaks when someone walks over the joist. The joist spans 14 ft and is an internal one. Close inspection does not reveal any rot, or borer damage. The adjacent joists are not damaged. We can splice another joist alongside the damaged one, because it will not show. We could nail or bolt a piece of joist about 8 ft long—4 ft extended on each side of the approximate center of the crack, but neither end would have a bearing. The best solution is to place another 14-ft joist alongside the cracked one with ends bearing properly. *Estimate.* One 14-ft joist, nails, a joist hanger, and replacement of two sets of bridging.

Example 2

The leading edge of the deck piece leading to the steps is badly torn as a result of wear and tear. The piece extends under both newel posts and a corner post. Close examination of the newels and rail assembly do not indicate damage. Further examination shows that the joists extend outward further than the opening of the stairs by one foot on each side. The best solution is to splice a new piece in place so that the newel posts will have new lumber to be fastened to. Work required includes careful removal of the newel posts and associated rails. Then cut and remove the defective piece, replace it with a new one, and reinstall the newels and rail assemblies. Follow with filling holes, staining, and sealing. *Estimate.* One deck piece, fasteners, new screws or bolts for the newels, filler putty, stain that will color the new piece to closely match the aged deck, sealer to protect the new wood.

Example 3

Let's assume that the kids (young or old) were horsing around and crashed into the perimeter seating. Three frames were torn loose, and another was cracked at the lap joint. In addition, the top cap joint was ruptured, splitting the back support. Work required includes removing the seat pieces, back pieces, and cap pieces, saving these for reuse. A minimum of four frames must be built. Others may need tightening. Then all new frames should be installed slightly (about $\frac{1}{2}$ in.) off center from the old ones to ensure sound screwing materials. Finally, the saved materials are reinstalled, and the stain and sealer are applied to the new wood to match the aged wood.

You may have noticed that the approximate sequence of repair is included in each example. This was done deliberately. There is a direct correlation between the assessment of material needs and the work that must be done. In almost all cases, as the examples show, more work must be done than the simple removal and replacement of the defective member or section.

If you make a checklist of elements of the deck and then use it to establish the exact condition, location, and degree of damage, it is very useful in making the estimates of materials and extent of repair.

REPAIR OF FRAMING SECTION

We treated the repair activities in the three examples very casually. In the event that it was difficult to apply the generalizations to all possibilities of repair, this section should help. There are three general tasks associated with each repair job. These are

1. Preparing for the removal of the defective pieces.
2. Removing and replacing the defective pieces.
3. Finishing the pieces to match the older ones.

The framing section consists of the joists, headers, sills and bridging, and the fasteners that hold everything in place. The deck may have stairs attached, and could have either railings and posts or perimeter seating. Let's assess each part separately, beginning with the sills.

Sills

A defective sill must be replaced. This will be the most difficult of all framing members to deal with. The *preparation for removal* of the sill consists of several activities. Weight of the floor joists and decking and everything on the deck must be lifted off the sill. This means that some form of shoring must be placed under the joists about 3 feet back from the sill or under the header attached to the sill to raise the floor assembly about $\frac{1}{2}$ to 1 in. The nut on the J-bolt must be removed.

The *removal and replacement* of the sill will probably require first cutting the sill near the bolt from under the deck. Then with the use of a crowbar, it is forced free from the header and joists. Then, by splitting the remaining pieces from around the J-bolt, the sill is removed. All nails must be withdrawn from the members. The new sill is cut to fit, and a slot is cut with a saw to access the J-bolt. The sill is placed properly and nailed as before. Finally, the washer and nut are reinstalled. Remove the shoring.

In this case there is no *need to finish* the sill. But we assume that treated materials are used. If not, a site treatment should be done before the piece is installed.

Headers

Headers cannot be spliced; they must be replaced. The *preparation for removal* of a header is always difficult. On one side of the deck all joists are nailed to the header; when the header is to be removed, shoring the joists is a must. When the header is not holding the joists, it is in fact the outside joist, and the decking is nailed to it with at least two nails per board. These nails must be pulled before the header is removed. In addition, railing bolts may be embedded in the header. These need to be removed, which means removing the railing assemblies and posts.

The *removal and replacement* activities include insuring the removal of all enhancements on the deck, removal of all nails from decking, freeing the bridging, and removal of nails connecting the header to joists or other headers. This should free the header. Next cut the new one and if necessary treat it before installing it.

Finishing the header is needed because it shows, and its newness will be evident for some years unless corrective measures are used. If the deck was stained, stain it again. If it was left to gray, use a stain or wash coat of gray to try to match the old color. Seal with the same sealer that you used before.

Joists

Joists can be either replaced or spliced. To prepare for work on the joists, the details of the examination must be studied. If there was or is wood borer damage different acts must be done. If the wood borers are gone for good, there is a great likelihood that a splice will be effective. If they are still present or if fungi are still present, the infected piece must be removed. In *preparation for removal* there will be only bridging to remove in splicing. But if replacement is required, the decking nailed to the joist must be loosened. No shoring is required.

For the *removal and replacement* all nails must be removed from the decking pieces, header, and joist hanger. Bridging on both sides must be removed entirely. Cut the joist in half and pull one half free of the joist hanger and the other free of the sill. Install the new joist (it will be difficult) and align it properly. Nails should be reinstalled from the header to the joist, through the joist hanger, and through the decking, using the same holes.

There is *no finishing required.*

REPAIR OF DECK SURFACE MATERIALS

The same three tasks apply here as in repairing the framing. They are

1. Preparing for the removal of the defective pieces.
2. Removing and replacing the defective pieces.
3. Finishing the pieces to match the older ones.

Since the decking pieces were installed with spacing between each, their removal and replacement would seem to be routine. But in most actual situations there are quite a few preparations needed before the removal can take place. *Preparation for removal* of decking will likely be in places of greatest use and greatest weathering and rot. If railings and/or perimeter seats are installed over the defective decking, they must be removed or at least freed sufficiently to remove the bad board(s). When these items are removed, care must be taken to avoid damage. Damage will result in added expense. When pieces are defective, their entire length should be *removed and replaced* even if some of its length is reusable. Several techniques are useful for accomplishing the task.

1. A nail puller tool is the desirable device to use.
2. If the pieces were screwed, an electric drill should be used to extract them.
3. Working from one end of the board, you will find that a crowbar or flat bar makes freeing the board easier. As the board is raised and released, some nails can be pulled free with a hammer.
4. Working from under the deck with a crowbar, you can loosen the board by driving the bar between the joist and flooring. Then the nails can be withdrawn with the crowbar or hammer.

Replacing the piece or pieces is simple. Measure and cut the new stock. Fit it in place and nail it to the joists and headers. If part of the old stock is visible, cut it to fit, half-lapping the joists, and install it with the underside up.

The *finishing process* may require a lot of work. Perimeter seats or posts and railings removed earlier must be reinstalled. If they were removed to make access, longer screws or bolts will probably be required, since the old holes are enlarged. If the same size screws are used, each hole in the decking can be partially filled with one or two wood match stems. In addition, the new pieces may need staining or painting, and the sealer should probably be used to prevent further decay and damage.

REPAIR OF ADD-ON FEATURES

The add-on pieces are the stair leading off the deck and perimeter seating and railings. These three are more subject to damage from wear and tear than other forms of damage because of their constant use and abuse. The rules apply to these items as well as to the framing and decking. Since all the materials are visible, the use of the splice is probably not a solution. More often the damaged pieces will need replacing.

Preparation for removal of the defective piece or pieces will be less extensive than removing deck and framing members. In the case of the stair stringer, the treads must be removed to gain access to the stringer. If posts in the railings are damaged, the railing assembly on each side of the post must be removed to make the task of post exchange possible. The same goes for seating that has damage. Once the defective piece or pieces have been exposed or freed, *removal and replacement* should begin. Bolts or screws should be removed first. The old piece should be used as a model if at all possible. Then the new piece should be cut and installed. However, the new lumber should be stained or painted before it is installed. Once in place, the adjoining treads, seats, or railing assemblies are reinstalled.

Then the *finishing process* should complete the job. Even if the new wood is already stained, added work such as filling holes and sealing the new wood with a protective coat should be done.

CHECKLISTS

There probably will be little occasion to devise checklists (C1, C2, and C3) as extensive as the following ones. However, they could be triggering devices that will ease the entire effort of deck repair and minimize the planning and estimating phases of the job.

CHECKLIST 1   Inspection of Wood Decks

Item	Condition and Location	Degree of Damage
1. Rail assembly		
2. Post or newel		
3. Post cap		
4. Seat frame		
5. Seat or back		
6. Seat cap		
7. Header(s)		
8. Joists		
9. Sill(s)		
10. Joist hangers		
11. Termite shields		
12. Step tread(s)		
13. Step stringer		
14. Step rail		
15. Stair newel		
16. Bridging		
17. Decking		

CHECKLIST 2   Extent of Repair and Estimate of Direct and Indirect Materials

Splice/Replace	Item	Dimensions and quantity		Unit	Price
e.g., Replace	post	4 × 4 4 ft	2	lin ft	$3.59
		Total cost			$_____

Framing

1. Will shoring be needed?	Yes_____	No_____
2. Is shoring in place?	Yes_____	No_____
3. Will framing member be replaced?	Yes_____	No_____
4. Is framing member free to be removed?	Yes_____	No_____
5. Is replaced member anchored securely?	Yes_____	No_____
6. Will framing member be spliced?	Yes_____	No_____
7. Is splice secure?	Yes_____	No_____
8. Has bridging been replaced?	Yes_____	No_____
9. Has member been treated?	Yes_____	No_____

Decking

1. Has add-on feature been removed to access decking?	Yes_____	No_____
2. Has decking piece been removed?	Yes_____	No_____
3. Has new deck piece(s) been fit and secured?	Yes_____	No_____
4. Has add-on feature been restored?	Yes_____	No_____

Add-on Railing

1. Has associate member(s) been carefully removed?	Yes_____	No_____
2. After removal of the damaged member, has the anchoring area been inspected and proved good?	Yes_____	No_____
3. Has new member been placed and secured?	Yes_____	No_____
4. Has associated member or assembly been reinstalled?	Yes_____	No_____

Add-on Seating

1. Have defective seat and backing members been removed?	Yes_____	No_____
2. Has defective frame been made free for removal?	Yes_____	No_____
3. Has replacement frame been installed?	Yes_____	No_____
4. Has replacement seat or back been installed?	Yes_____	No_____

Add-on Stairs

1. Has defective tread been removed and replaced?	Yes_____	No_____
2. Has newel post and railing been removed to access tread?	Yes_____	No_____
3. Has new tread been installed?	Yes_____	No_____
4. Have all treads and railing assembly been removed to access defective stringers?	Yes_____	No_____
5. Has a replacement stringer been cut and installed?	Yes_____	No_____
6. Have the newel posts and railing assemblies been reinstalled?	Yes_____	No_____

Finishing and Protection

1. Has the new exposed wood been colored to match aged members?	Yes_____	No_____
2. Have all holes been refilled?	Yes_____	No_____
3. Has a protective coating been applied to new wood?	Yes_____	No_____

Clean-up

1. Have all tools and machines been accounted for?	Yes_____	No_____
2. Have brushes or sprayer been cleaned?	Yes_____	No_____
3. Have the grounds been cleaned and restored?	Yes_____	No_____
4. Have workbenches and sawhorses been stored?	Yes_____	No_____

9

The Basic Design and Construction of the Porch Floor

OBJECTIVES

- Plan for the construction of a wood porch floor capable of supporting a roof and 40 psf live load.
- Design the specifications and materials listing for the porch floor.
- Define the foundation requirements and materials necessary to construct it.
- Make selections of lumber adequate to support the design parameters.
- Generally organize the sequences necessary to construct the floor assembly.
- Show the trimming of the porch floor assembly.
- Finalize the materials listing.

BACKGROUND

The subject of this chapter is building a porch floor assembly that will support a live load of 40 psf and later support a roof, since all porches have roofs. The roofing of the porch will be a subject in this section but in another chapter. Compared with the deck, which was the subject of Chapter 7, this design will be different because the porch floor will require a girder. We will learn how to design and build one and where to place it. In addition, the flooring will be different—tongue and groove. The porch will also have trim, whereas the deck did not.

There are two methods of supporting the framing and flooring as well as anticipating the force of the roof on the foundation selected. We could use piers and plan for the framed lattice panels to fill in between them. If so, we would want them strategically placed to coincide with the columns on the porch. Or, on the other hand, we could build a foundation from block or brick. If this option were selected, columns could bear anywhere along the foundation. All we would have to do is to make access to the underside of the floor and later close it up with a door. Since cement block piers were covered in an earlier chapter, we could refer to that area if the option is to use them for the piers. Likewise, we would refer to an earlier chapter for details on foundations of block construction. However, the use of the block is not necessarily that attractive, so we shall assume that the piers are made of brick where they are exposed and cement block where they are not. If you were to elect a full foundation of brick, adaptation of the information on block foundations and the bricklaying technique used in this chapter would be combined.

What are some terms we should become familiar with in this chapter? The *girder* is one. Different grades of framing materials will be used, including *machine rated grades*, and *common*. We will use *kiln-dried lumber*, as opposed to *air-dried* or *green*. Graded flooring will also be selected and used. Terms we already should know include *joist, headers, joist hangers, bridging, batter boards, concrete footings, foundation lines, finished floor height, slope of floor, mortar, striking joints, J-bolts*, and *termite shields*.

This is a complex project. Skill and knowledge of layout, batter board installation, masonry, bricklaying, mixing mortar, framing with the inclusion of a girder, installing tongue and groove flooring where nails do not show, and adding trim all contribute to the difficulty. In addition we must plan where the columns are to be located, which will indicate where to locate the piers. Many of the tasks can be done without assistance. The one where assistance could best be used is in the construction of the girder and its placement.

We need two views of the project—the floor plan and the elevation. (See Figure 9-1.) The floor plan provides the usual information about footings and piers, as well as framing considerations. The elevation drawing provides us with height details and shows us where to add the molding.

We use standard conventions beginning with a specifications section, fol-

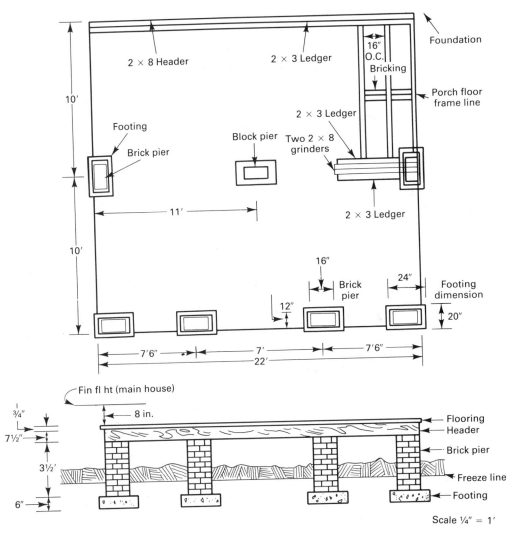

Figure 9-1 Porch floor and elevation plan.

lowed by a materials assessment table, and then proceed with the construction and conclude with the materials invoice.

There is a great deal of satisfaction in building this part of the porch. It will look really beautiful, and will serve well for many years. Now let's begin by examining the specifications.

SPECIFICATIONS

Carefully read the specifications in Table 9.1 to grasp the variety of requirements for the construction of a porch. As before, we proceed with a generic porch floor. You, of course, would adapt these specifications to the local requirements. The details in Figure 9-1 coupled with specifications provide the large picture. Those who fully understand these can modify the data to suit the conditions of their home and proceed to the construction sections. Those who need more understanding should begin with the materials assessment.

TABLE 9.1 Specification Listing
PROJECT: *Building the Porch Floor Assembly*   **DATE:** _____

General Description

A porch floor made from kiln-dried lumber and framing materials will be constructed $7\frac{1}{2}$ in. below the finished floor height of the main floor of the house. It will be 22 ft long by 20 ft wide (outward from the house. It will be able to support a live load of 40 psf. The frame will be supported by brick piers that rest on concrete footings. There will be four piers equally spaced across the 22-ft length, and one pier on each end that will support the girder and the floor and later will transfer the force from the roof directly through the columns. The flooring will be a tongue and groove fir, toenailed, and will extend over the framing sufficiently to permit molding to fit under the overlap. Termite shields will be used, as will joist ledgers. In addition, one set of bridging will be installed in each 10-ft half of the floor.

Specifications

Item	*Specs*
Dimensions	20 ft $\times$ 22 ft
Footing and pier dimensions	20 $\times$ 24-in. footings, 16 $\times$ 12-in. brick piers with joints struck, footing below freeze line, brick same as house veneer, 1 block pier
Framing technique	L-type sill and header and center girder flush with the tops of the joists
Girder	Double 2 $\times$ 8s No. 3 or 2 common KD supported by three piers; the center one may be constructed from cement blocks
Joists	Southern pine MSR for 40 psf LL and 10 psf DL, spaced 16 in. o.c.
Sill and header	Southern pine MSR 2 $\times$ 6 sills, 2 $\times$ 8 headers
Joist ledgers	All joists will bear on a 2 $\times$ 3 joist ledger or sill
Bridging	One row of X bridging will be installed midway between outside header and girder and wall and girder
Flooring	1 $\times$ $3\frac{1}{2}$-in. T&G fir, toenailed
Flooring overlap of frame	2-in. ends and outside edges
Trim	$1\frac{3}{4}$ in. bed molding or suitable substitute
Primer and paint finish	1 coat sealer, 1 coat primer, 2 coats paint porch and deck quality
M-type mortar mix and sand	Mortar for brick

MATERIALS ASSESSMENT

Table 9.2 provides us with an overview of the materials that will be needed to complete the generic porch floor assembly. If you have studied other chapters, you know that the direct materials are used in the construction of the porch, the indirect materials are needed to assist in the construction, and the support materials are tools and the like that make the construction possible.

TABLE 9.2 Materials Assessment
PROJECT: *Porch Floor Assembly and Foundation*   **DATE:** _____

Direct Materials

Type or Description	*Use or Purpose*
Concrete by the bag	Footings
Cement blocks and bricks	Piers
Mortar mix and sand	Cement blocks and bricks
Termite shields	Protection against wood borers
Framing lumber	Sills, joists, girder, and headers
Tongue and groove flooring	Floor for the porch
Molding	Improved the finished look
Bridging	Stiffen the floor assembly
Nails and bolts	Fasteners

Indirect Materials

Type or Description	*Use or Purpose*
Batter boards and stakes	Identifies reference heights and perimeter dimensions
1 × 6 lumber	Footing forms
Mason line	Aids in establishing footings and piers
Mortar board	Makes brick and block laying simpler
Nails	Fasteners

Support Materials

Type or Description	*Use or Purpose*
Carpentry tools	Carpentry construction
Mason tools	Masonry construction
Shovel and hoe	Aids in preparing areas for footings, mixing mortar and concrete, and general digging
Power saw and drill	Eases the work
Sawhorses and planks	Makes the work safer
Radial arm saw (optional)	Eases work of cutting wood

GROUND PREPARATION AND MASONRY TASKS

We must assume that the ground where the porch is to be built is already below the house's finished floor by several feet. If it were not, we would probably build a slab floor. Ground preparation therefore consists of the following tasks:

1. Remove all vegetation and apply a weed killer.
2. Locate the footings with stakes.
3. Establish heights with batter boards.
4. Dig out the areas for the footings.
5. Build the forms for the footings and install them.
6. Mix concrete and fill the footings.
7. Construct the center pier with blocks and the six perimeter piers with bricks. Strike all joints.
8. Insert J-bolts where sills are to be installed.
9. Clean up all masonry tools and mortar board.

No discussion is needed concerning the removal of vegetation. For task 2 close examination of the information in Figure 9-1 shows us where the footing stakes are to be located. Each corner or center of each pier is shown on the floor plan. For the precise details on how to locate the stakes, refer to Chapter 5.

The elevation details in Figure 9-1 show that all piers are the same measurement from the finished floor height. There is a very slight slope to the porch—$\frac{1}{2}$ in. in 20 ft. The batter boards should have been set for this slope. Also note that the footings are below the freeze line. Between the two parts of the drawing all information about the footings is shown.

Figure 9-2 shows the form needed for the brick piers and for the block pier. Each brick pier is 16 × 12 in. with the 16-in. side parallel to the header and end

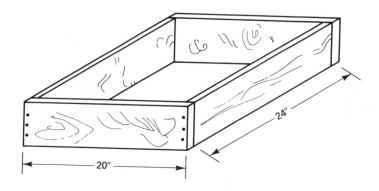

Figure 9-2 Footing form.

joists. The one block pier is in line with the girder. These details are shown in the floor plan drawing for the foundation. The footings, therefore, must be 4 in. wider than the piers on all sides. That makes the ones for the brick 24 × 20 in. and the one for the block 24 × 16 in. All will be 6 in. deep.

Be sure to set each form as exactly as possible for height and for position. The four brick piers on the outside are set about equal distances apart as per specifications and as shown in the plan. The 7-ft opening in the center is for the steps. When steps are built later between the two center posts, the posts on each side of the steps will act like newels, and the steps will be about $7\frac{1}{2}$ ft long. The piers should also be in line with porch lines, but if they are off $\frac{1}{2}$ in. or slightly more, it will not be critical.

Since there are seven footings, six brick piers and one block pier, hand mixing will likely be done on site. Let's estimate how many bags of premixed concrete we will need to fill the footing forms. Each bag will provide $\frac{1}{2}$ cu ft of concrete. Seven forms about 2 × 1.875 × 0.5 = 1.875 cu ft per form for a total of 13.2 cu ft. This equates to 28 bags.

After filling each footing formed area, screed the surface flush with the form's top edge. There is no need for rebars in either the footing or extending up through the piers. The piers extend only about $3\frac{1}{2}$ ft up from the footing.

The bricklaying pattern is shown in Figure 9-3. Because of the size of the piers, no bricks need to be cut. Carefully note this. To ensure that each pier is just the right height, a story pole or layout stick showing each course should be used. A 4-ft mason level should be used to maintain vertical plumb and horizontal level. After several courses are laid, strike the joints with a striking tool. Then continue laying more brick until the pier is complete.

J-bolts are needed in each of the four outside piers (22 ft length). None are needed for the piers that support the girder. When installing the J-bolt, stuff paper into hollow core of the brick piers and push it down about a foot. Then you do not have to fill the entire space with mortar. Fill the remaining space with mortar and push the J-bolt in the mortar so that it extends above the last course of brick $2\frac{1}{2}$ in.

Once the mason work is complete, the ground should be leveled to make for a safe work area. Also clean cement and concrete off the tools, mixing vessel, and mortar board.

Let's review. Batter boards establish the finish floor height and pinpoint the locations of the piers. The footings for the piers must be set exactly right for height to ensure uniform brick mortar joint thicknesses. Proper portions of water added to the mixture assures quality concrete. The piers must be laid for the right height and aligned properly along the porch lines so that the framing will set properly. Each brick pier must have all joints struck, and J-bolts must be installed in four piers. See Chapters 1 and 5 for batter board installation and Chapter 5 for pier construction details if this data is insufficient.

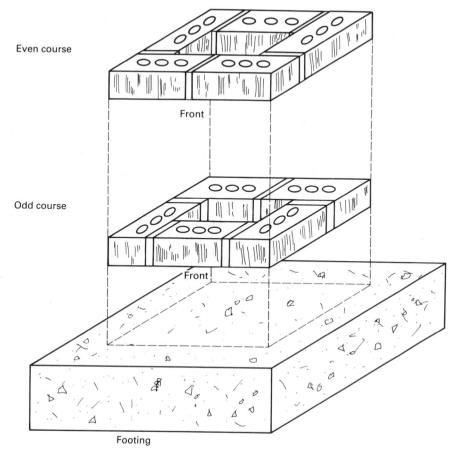

Even course

Odd course

Front

Front

Footing

Figure 9-3 Bricklaying pattern.

BUILDING THE FRAME FOR THE FLOOR

We must begin with installing the termite shields and building the girder. We will also discuss how to build a ledger for joist support versus using the joist hangers. Here is the list of tasks for this part of the project:

1. Cut and form the seven termite shields from aluminum.
2. Prepare the girder with ledgers and install it on the center piers.
3. Install the 2 × 6 sills 1½ in. in from the outer edge of the piers.
4. Cut and install the 22-ft headers—one against the house foundation and the other nailed to the sills. The ledger will be installed on the header fastened to the house.

5. Cut and install the outside joists/headers on both 20-ft sides.
6. Lay out the position of each joist.
7. Measure and cut each joist for length and cut out the notches in each for the ledger.
8. Install the joists.
9. Install the cross bridging.
10. Install the flooring.
11. Install the molding under the flooring overhang. *Note*: If lattice is to be installed, do not install the molding until after the lattice is in place.
12. Seal the exposed materials with a wood protector.

The girder should be built as shown in Figure 9-4 from 2 × 8s with a 2 × 3 ledger on each side. Its total length must be 3 in. less than the full 22 ft of the porch. This allows for the nailing of the end joists/headers to the ends of the girder. Joints on the girder should be spaced at least four feet apart. Fourteen-ft 2 × 8s No. 3 common Douglas fir (North) or Southern pine pieces are a good choice.

I'll get a little technical now so that you can understand why we will need to use good lumber for the girder and joists. The girder must carry the dead load of the floor (DL) and the live predictable load (LL). Our specifications state 10 lb/sq ft DL and 40 lb/sq ft LL. One-half of the floor's width, on each side of the girder, must be supported by the girder. This means that the total force on the girder can be as much as 10 × 22 ft times 50 lb/sq ft, for a total 11,000 pounds of force. But we are placing a pier halfway between the ends, which aids in carrying the load. The actual free span of girder will be about 10 ft 6 in. Because of this we can use a

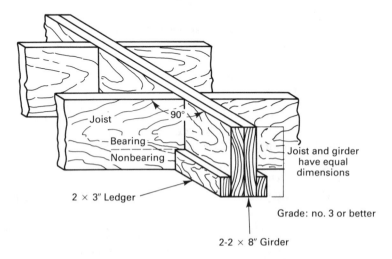

Figure 9-4 Girder and ledger construction.

No. 3 grade KD Douglas fir-larch, Douglas fir-(North) or Southern pine. If all you can buy is a No. 2 grade, that's better. These grades of lumber all have the appropriate modulus of elasticity, *strength*, and fiber in bending, *stiffness*.

Once the girder is constructed and trimmed for length, it must be placed on the three piers, on top of the termite shields. Because of its weight and position, it does not need to be secured to the piers.

Next cut and install the 2 × 6 sills on the outer piers. These must be bolted in place and must be held back from the outer edge $1\frac{1}{2}$ in. to allow for the header to sit on the pier. Install the termite shields first.

Follow this activity by installing the header against the sill and nailing it to the sill. Then install the other one against the foundation with proper anchor bolts.

Box in the frame with the outside joists/headers. Pick out good-looking ones and be sure to make good, tightly fit joints. Referring to Figure 9-1 again, lay out the position of the joists at 16 in. o.c. (on center). Either step off the markings, or for a more accurate method, use a 25- or 50-ft tape and mark the 16 in. points. Make all measurements from the same end on the outside header, inside header, and girder. Place an X on the same side of each mark.

Measure and cut the joists for length; where the ledgers are, cut a notch on the bottom edge. See Figure 9-4 for this detail.

As each joist is nailed in place, a combination square must be used to ensure that each joist is accurately set for plumb. Toenailing must be used. Here's why! Nails through the outer header will detract from the finished appearance, and there is no way to use any other nailing technique when nailing into the girder and inside header. However, if lattice panels are to be installed and overlap the lumber, then 16d common nails can be used. Due to the design of this generic porch floor, the lattice panels will be fitted beneath the joist/headers and between the brick piers, so toenailing is required.

When all the joists are nailed in place, the bridging should be installed. One row should be nailed in place midway between the girder and each header. Again refer to Figure 9-1.

DECKING THE FLOOR AND ADDING TRIM

Tasks 10 and 11 remain to be done. The flooring is tongue and groove fir, as shown in Figure 9-5. To make a really superb job several standards must be met.

1. No nails must shown when the task is complete.
2. The end joints of each flooring piece must all break on the joist.
3. The shoulder on each piece must be tight against the opposite side.
4. The overhang must be $2\frac{1}{2}$ in.
5. The alignment of the pieces from end to end must be straight, not bowed.

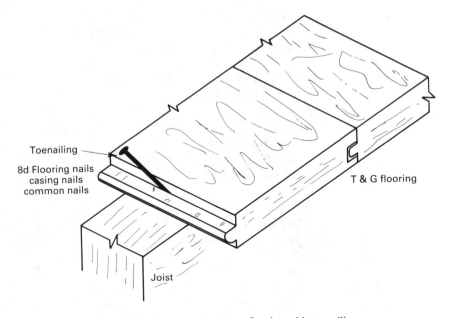

Figure 9-5 Tongue and groove flooring with toenailing.

Notice in Figure 9-5 that one edge has a groove while the other has a tongue. The tongue is slightly smaller in width than the depth of the groove. This makes it possible to tightly draw up the boards. See the toenailing technique? By driving the nail as shown, its head will draw up the board into the previous one. The trick is not to break off the tongue while driving the nail home. I use a nail set or the head of another nail to draw up the board.

Here's what you should do to install the flooring. Use a chalkline to make about six lines across the joists—one each three feet. These will be reference points. After several rows of flooring are installed, measure to the first line to confirm the accuracy of the installation. If, for example, the measurement reveals a $\frac{1}{8}$-in. difference, the next several rows will need to be drawn up more tightly where the short measure resulted and more loosely drawn up where the measure was long. Yes, it is possible to do this!

To ensure that the line along the ends is overhanging the joist/headers exactly $2\frac{1}{2}$ in., they should be trimmed (cut) after all pieces are installed.

Last, the molding is cut and installed with 6d or 8d casing nails, using the toenailing technique. Several moldings can be used, as shown in Figure 9-6. Each of these should be mitered to fit the outer corner returns.

Finally, task 12 directs us to seal the exposed lumber with a wood sealer to prevent damage. In fact it is a good idea to follow the sealing action with several coats of good quality paint for porch floors.

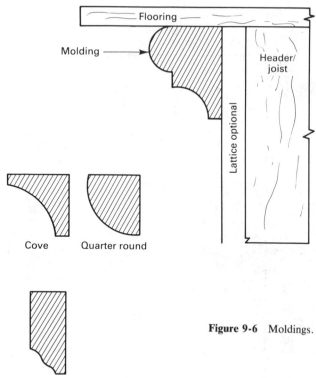

Figure 9-6 Moldings.

MATERIALS LISTING

Table 9.3 (see page 130) shows the materials listing as it would appear on an invoice. The quantities are for the generic porch floor assembly and supporting piers.

SUMMARIZING THE PROJECT

This project included the use of a girder so that you can become familiar with such design. It also covered brick piers, which are different from the block kind. The project also covered tongue and groove flooring rather than decking. Finally, several aspects were lightly treated since they have been covered in earlier chapters. If it is necessary, you can refer back to them for specific details such as locating grade and pier stakes and setting batter boards.

TABLE 9.3 Materials Invoice
PROJECT: *Porch Floor Assembly and Foundation*   **DATE:** _____

Quantity	Type	Total
28 bags	Concrete mix	28 ea
6	8 × 8 × 16 cement blocks	6 ea
490	Bricks	500 ea
4 bags	Mortar mix type M	4 bags
$\frac{1}{2}$ yd	Washed sand	$\frac{1}{4}$ yd
12 ft	16-in. aluminum (termite shields)	12 lin ft
4	2 × 8 14 ft No. 3 or 2 common KD pine	56 lin ft
4	2 × 8 8 ft No. 3 or 2 common KD pine	32 lin ft
34	Joists, 2 × 8 10 ft No. 3 or 2 common KD pine	340 lin ft
20 lin ft	2 × 6 No. 3 or 2 common KD pine sills	20 lin ft
500 bd ft	1 × 3 fir or pine T&G flooring	500 bd ft
70 lin ft	Bed molding or substitute	70 lin ft
23	1 × 3 12 ft spruce (bridging)	276 lin ft
3	2 × 4 12 ft (batter board stakes)	36 lin ft
2	1 × 6 10 ft (batter boards)	20 lin ft
7	1 × 6 8 ft (forms)	56 lin ft
4 lb	6d common nails	4 lb
15 lb	8d common nails	15 lb
10 lb	10d common nails	10 lb
4 lb	16d common nails	4 lb
1 gal	Wood sealer	1 gal
2 gal	Primer paint	2 gal
2 gal	Porch and deck paint	2 gal
1	$3\frac{1}{2}$-in. paint brush	1 ea

Rental Equipment	Duration of Rental
Cement mixer (optional)	2 days
Radial arm saw (optional)	1 day

10

Design and Construction of the Porch Roof

OBJECTIVES

- Identify the principles necessary to build a gable, hip, valley, and shed roof.
- Plan for the construction of the roof to cover the porch floor with an A-framed (gable) roof and ceiling.
- Plan a specifications and materials assessment for a generic A-frame roof and ceiling.
- Establish the conditions necessary to have the roof blend with the architecture of the house.
- Identify the trim customarily used to build the cornice.
- Identify the sequence of tasks and materials used to complete the ceiling.
- Finalize the materials listing with computations included.
- Ascertain the cleanup tasks and safety tasks associated with this type of project.

BACKGROUND

This chapter deals with the construction of a porch roof and ceiling. As the chapter provides information, all aspects concerning this effort will be covered. A frame is made from headers that must support the trusses and ceiling. In the design, there must be a methodology that ensures that the house cornice and overhang characteristics are carried onto the porch roof.

Three roof designs are customarily used on porch roofs. They are the gable or A-framed, the hip, and the shed styles. The one selected for the generic project in this chapter is the A-framed style. Selection of this roof style provides us the opportunity to gain a base of knowledge about roof construction using trusses. This base of knowledge can be transferred to the other two types of roof design. For a knowledge of roof construction using rafters, ridge boards, and collar ties, refer to *Carpentry: Framing and Finishing*, Byron W. Maguire (Prentice Hall, Englewood Cliffs, New Jersey, 1989).

Later in this section we study the three types of design to learn some of their special characteristics.

Generally speaking, building a roof requires a great deal of physical stamina. People with a fear of heights may need to overcome this or abandon the project. You must be physically able to:

1. Work above ground and work on the slope of the roof.
2. Carry heavy trusses and headers off the ground to frame and build the roof assembly.
3. Handle full $\frac{7}{16}$-in. sheets of plywood sheathing on the sloping roof.
4. Install half sheets of $\frac{1}{4}$-in. plywood overhead on the ceiling to finish the ceiling.
5. Handle cornice materials while nailing each into place.
6. Erect frame headers where there are no columns in existence.
7. Build scaffolds and work from ladders and sawhorses where materials are installed about shoulder height.

This list is fairly complete and is intended to amplify the physical characteristics and exertion required to complete the job. For some of the work a professional carpenter can work unassisted. But it is far safer to have a minimum of two workers on the job at all times. The work goes along more smoothly and considerably more safely. Get a buddy to help!

Figure 10-1 shows examples of the three roof designs. We use these examples to illustrate the terms commonly used in this chapter. Figure 10-1a shows a gable roof design. When the roof is exposed, the trusses revealed are all *common*. Each truss is a unit. The lower member (*chord*) is the ceiling framing replacing the ceiling joist, and the slanted one acts as the rafter. When you install

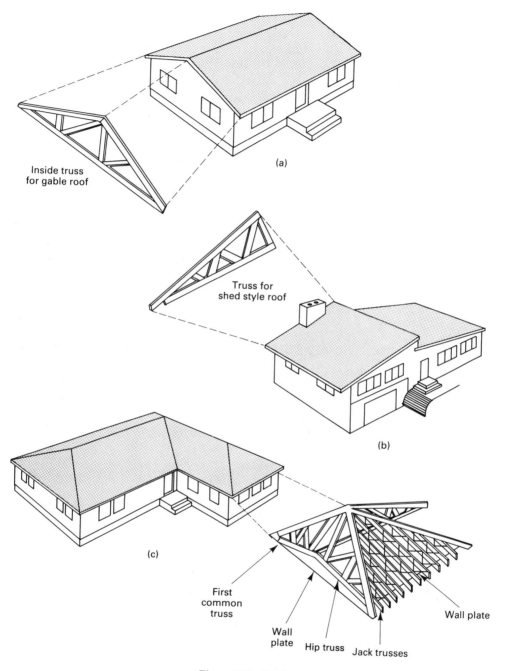

Inside truss
for gable roof

(a)

Truss for
shed style roof

(b)

(c)

First
common
truss

Wall
plate

Wall plate

Hip truss

Jack trusses

Figure 10-1 Roof styles and trusses.

trusses, there is no need for the ridge board. The open end of the gable is filled in with *gable-end studs*. These are usually installed on 16 in. o.c. and come from the mill already installed in the outer truss. Figure 10-1b shows a shed roof. The rafters in a shed roof are usually installed with a *pitch of 3 in 12*, although the slope may be slightly more or less. A *3 in 12 pitch* means that the rafter slope rises 3 in. for each foot (*12-in. run*) of rafter run. Just like the A-framed trusses, the shed roof trusses may be constructed in a mill. The ends have studs installed on 16-in. centers. One end truss must be built for each end, since a shed design has two open ends. Figure 10-1c shows a *hip roof*. In a stick-built roof there would be two hip rafters in one section of the roof. There would be *hip-jack rafters* as well. These extend from the plate or header to the hip rafter. None ever reach the ridge board. If this roof were made from trusses, there would be quite a few different pieces to the roof, as shown in Figure 10-1.

Where the roof in our generic project is connected into the main roof, the shingles must be removed to expose the sheathing. Special trusses are built to create valleys and continue the A-frame design. All of these parts of the project are covered in more detail later.

Cornice consists of several different members. The *fascia* is the most exposed board, as shown in Figure 10-2. The board under the overhang of the rafters is called a *soffit*. Most of the time the soffit is nailed to *lookouts*, which are nailed level from fascia to header or plate. In our generic project the lower chord will extend 12 in. past the header and act as a lookout for nailing the soffit to. The *frieze board* is a piece that fits up against the soffit and extends over the top course of brick or last row of siding on a house. In our generic project, we use a molding as a frieze board to trim the porch headers. Standard cornice principles are used. These include making a groove in the fascia for the insertion of the soffit, adding cutouts in the soffit pieces for the ventilation screen, and making sure that there is sound nailing in corner areas for all parts of the cornice. Figure 10-2 shows a detail of the fascia with groove. This groove serves two purposes: (1) It improves the overall appearance of the cornice; (2) it makes it much easier to install the soffit and fascia.

The building principles we use are varied but not that difficult to understand or put into practice. We are dealing with force from both dead and live loads and may need to concern ourselves with 7-day snow loading as well. So the selection of materials for headers must be made on a scientific basis. Erection of the perimeter headers must properly tie into the existing house. The trusses are made to standard specification at the mill and delivered to the job site. They will be able to sustain the loads. The principles of erecting them include not only their positioning on the headers and existing roof, but using the level to plumb each as it is installed. Spreaders are also used to aid in alignment.

Other principles must be employed. Nailing schemes must be followed in every different situation. All nails must be appropriate for the job. Sheathing joints must break joints to add strength to the roof. Strip shingles must align

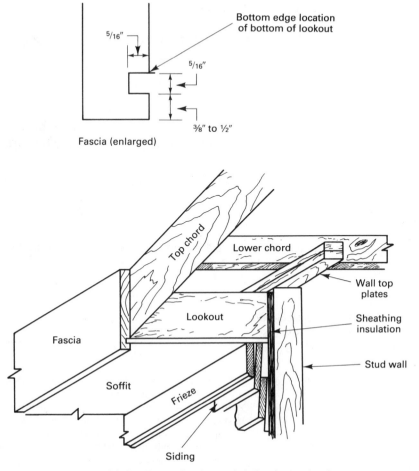

5/16″

Bottom edge location
of bottom of lookout

5/16″

3/8″ to 1/2″

Fascia (enlarged)

Top chord

Lower chord

Wall top
plates

Lookout

Sheathing
insulation

Fascia

Stud wall

Soffit

Frieze

Siding

(a) Usually top chord extends below lower chord

Figure 10-2 Customary truss overhang and cornice construction.

horizontally and vertically. The valley materials must be installed to ensure a waterproof roof.

One serious problem we face is the chance that rain may enter the open main house while the roof is exposed. This must not happen, so a good day must be selected for raising the roof over the main house and dry it in before the rains come. (*Dry it in* means cover the roof, in this case, with 15 lb felt to prevent rain from getting into the ceiling/attic area.)

By selecting the truss style versus the stick-built rafter and joist-style roof, we have reduced the amount of planning and technical requirements. It might even make the project more pleasurable to build. The finished project can be one to be proud of.

Now let's begin with the generic porch roof and the specifications.

SPECIFICATIONS

Several of the parameters pertaining to the project have been identified in the background section. Table 10.1 places those and others in the form of a specification.

MATERIALS ASSESSMENT

Once again we use the standard form for the assessment of materials required to complete the job. Table 10.2 provides these.

TABLE 10.1 Specification Listing
PROJECT: *Constructing the Porch Roof Assembly*   **DATE**: _____

General Description

The project will be constructed with No. 2 common KD southern pine or Douglas fir framing materials and premanufactured trusses. The porch ceiling will be covered with $\frac{1}{4}$-in. AC grade fir plywood cut into either 4 × 4-ft or 2 × 4-ft pieces. Sheathing grade plywood $\frac{7}{16}$ in. thick will be used for the roof, and strip shingles will cover the sheathing. The overhang will match the existing house at 12 in. The cornice, consisting of a fascia, soffit, and frieze, will match the main house. The new roof will tie into the main roof at 90 degrees, and an opening will be cut into the main roof sheathing to permit access as well as ventilation. All exposed materials will be primed and painted. The gable end will be covered with reverse board and batten fiber board. The roof shall have ridge vents and soffit vents. The soffit vents will be spaced 6 ft apart.

Specifications

Item	Specs
Dimensions	20 × 22 ft A-framed roof
Pitch	6–in–12
Framing to support trusses	2 × 6s doubled and spaced with 2 × 4
Truss spacing	24 in. o.c.
Ceiling type and grade	$\frac{1}{4}$ in. exterior, AC grade plywood
Roof type and grade sheathing	$\frac{7}{16}$ in. exterior sheathing grade
Shingle type and weight	12 × 36 strip fiber glass, graded 25 yr
Cornice type	Closed with 12-in. overhang

TABLE 10.2 Materials Assessment
PROJECT: *Constructing the Porch Roof Assembly*   **DATE:** _____

Direct Materials

Type or Description	*Use or Purpose*
Trusses	Main roof and ceiling frame
2 × 6s	Frame headers
2 × 4s	Supports, braces, p/o header frame, look-outs
1 × 8s	Fascia boards
$\frac{1}{4}$ in. ext plywood	Ceiling and soffit
$\frac{7}{16}$ in. sheathing plywood	Roof
Molding	Frieze
Reverse board and batten	Gable end cover
Ridge and soffit vents	Air circulation system
$\frac{1}{4}$ round	Molding for ceiling
Shingles	Roof
Aluminum	Flashing for valleys
Felt	Dry in roof
Nails	Roofing, finish and common
Paint	Undercoat and final coat

Indirect Materials

Type or Description	*Use or Purpose*
2 × 10s	Scaffold planks
2 × 4s	General bracing and temporary columns
1 × 4s	Spacers, braces—temporary
Nails	16d and 8d common fasteners

Support Materials

Type or Description	*Use or Purpose*
Carpentry tools	Construction
Ladders	Access to roof and general use
Saw horses and work bench	Work surfaces
Portable power saw and radial arm saw	Eases cutting materials
Paint brushes, rollers or spray outfit	Painting

LAYOUT OF MATERIALS

Working Drawings

Figures 10-3 through 10-12 provide the ideas required to build the generic porch roof assembly. For our generic project they show the following:

1. The design of the perimeter headers (Figure 10-3)
2. The design of the truss (Figure 10-4)
3. The placement of the truss on the header (Figure 10-5)
4. The approximate placement of the trusses that are nailed to the existing roof (Figure 10-6)
5. The design of the gable-end overhang and fly rafter (Figure 10-7)
6. Installing the sheathing plywood (Figure 10-8)
7. Installing the shingles (Figure 10-9)
8. The design of the cornice (Figure 10-10)
9. Gable end closed box cornice (Figure 10-11)
10. Installing the reverse board and batten
11. Ceiling paneling (Figure 10-12)

Each of the parts of the drawing is used in one or more of the descriptions later as the tasks are identified and explained.

Preliminary Layout of Materials

The layout of the headers is the main work done on the ground or, preferably, on the porch floor. We must consider where the posts will be installed when the headers will be made from several pieces. Since the generic porch roof is to be built over the porch floor assembly discussed in Chapter 9, we know that there will be six posts. One post is placed over each pier. We mark their exact location with pencil. Then we can use those references as aids in the design and construction of the header assembly. Joints in the header sections need to be offset 3 to 4 ft and if possible to break relatively near the position of a post location. However, we will use full-length headers for the project; the post positions are more for reference than for supporting joints in the header. The best solution for construction of the headers is to use 20-ft 2 × 6s for the sides and 22-ft pieces for the front and avoid splicing headers.

Again with reference to the porch floor (see Figure 9-2) that we described in Chapter 9, the headers' outer edge/side must line up with the header/joists in the porch floor assembly. This reference establishes the placement of the header against the house framing. It is therefore possible to fabricate the header assembly or assemblies on the porch floor and use the floor as the reference. Easy solution! Yes, but it may require some consideration. Since the porch floor is about 8 in. below the finished floor height of the main house, the foundation should be exposed above the floor. Customarily, the framing (studs and walls) is flush with the foundation. Measuring from this reference should be the same as measuring from the exposed wall plates at the ceiling level of the main house. But you will need to verify this before building the header assemblies. Looking at the

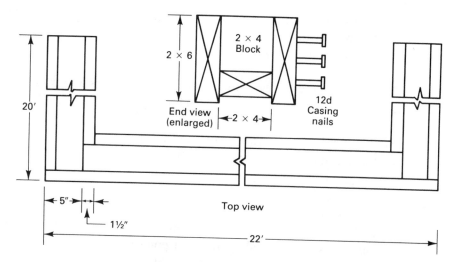

Figure 10-3 Porch roof header assembly, details.

end view in Figure 10-3, we see that the two 2 × 6s are spaced with a 2 × 4. Blocks of 2 × 4 are used to maintain the parallel positions of the headers. The horizontal 2 × 4 member should be recessed about $\frac{1}{4}$ to $\frac{1}{2}$ in. Set a combination square for $\frac{1}{2}$ in. and use it as a guide as each part of the 2 × 4 is nailed to the 2 × 6. Then nail the inside 2 × 6 to the other edge of the 2 × 4s. The end of the assembly near the wall must be flush. The inner 2 × 6 on the other end of the assembly must be cut shorter to allow for mating with the front header assembly.

Next, the corners must fit. Since there will be three sections to raise, we need to plan and construct each to fit in place. Note in Figure 10-3 how each side section intersects with the front section.

This preliminary work must be done if the headers are to fit into place properly.

When the trusses are delivered to the job site, place them such that a minimum distance exists between them and the porch. Also place them in the order of their installation. The one with the gable end studs should be on the bottom of the pile.

FRAMING, SHEATHING, AND SHINGLING

If you have been studying the entire chapter, you know that in the previous section preliminary work was done on designing the headers. If you are entering your specialized project at this point, let me suggest that you first read the previous section and then return here. It should take only a few minutes.

In this section a great deal of the project will be discussed and examined. Let's begin with the usual convention by listing the tasks that must be accomplished. Where two people are required, a (2) follows the task:

1. Remove the existing cornice to reveal the rafters and wall.
2. Remove the upper rows of the siding to the point where the headers will fit against the house wall.
3. Prepare the header framework and erect it. (2)
4. Lay out the positions of the trusses and erect the ones over the porch floor.
5. Install the 2 × 4s across the ends of the trusses. (2)
6. Mark the area on the main roof where the shingles are to be removed and then remove all shingles.
7. Use a mason line or chalkline to ascertain the ridge point on the main roof and the two lower valley intersect points.
8. Cut an access port into the main roof.
9. Install the remaining trusses. (2)
10. Sheath the roof with plywood. (2)
11. Dry-in the roof with 15# felt. (2)
12. Shingle the roof.
13. Build the cornices. (2)
14. Add the reverse board and batten siding. (2)
15. Install the ceiling. (2)
16. Prime and paint the exposed wood.

Use Figure 10-2 as a reference if you need explanation of terms used in the next several paragraphs. Locate natural joints in the existing fascia boards on the side of the house where the porch is. If possible, use these to decide which ones to remove. If this technique is inconvenient or impossible, the fascia must be cut in two places. Use a plumb bob and, while holding the string end against the fascia, move it around until the plumb bob point is even with the outer edge of the outside joist/header of the floor assembly. (If you are building the roof over a slab floor, make the point 6 in. in from the outside edge of the slab.) When in position, mark the fascia. Repeat the technique on the other end. These marks represent the outer edge of each header.

The specifications call for a matching 12-in. overhang. We could measure back 12 in. (outside the porch floor), draw a line on the fascia with a pencil and combination square, and cut the piece. However, this may not be the best method. Let's give ourselves some room to build the roof. We need to get to the wall's framing. So locate the next rafter end outside the mark. Then draw a line and cut the fascia so that half the rafter end is exposed when the fascia is removed. (*Note*: If the rafter ends are covered with 2 × 4s, we can cut the fascia anywhere.) Repeat the task on the other end, and then remove all fascia between the cuts.

Next plan to cut and remove the frieze board. Use the same procedure by looking for joints in the frieze board that are outside the roof assembly area. It is much better to remove this piece of cornice than to cut it, since the cutting must be done, in part, with a chisel.

The soffit is now exposed, and it too must be removed. Find the closest lookout or lower truss chord where the fascia was cut. If there is a natural end to the soffit piece, plan on using that as a break. If one is not close by, select a point and mark the soffit for cutting. Remove the soffit pieces. In most modern homes these pieces are 8-ft-long ¼-in. pieces of plywood and should be relatively easy to remove. Now we have the area exposed, and task 1 is finished.

Task 2 requires us to remove outer covering to make access to the wall framing and sheathing. If the covering is siding, then we will need to remove enough rows to permit the 2 × 6 header assembly to butt against the framing. For the generic project we want the top of the header placed such that when the truss is set on top of it, the height of the sloping member (top chord) is level with the top end of the main roof rafter. This should also make the end of the lower chord level with the lookouts. Therefore, because of the design of the truss, the top edge of the header should butt up to the lookout's lower side. This means that we would need to remove only one or two rows of siding.

If the outer covering of the wall is brick, we need to remove the soldier course and maybe one more course of brick. Be very cautious here. You do not want to remove bricks when there is no need, because they have to be relaid.

If vertical siding is the outer covering of the wall, carefully lay out where the headers go. Then cut just enough to permit the header assembly to slide through to the house framing.

Finally, cut away the sheathing to expose the framing of the wall. In all probability the sheathing will be fiber board or insulated fiber board, and this can be cut with a wood chisel.

Header Installation

Let's assume that the headers have been laid out on the porch floor (Figure 10-3). This means that the two 20-ft ones have been trimmed to allow the 22-ft one to intersect with them.

Before we can install the headers, we need temporary posts. Cut four 2 × 4s for temporary posts for each side section/end and two more for the support of the front header. Plan to place one at the approximate 10-ft point, one near the end under the side headers, and the others evenly spaced under the front header.

Plan where to anchor the header to the wall. Decide if there is enough wood to use toenailing, or if it would be better to use metal ties such as joist hangers. After deciding, raise the first side header up and place it against the wall. Place

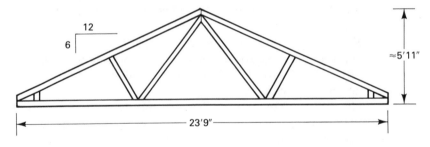

Figure 10-4 Truss for generic project.

the temporary post under the header and tack-nail each in place with 8d common nails. Then use a 1 × 4 12 ft long as an angle brace and make the 2 × 4 near the outer point relatively plumb. (Don't worry; it can be made absolutely plumb later.) Fasten the header in the exact location. Repeat the technique with the other side header assembly.

Now that both side headers are in place, raise the outer one into place and prop it up with the two 2 × 4s cut for the job. Since part of the nailing is through the end of the outer 2 × 6 into the outer 2 × 6 on each side, one of you will probably use an extension ladder from the ground to nail the pieces together. The inside ones can be nailed from a step ladder.

The frame is up. Now final positioning and squaring are done. Two checks are made and braces of 1 × 4 are used to ensure accuracy of the final nailing. First, square the frame. Begin by trying the frame square method. Hold the square inside each corner. This may work, but it probably won't. The best way is to use the 3–4–5 (12–16–20) technique with the main house wall as the 16-ft reference.[1] First nail a 1 × 4 piece from the main house plates to extend over the header at about the 12-ft point. (Form a triangle.) Then square this side, with the main house wall. Repeat the process on the other header section. In this way we are sure that the frame is correct. Next nail two shorter 1 × 4s across the outer corners of the headers to ensure that the front header is square with the sides and is straight. These last two braces should be nailed under the headers to be out of the way of the trusses. Next verify that the height is accurate. It should be, but check. Use shims to raise and trim the temporary post to lower the frame as necessary. The frame is up, secured and squared, and at the right height.

Installing the Trusses

The trusses delivered from the mill should look very similar to the one shown in Figure 10-4. Task 4 is the layout of the trusses on the headers and installing them. The specifications call for trusses on 2-ft centers. Start the layout from the

[1] Note: Please refer to the Pythagorean theorem in Chapter 1.

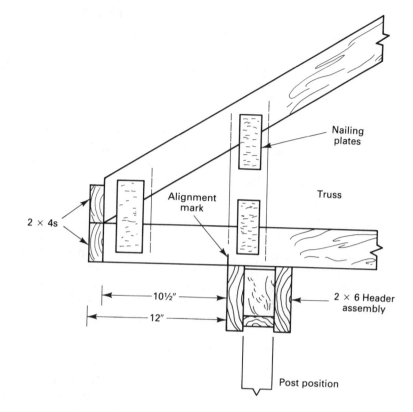

Figure 10-5 Location of truss on porch header, details.

outside header. The end header must be flush with the outer header. Step off the 2-ft increments with a folding ruler or tape and mark them. As an aid to installation, partially drive an 8d common nail at the place where each mark has been made.

With reference to Figure 10-5, make a mark on each truss 10½ in. back from the end. This is the point where the truss lines up with the outer edge of the header.

To erect the truss, we need to have ready a 1 × 4 about 10 ft long, an extension ladder, a level, and a step ladder. The first one to erect is the one closest to the main house. It will be braced with the 1 × 4 to the main roof. Follow the sequence:

1. Raise the truss onto the opposite headers.
2. Position it against the correct side of the guide 8d nails and even with the pencil marks.

3. Toenail the truss to the 2 × 6 headers with 12d or 16d common nails.
4. Tack-nail the 1 × 4 into the top chord about a foot or two down from the ridge with the opposite end extending to the main roof.
5. Using the level against the truss, plumb the truss and nail the loose end of the 1 × 4 into the roof.

Truss number one is in place.

Installing the remaining trusses duplicates the above except for the bracing. Short 1 × 4s (about 5 ft long) should be used to secure the top of the truss in alignment. Simply nail the brace from the first to the second and so on as each new one is raised in place and plumbed.

Main Roof Preparation

Now that the common trusses are in place, we can prepare the main roof for the valley trusses. First, as shown in Figure 10-6, we must remove the shingles in an area wider and higher than the new extension will occupy. Later we will build the valley and replace the shingles. Under the shingles is felt (tar paper), and some of this must be removed. We use a mason line and a chalkline to define where to cut the felt.

Nail one end of the mason line to the peak of the fifth or sixth truss already installed. Extend the line over the main roof tightly, until the end you are holding is in contact with the felt and the line is perfectly aligned over the peaks of the trusses and is just barely touching. The point where the line touches the roof is the peak of the valley. Drive a nail there.

Next we establish the valley lines. Let's go down to the corner where the main roof overhang and the truss overhanging the header almost touch. We need to define the exact point where these two will ultimately meet. To do this nail a short (4-ft) piece of 2 × 4 across the top edges of the top chords so that it extends almost to the main house framing. Then with a straight edge or scrap of 1 × 4, mark the intersection point from main lookout/rafter overhang to the temporary 2 × 4 piece. This point is the lower point of the valley. Great! Now put one end of the chalkline over the nail at the peak of the valley and stretch the line until it is tight and aligned over the mark at the lower end. Snap the line; one valley is defined. Repeat the process on the other side. Trim the felt inside the chalklines about 2 ft and remove the paper.

Next cut away the plywood sheathing to create the access port between the main roof and the porch roof. This is necessary for several reasons. First, electrical service to the porch must pass through here. Further, every roof needs ventilation, and this aids in that process. At some later date you may want to close in the porch with glass and maybe French doors. That means there will be a need to provide heat and air conditioning. Ducting will have to be passed through the

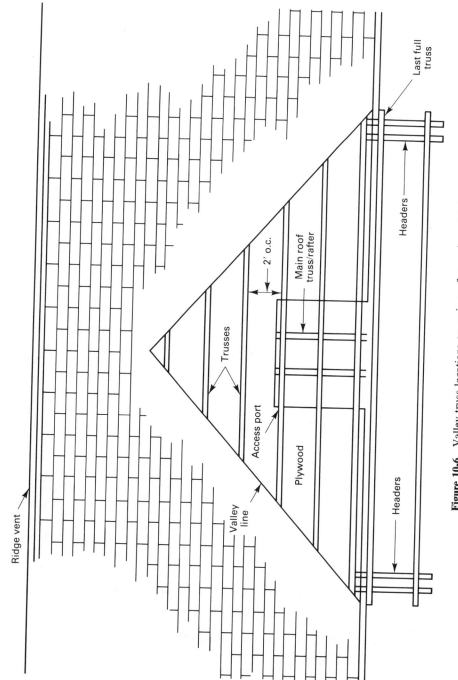

Figure 10-6 Valley truss locations on main roof, top view, details.

Ridge vent

Valley line

Trusses

Access port

Plywood

2' o.c.

Main roof truss/rafter

Headers

Headers

Last full truss

port. If the porch is converted into a sun room, its ceiling will need insulating. Again the port will be needed for access to blow in the material. Enough said.

Main Roof Truss Installation

With the aid of Figure 10-6, which is a top–down view, locate the positions of the remaining trusses to complete the porch roof. These need to be spaced 2 ft o.c. as the others were. Starting with the largest one, position it and nail it to the main roof rafters with 16d common nails. Plumb it and brace it plumb. Repeat the technique for the remaining trusses.

Gable End Truss
and Fly Rafter Installation

If the weather is still good, we can install the gable end truss and fabricate the fly rafter assembly. Let's assume the conditions are good. (By the way, if there is a chance of rain, by all means sheath in the roof and dry it in with new 15# felt.)

Install the end truss flush with the outside edge of the outer header. Nail it securely to the header and then plumb and brace it.

Before building the fly rafter assembly, we must install the 2 × 4s that will be behind the fascia. Refer again to Figure 10-5 and notice that there are two 2 × 4s nailed to the ends of the trusses. The ends near the house should extend into the 12-in. overhang at least 2 in. The outer ends should extend at least 12 in. past the end truss. The fly rafter will be nailed to these pieces.

Now look at Figure 10-7. It shows the fly rafter assembly. Some carpenters use the sheathing as the support to hold the fly rafter in place. We will do a much better job, one that will hold up without sagging.

We could have ordered the end truss $3\frac{1}{2}$ in. lower than the others, and then we could have just nailed the lookouts on top of the top chord. But we did not, so we must make notches into the top chord for the lookout to fit into. Let's make a notch about half the width of the 2 × 4 lookout (about $1\frac{3}{4}$ in.). Then we should cut one lookout long enough to be nailed against the first common truss, pass through the end truss, and extend $10\frac{1}{2}$ in. out into space. After cutting it for length, mark it to make the opposite notch, and try for a fit. When it fits, use it as a pattern to make enough to complete each side of the gable end overhang. Then nail them in place.

Next, cut two 2 × 4s for fly rafters, fitting the pieces with properly fitted joints. Then nail each one in place. This ends the basic framing for the roof. We still have to add the cornice, but let's delay that and proceed with sheathing the roof and drying it in.

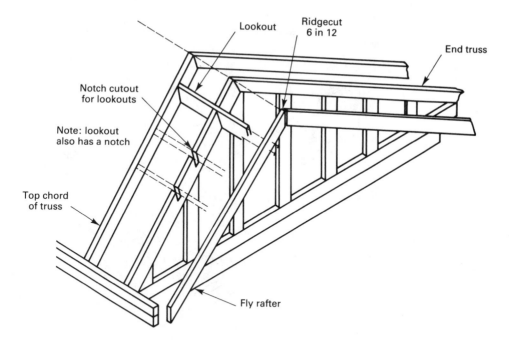

Lookout

Ridgecut
6 in 12

End truss

Notch cutout
for lookouts

Note: lookout
also has a notch

Top chord
of truss

Fly rafter

Figure 10-7   Gable end overhang and fly rafter construction, details.

Sheathing the Roof

The specifications call for $\frac{7}{16}$-in. sheathing plywood; Figure 10-8 gives a view of getting started. These pieces are 4 by 8 ft large. The number of pieces needed to cover both sides of the roof is calculated as follows.

Step 1. Determine the square feet of roof to cover on each side up to the beginning of the valley.

Solution. **A.** Using a tape measure, measure the length of the top chord and the length of the 2 × 4 nailed to the ends of the common trusses. First multiply the number of feet, then divide the product by 48 (the number of square feet per sheet of plywood.)

B. Each 12 in. of run along the outer header creates $13\frac{1}{2}$ in. of length up to the top chord. Since we know that one-half of the 22-ft span of the porch is 11 ft and the overhang is 1 ft, the total length is 12 ft. Therefore, $13\frac{1}{2}$ in. × 12 ft equals the length of the top chord, or 13 ft 6 in. Further, we know that the side header extends out 20 ft, but 1 foot reaches under the 12-in. overhang of

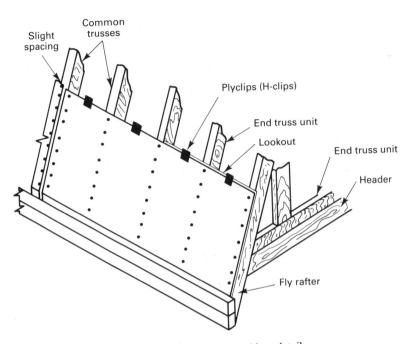

Figure 10-8 Plywood sheathing, details.

the main roof. (This subtracts 1 ft.) But the overhang on the gable end is 12 in. (We gain back the 1 ft.) So we calculate the number of sheets as follows:

13 ft 6 in. × 22 ft = 297 sq ft, or 8.18 sheets of sheathing per side

Step 2. Determine the number of square feet of roofing on each valley.

Solution. Knowing what we already know makes the calculation of sheathing easy. We designed an equally-pitched valley. This means that both the pitch on the main house and that on the porch are the same. Since the length of the top chord is 13 ft 6 in., the ridge of the porch roof extends over the main roof by the same amount. Therefore, we merely square 13 ft 6 in. and have our requirement for both sides of the valley extension. (*Note*: One-half of the product is all that is needed for each half of the roof.)

(13 ft 6 in.)² = 182¼ sq ft, or about 4 sheets of sheathing

Step 3. Summing the requirements, we have:

Common area 1 + 2 + valley extension + 10% for waste

8.18 + 8.18 + 4 = 20½ sheets + 2 sheets for waste = 22 to 23 sheets

To install sheathing we must follow several rules:

1. H clips must be installed between each truss, as shown in Figure 10-8.
2. Sheathing boards should touch lightly at the joints or may be spaced about $\frac{1}{16}$ in.
3. Joints from one row to the next must be offset at least one truss.

Install the sheets beginning at the lower end of the trusses and do not overhang the 2 × 4s or fly rafter. Nail them in place with 6d common nails spaced about 4 in. up the ends and about 6 in. up intermediate trusses. Measure the length of pieces that will fit into the valley and cut these on the ground; it's safer. Also cut the last piece at the ridge on the ground. Keep it $1\frac{1}{2}$ in. down from the ridge to allow for ridge ventilation.

As soon as the plywood is installed, install the 15# felt. Overlap each piece in the direction of rainfall by about 2 in. and about 12 in. where vertical laps are made. Nail the paper with flat circle metal pieces under the nails or buy nails especially made for nailing felt paper.

Shingling the Roof

There are several tasks that need to be done to complete the job of shingling the roof:

1. Prepare the valley.
2. Install the strip shingles.
3. Install the ridge vents.

I have elected to place the subject of shingling the roof at this part of the construction even though we have not yet built the cornice. If there were no threat of damage to the main house from violent storms, which would rip off the felt and allow rain to spoil ceilings, this job would follow the cornice construction. So we must make allowances for the cornice fascias as part of the job.

First we need to establish the valleys. Begin with the laying of a strip of felt from the lower edge to well past the peak of the valley. Split the difference—one-half the width of the paper on each slope of the valley. Nail this in place. Next unroll the aluminum flashing so that it extends below the valley and above the valley, and trim it off. Center it and crease it along the center so that it fits neatly into the valley. Nail it with roofing nails about every four feet near the outer edge. DO NOT ever nail in the valley. Some builders want an extra measure of protection, so they cut another piece of felt for valley length and then rip it into two halves lengthwise. One half is placed so that it overlaps the edge of the aluminum about 4 in. or so and is nailed on the roof but not into the flashing. Other builders do not do this, and the roof seldom, if ever, leaks. It's your choice!

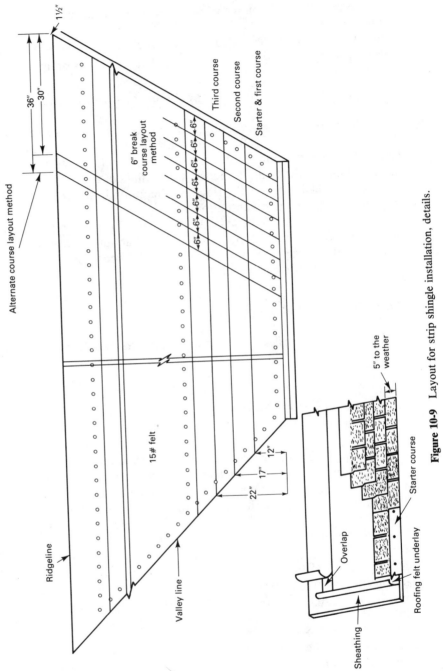

Figure 10-9 Layout for strip shingle installation, details.

1½"

36"

30"

Alternate course layout method

Ridgeline

15# felt

Valley line

22"

17"

12"

6" break course layout method

6" 6" 6" 6" 6" 6" 6" 6" 6"

Third course

Second course

Starter & first course

5" to the weather

Overlap

Starter course

Sheathing

Roofing felt underlay

Before we can begin installing the strip shingles (task 2), we need to make some decisions regarding the cornice and overhang of the shingle. We know that the cornice is made from 1-in. stock ($\frac{3}{4}$ in. actual). Therefore, the starter course should be set so that there is a $\frac{1}{2}$- to $\frac{3}{4}$-in. overhang beyond the fascia. Let's set the total overhang at $1\frac{1}{2}$ in. ($\frac{3}{4}$-in. overhang + $\frac{3}{4}$-in.-thick fascia).

Refer to Figure 10-9. Since the shingle is 12 in. wide, we can establish where to snap the chalkline to use as a guide in installing both the starter and first row of shingles. (12 in. $-$ $1\frac{1}{2}$ in. $=$ $10\frac{1}{2}$ in.)

While we have the chalkline in hand, let's make several more lines. Measure up from the first line 5 in. several times and snap the lines. Also snap two lines in the valley. Let's make each line $\frac{3}{4}$ in. back from the center line of the valley. This simplifies marking the shingles for cutting. Now let's move over to the gable ends of the roof and make several more lines, which will help keep our vertical alignment. Again see Figure 10-9. The reason for the fractions of an inch is the same as for the starter course. We must account for a $\frac{3}{4}$-in. overhang + a $\frac{3}{4}$-in. gable end fascia. About six or seven lines will do if the shingles are laid $\frac{1}{6}$ (6-in.) back from each other. If alternate rows are full and $\frac{5}{8}$ shingles, two lines are used, one at 36 in. minus ($-$) $1\frac{1}{2}$ in. back from the edge of the sheathing, and another 30 in. minus ($-$) $1\frac{1}{2}$ in. (Net: $34\frac{1}{2}$ in. and $28\frac{1}{2}$ in.)

Periodically snap lines to maintain accuracy vertically and horizontally. As each row reaches the valley, mark each shingle, using the chalkline for the reference, and cut it with a pair of snips. Nail close to the valley but no closer than 6 in.

When both halves of the roof are shingled to the ridge, install the ridge vents as shown in the simple instructions supplied with the vents.

CORNICE AND CEILING

Building the cornice for the first time is difficult. There is no other way to say it. So many pieces must fit well to each other. Materials can be consumed very quickly due to faulty cuts. But let's not be negative. We proceed with the job. The tasks are

1. Prepare the fascias with a groove for the soffit.
2. Rip the soffit plywood pieces to the proper width.
3. Replace the old soffit that was removed earlier.
4. Replace the old fascia that was removed earlier.
5. Replace the old frieze boards.
6. Install the vents in the new soffit pieces.
7. Install the soffits on the sides.
8. Install the fascia on the sides.

9. Finish the framing on the gable ends.
10. Install the soffits on the gable ends.
11. Install the gable end fascia.
12. Install the extra piece on the gable end and the rest of the cornice at the lower end.
13. Install the reverse board and batten siding.
14. Install all the frieze boards.

Figure 10-10 shows us the pieces of the cornice as they will look when installed from the end view. Cut the groove into the fascia with several passes of the saw or a router. The joint made at the valley junction should be a butt type. That's easy to fit. There will be a joint in each side; this one should be a 45-deg miter. It makes a much finer joint. Trim the end even with the 2 × 4s that are even with the fly rafter. As you install the fascia, use a scrap piece of plywood to maintain the exact position—up and down.

Now let's install the gable end fascia. We must make a groove in this piece, too. It should be just below the position of the lookouts. Then install this piece. The ridge cut must be vertical, and the lower end must overlap the horizontal fascia and must be trimmed along its line.

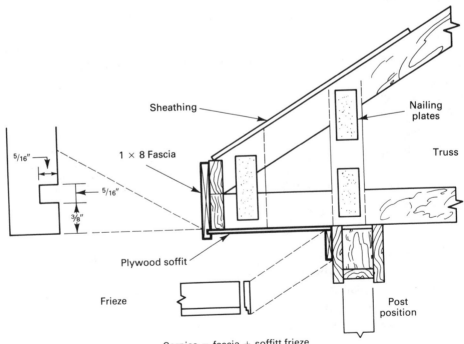

Cornice = fascia + soffitt frieze

Figure 10-10 Cornice design for horizontal side cornices, details.

Next we add framing for the horizontal soffit and a vertical piece of soffit material, which will create a box. First make an added piece and nail it to the underside of the gable end fascia as shown in Figure 10-11. Toenail a short 2 × 4 to the truss and nail its outer end through the added piece. Nail a second 2 × 4 as a lookout as shown so that its one surface provides nailing surface for the vertical $\frac{1}{4}$-in. plywood piece. Nail a second one as a lookout against the plywood. This provides a nailing surface for the lower piece of gable end soffit.

Next, cut and install the soffits.

Finally, install the frieze boards. Begin with replacing the ones taken off the house. Then take the molded frieze and cut it to fit under the soffit. Nail these with 6d finish or casing nails. Set the nails. The frieze cannot be installed on the gable end until the siding is installed. Let's talk about that.

Siding Installation

Vertical reverse board and batten is sold in 4-ft by 8-ft sheets about $\frac{1}{2}$ in. thick. The sloped piece should fit against the soffit. The lower end should extend over the joint $\frac{1}{2}$ in. to preclude rain entering the porch through the truss–header joint. Plan the work to ensure that the vertical joints in the siding are over a stud.

When all siding pieces have been installed, install the two gable end frieze moldings.

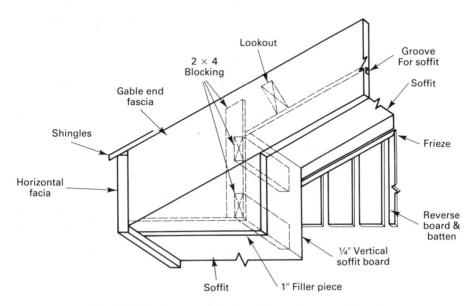

Figure 10-11 Cornice design for gable end lower end, details.

Ceiling Installation

Exterior plywood should be used for the ceiling as per the specifications. Other materials could be used as well, but for the generic porch ceiling we will discuss the plywood style.

One method is to cut each piece of plywood 4 × 4 and bevel all four edges with a block plane. These pieces would create a pattern in the ceiling. An alternative would be to cut each panel 2 × 4 and bevel all four edges. This would make a different pattern but also very nice. Since the porch is 20 ft wide less the dimension of the front header, some trimming will be needed to make end pieces equal; see Figure 10-12. The same technique applies to the first and last rows. *Note*: The 20-ft dimension is reduced by two header thicknesses. Usually 4d finish nails are used to install the plywood pieces. Following the installation of the ceiling, quarter round or cove molding must be installed along the ceiling line. Either miter the corners or cope them as required.

The job is done, and it should look great. Now seal the wood with primer and paint as soon as possible.

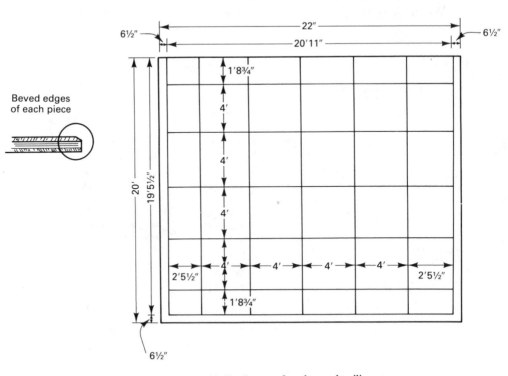

Beved edges
of each piece

Figure 10-12   Layout for plywood ceiling squares.

SAFETY

Let's talk for a minute about safety, which needs serious consideration. With the exception of some small amount of ground work, most of the tasks in this project are done above ground and above the porch floor. At every opportunity the porch floor and surrounding ground area should be cleared of loose building materials. Building materials on the ground and porch floor create uneven surfaces. These are difficult to land safely on if one of us loses balance and must jump to safety. Also, *falling materials are not forgiving*. This means that constant attention by all builders is absolutely essential. Further, avoid the practice of throwing building materials off the roof. Even though you may not strike a person intentionally, sometimes it happens.

Safe handling of trusses, headers, and sheathing is made difficult because of the sizes of these parts. Two people must be available for handling them. Bracing must be constantly applied to secure headers and trusses as they are erected, not some time later.

Another real problem to be concerned with is the use of the power saw while on the roof. Do not turn it on until you are sure that you have solid footing.

Finally, watch out for falling tools. Many people have been struck and injured by falling hammers, squares, chisels, and saws.

CLEANUP

We know that the job is never done until the paperwork is done. In regard to our project, it is not done until the cleanup is done. There will be a lot of nails lying around on the ground, no matter how careful we are to avoid dropping them. These are difficult to find in grass and gardens, and only a rake will help find them. All short scraps of wood and plywood, shingles, and tarpaper should be made small enough to be bagged. Tools should be accounted for and cleaned. Ladders, sawhorses, and work planks must be put away. Finally, the porch should be swept.

MATERIALS LISTING

Table 10.3 provides an inventory of the materials needed to build the generic porch roof assembly. As with others found in other chapters, this can be modified to your own specifications.

TABLE 10.3 Materials Invoice
PROJECT: *Constructing the Porch Roof Assembly*   **DATE**: _____

Quantity	Type	Total
4 ea.	2 × 6 20 ft No. 1 Douglas fir—northern or southern pine KD	4 ea.
2 ea.	2 × 6 22 ft, same grade	4 ea.
1 set	Roof trusses (separate contract)	1 set
2 ea.	2 × 4 16 ft No. 2 common KD southern pine (fly rafters)	32 lin ft
6 ea.	2 × 4 8 ft same grade (posts)	48 lin ft
16 ea.	2 × 4 12 ft same grade	192 lin ft
2 ea.	1 × 8 16 ft No. 2 common KD fir or southern pine	32 lin ft
4 ea.	1 × 8 12 ft same grade	48 lin ft
6 ea.	1 × 4 12 ft No. 2 common pine	72 lin ft
80 lin ft	Molded frieze board	80 lin ft
3 sheets	4 × 8 $\frac{1}{4}$-in. AC grade ext (soffits)	3 sheets
18 sheets	4 × 8 $\frac{7}{16}$-in. CD grade sheathing	18 sheets
9 sheets	4 × 8 $\frac{1}{4}$-in. AC grade ext (ceiling) plywood	9 sheets
86 lin ft	$\frac{3}{4}$-in. $\frac{1}{4}$ round	86 lin ft
1 roll	18-in. aluminum flashing	1 roll
9 rolls	No. 15 felt	9 rolls
8 sq	25-yr strip shingles	8 sq
5 lb	Nails for felt installation	5 lb
10 lb	1-in. roofing nails	10 lb
12 lb	16d common galv nails	12 lb
5 lb	8d common galv nails	5 lb
3 lb	8d fin galv nails	3 lb
10 lb	12d casing galv nails	10 lb
5 lb	4d fin galv nails	5 lb
2 gal	primer	2 gal
2 gal	Exterior paint	2 gal

Rental Equipment	*Duration of Rental*
24-ft extension ladder	1 week

11

Design and Installation of the Porch Columns

OBJECTIVES

- Plan for the construction and installation of the columns for the porch.
- Plan a specifications and materials assessment.
- Establish the conditions for anchoring the columns.
- Identify the principles necessary to build the columns and install them.
- Identify the trim customarily used with on-site-built columns.
- Finalize the materials listing with computations included.

BACKGROUND

In this chapter we study the tasks associated with building columns on-site versus buying ready-made ones from a building supply house. We use the generic porch as a model. In Chapter 10, we built a roof assembly over a porch floor assembly and left the project without any finished columns. In that design we anticipated that six columns would be used to finalize the porch. In this chapter we design one column and illustrate how to construct it. To complete the porch we would have to build six columns.

The job is not all that difficult, but it does require understanding and skill to perform the various tasks. These are advanced skills possessed by craftsmen. This type of work is classified *finished work*. We use the best materials available, even though the wood will be painted.

Several elements of the design must ensure longevity of the columns. Every design consideration and characteristic must account for quick runoff of rain water to avoid rot and decay. The design must also be such that the column will adequately support the weight of the roof assembly. Another aspect that must be considered is the style of the column. It must carry on the theme or the style of the house. These considerations are discussed in this chapter.

There are two techniques that apply to building on-site columns. One way is to build each one in place. The other is to build each on a bench and then install it. Each way has its good points and a certain set of conditions to meet. Ultimately there is no practical difference in the outcome.

SPECIFICATIONS AND MATERIALS ASSESSMENT

We continue the format of previous chapters. The specifications are provided in Table 11.1. Due to the simplicity of the overall job, no special information from the specifications has to be provided. Rather, we use the data during the construction section. Table 11.2 (page 160) lists the materials for the generic columns we study in the next section. As listed, the table saw is one tool that will almost ensure success.

LAYOUT AND CONSTRUCTION

Columns that are built on-site require skill with wood and smoothing tools. Sometimes they are built to match a period in time, such as colonial, southern, western, and New England. Other characteristics include the sizing of the column. Finally, the use of crowns and bases or base moldings is selective. These range from very plain and functional to very ornate.

TABLE 11.1 Specification Listing
PROJECT: *Constructing the Porch Columns*   **DATE:** _____

General Description

Six columns will be constructed on site to support the roof assembly. These will each have a doubled 2 × 4 core and first-quality 1-in. stock encasing the 2 × 4s. There will be a base about $5\frac{1}{2}$ in. high with the top edge sloped in the direction of the rainfall. The crown will be simple and will fit against the porch headers. Its lower edge will be molded with an ogee or cove pattern. Further shoe style molding will finish off the crown.

Specifications

Item	Specs
Dimensions	Approximately 5 in. square by about 8 ft high
Core materials	No. 2 common KD fir or southern pine
Casing materials	Clear grade 1-in. stock
Nailing	Casing and finish nails will be used for 1-in. stock and molding
Installation	Columns will be nailed to the headers and to the floor
Base design	Top edge slopes $\frac{3}{8}$ in. in the direction of the rain
Crown design	Lower edge molded with ogee or cove, upper edge trimmed with shoe molding
Prime and paint	Exterior grade latex-based paints

For our generic project we are going to construct a style of column that is decorative, yet not ornate. It has a 2 × 4 core and 1-in. clear pine casing. A *casing* is like an envelope in that four pieces close in the 2 × 4s.

Figure 11-1 shows us the generic column. We have to build it to fit under the header on the porch frame and stand on the floor. If you have been studying the chapters in their order, you know that we planned to have the six columns installed over the six piers that support the porch floor assembly. If you are entering the program here, one of the purposes for a column is to transfer the force from the roof to the footings. The force from the roof is borne by the headers and plates, which in turn is collected onto the columns and transferred to the piers to the footings and ground. This alignment is important to remember.

Figure 11-1 also provides several detail sections: the top view, the crown details, and the base molding. We discuss these in detail later in the chapter. First let's make a decision. Should we build the columns in place or on the workbench? Some find it better to make them on the bench, where planing and

TABLE 11.2 Materials Assessment
PROJECT: *Constructing the Porch Columns*   **DATE:** _____

Direct Materials

Type or Description	*Use or Purpose*
Double 2 × 4s	Basic support for the roof
1-in.-thick clear stock	Casing for the core 2 × 4s
Shoe molding and cove	Part of the crown design
Nails	Fasteners
Primer and paint	Paint columns

Indirect Materials

Type or Description	*Use or Purpose*
2 × 4s	Temporary posts

Support Materials

Type or Description	*Use or Purpose*
Sawhorses and planks	Workbench for dressing, cutting, and shaping materials
Table saw	Rip and cross-cut stock
Carpentry tools, including 12-in. plane	Construction
Miter box	Cut molding
Router and ogee blade/bit	Mold the crown pieces
5-ton house jack	Raise the headers to allow placement of the columns

fitting the pieces is easier. Others would have no trouble building them in place. In fact, the advantage of building them in place is that the core 2 × 4s can be installed and plumbed before the casings are installed. On the other hand, the completed column is easily placed by simply jacking the headers up, placing the column in position, and lowering the headers. For our project we shall build them at the bench and then insert them in place.

The tasks we will perform are as follows:

1. Determine the total length of the column.
2. Prepare six cores.
3. Install the casings around the six cores.
4. Build the crowns.
5. Build the bases.
6. Install the columns in place.

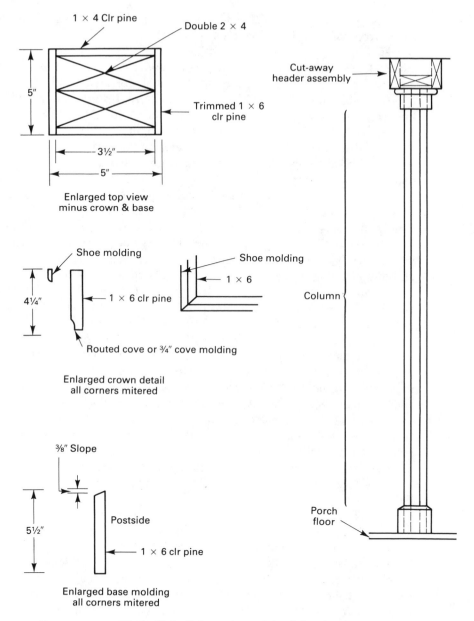

1 × 4 Clr pine

Double 2 × 4

5"

3½"

5"

Trimmed 1 × 6
clr pine

Enlarged top view
minus crown & base

Shoe molding

4¼"

1 × 6 clr pine

Routed cove or ¾" cove molding

Shoe molding

1 × 6

Enlarged crown detail
all corners mitered

⅜" Slope

5½"

Postside

1 × 6 clr pine

Enlarged base molding
all corners mitered

Cut-away
header assembly

Column

Porch
floor

Figure 11-1   Column plan and detail drawings.

Let's assume that the actual measurement of the columns is exactly 8 ft from the floor to the underside of the headers. We will put a filler piece of ½ in. to make sure that the 2 × 4 core pieces are in full contact with the header assembly. An alternative would be to extend the core ½ in. above the casing and crown.

Let's cut 12 pieces of 2×4 8 ft long and nail them in pairs with 12d common galvanized nails. This will give us six cores.

For task 3, the casing consists of four pieces per column (see the detail in Figure 11-1). We should buy clear stock ponderosa pine. It is easy to work with and does not split easily. Other species that are also good to work with are cypress, white pine, hemlock, and spruce. *Note:* Spruce is not readily available knot free. We need to buy 12 pieces of 1×4s 8 ft long, two for each column, and 12 pieces of 1×6s 8 ft long, two for each column. The 1×4s should be the same width as the 2×4s, $3\frac{1}{2}$ in. These are nailed to the core as shown in Figure 11-1, with 6d galvanized casing nails. Recess each with a nail set and above all do not make any hammer marks.

Next measure the width of the column from outside to outside of the casings. It should be 5 in. but may be slightly more. Set the table saw or guide on the hand power saw for $\frac{1}{16}$ in. wider than needed. After ripping the 12 pieces, plane each one smooth with a surface plane. I always bevel the planed side toward the inside slightly. Then, if necessary, I have extra materials to make a final sweep with the plane after the pieces have been nailed to the other casings.

Now nail the pieces to the casings already installed. Set the nail heads. Begin with making one side flush. Then all final planing will be relegated to only one side. Dress any overlap with the smoothing plane.

Task 4 directs us to build the crowns. The enlarged detail in Figure 11-1 shows two methods: Either we make the basic crown piece from 1×6 trimmed to $4\frac{1}{4}$ in. and we route a cove molding into it, or we buy 1×4 and add $\frac{3}{4}$-in. cove molding. I would opt for the use of cove. Each piece of 1×4 must be measured and cut on a 45-deg angle. A table saw is the best tool to use for the job. First cut 24 pieces 8 in. long; then set the saw for 45 deg, and cut one end of each piece. Next measure the exact length of one side and cut 12 pieces at 45 deg to this length. Number these 1. Repeat the process for the adjacent side and label these 2. Nail the four pieces even with the top of the core.

Using a miter box, cut and nail the cove and shoe moldings as shown in the details of Figure 11-1. Use 4d finishing galvanized nails for the job.

Task 5 directs us to build the base molding. For this we use 1×6 materials, and the first part of the job is to bevel and dress the top edge. A requirement we must meet is to build a base with a top edge that slopes in the direction of rainfall. We set the saw for a 3.8-in. bevel. After cutting the full-length pieces with the bevel, we dress it smooth with the plane. Then we can cut the 24 pieces we need for the base molding. Let's repeat the process we used for the crown. All corners must be mitered. Nail all pieces with 6d galvanized casing nails.

The columns are now done. The installation can begin. The subtasks are

1. Locate the positions of each of the columns.
2. Install the corner columns first.
3. Install remaining columns.

Locating the Columns

The simplest method of locating the exact position of the corner columns is with the use of a plumb bob, as shown in Figure 11-2. Using the outer corner of the headers, drop the point until it is just above the floor. Mark the precise point on the floor. Make two more marks $\frac{5}{8}$ in. in from this point, parallel to the floor edges. This 90-deg angle is the exact corner of the base molding.

Next, take a chalkline and snap three lines. Snap one across the front of the porch floor from pencil line to pencil line. Second and third lines are snapped along the sides of the porch. Make a parallel pencil mark at least 10 ft from the front back and an equal distance in to the first pencil marks made after using the plumb bob.

Next, measure along the front edge to divide the space in half, and then from the center point measure $3\frac{1}{2}$ ft either side for a total opening of 7 ft between columns. Place an X to the left and right of these marks. Then use the plumb bob to find the corresponding points on the header. Mark a point $\frac{5}{8}$ in. toward the center. Each is the plumb point for the crown.

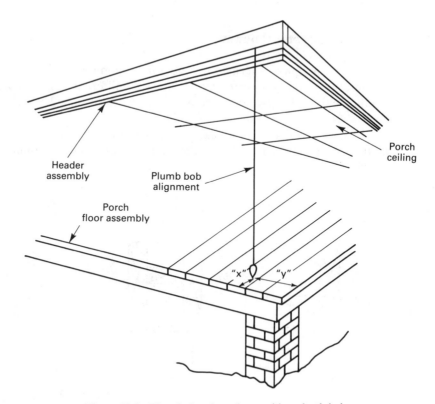

Figure 11-2 Pinpointing the column with a plumb bob.

Finally, measure 10 ft back from the edge of the porch, and make a mark that touches the chalkline. Use the plumb bob and make a corresponding mark on the header. Then measure back to the porch front $\frac{5}{8}$ in. and make a pencil mark. This is the exact mark for the crown. Repeat the sets on the opposite side.

All six columns are located.

Installing the Corner Columns

A temporary column was installed during the construction of the porch roof. This must be removed, and the finished column must be installed in its place. Using another 2 × 4 and a jack, install a second temporary post near the corner. Raise the roof until the first temporary 2 × 4 is free of stress. Remove it and replace it with the first finished column. Align the column with the marks, and check your work with a spirit level. Release the jack, and then use the toenailing technique to secure the column to header and floor. Set all nails, and do not make hammer marks.

Repeat the process for the remaining five columns.

This job is done.

The 7½-in.-Diameter Column

All of the techniques described for the 5-in. column apply for the 7½-in.-diameter column except the core structure. It must be different. Figure 11-3 provides us with the details. The two core members are a 2 × 6 and a 2 × 4 that form an **L** or two 2 × 6s and a 2 × 4 that form an **H**.

If the **L** form is used, blocks of 2 × 4 are nailed every foot apart to ensure that the casing materials will have ample nailing and that the column will stay true and will not twist.

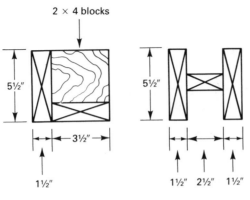

"**L**" Design core   "**H**" Design core   **Figure 11-3** "L" and "H" column core structures.

CLEANUP AND SAFETY CONCERNS

There will not be much to clean up in comparison to other phases of building a porch. But there is a need to keep the work area free of scraps of wood. The porch floor should already be cleaned as part of work already completed. If not, do it before making the columns.

Coincidental with a clean work area is the need to take safety measures. One very important measure is to place the table saw on the porch floor (preferably) or on a cleared area on level ground. The porch roof protects the saw and permits work on the columns during rain or other bad weather. Sawhorses and planks forming the work/assembly bench should be set away from the edge of the porch floor *and* in such a manner that the bench is between you and the floor edge.

The use of a house jack with a temporary 2 × 4 that raises the roof assembly just enough to install the column is dangerous. A true alignment of both needs to be made plumb. In this way the force is directed directly upward and not outward at the junction of 2 × 4 and jack. Be very careful!

Use ordinary caution when installing the columns. You will be working at the edge of the floor assembly. An inadvertent step in the wrong direction could result in a serious accident. Ordinary caution must also prevail around the table saw when it is running.

Somewhat more than ordinary caution is necessary if the cove molding is machined into the crown material. Since the pieces used for the crown are not very large (about 8 in. square) extreme care must be taken when using the router. If you are routing the cove into the crown without assistance, you will need to either install the router in its table and clamp the table to the workbench plank or to the edge of the table saw. This permits freedom of both hands for control of the crown as the four edges are routed. If no router table is used, the crown must be clamped to the table saw top or to the plank in the workbench. Doing it this way is safe but restricts the number of sides routed to two. Then the piece must be repositioned and reclamped to route the remaining two sides. Under no circumstances attempt to hold the crown with one hand while operating the router with the other. This tool has a blade that rotates at 25,000 revolutions per minute.

Finally, avoid accidents by using sharp saw blades, sharp wood chisels, and sharp blades in the smoothing planes.

MATERIALS LISTING

We built six columns for the generic project. The materials invoice shown in Table 11.3 provides us with a detailed listing of the actual material used to make these columns.

TABLE 11.3 Materials Invoice
PROJECT: *Construction of six porch columns*   **DATE**: _____

Quantity	Type	Total
12 ea.	2 × 4 8 ft, No. 2 common KD southern pine or fir	12 ea
12 ea.	1 × 4 8 ft, clear ponderosa pine or cypress	32 bd ft
12 ea.	1 × 6 8 ft, clear ponderosa pine or cypress	48 bd ft
1 ea.	1 × 4 16 ft, clear pine or cypress (crown)	1 ea.
1 ea.	$\frac{3}{4}$ in. 16 ft, cove molding	1 ea.
	OR	
1 ea.	1 × 6 16 ft, clear pine or cypress (crown and molding)	1 ea.
2 ea.	$\frac{3}{8}$ × $\frac{3}{4}$ shoe molding, 10 ft	20 lin ft
1 ea.	1 × 6 ft clear pine or cypress (base)	1 ea.
1 lb	12d common galv nails	1 lb
1 lb	4d fin galv nails	1 lb
4 lb	6d casing galv nails	4 lb
1 ea.	Combination saw blade	1 ea.

Rental Equipment	Duration of Rental
5-ton house jack	4 hr
Table saw	1 day

12

Screening the Porch

OBJECTIVES

- Plan for the screening of the porch.
- Identify the cabinetmaking techniques needed to construct the screen panels.
- Identify the sequence of steps used to construct each panel.
- Explain the installation techniques for panels and door.
- Prepare a materials listing.
- Define the finishing tasks, including painting.

BACKGROUND

Figure 12-1 provides a perspective view of the finished screened porch. This project is very complex; it requires some cabinetmaking skills and knowledge as well as excellent carpentry skills. However, the project is worth doing and doing well. We shall discuss some of the principles of screening a porch, including the do's and don'ts. Some preplanning is required, and some special tools are used, including a dowel centering tool, drill, staple gun, and bar clamp.

Style must be incorporated into the design. This can vary from unpretentious, as shown in Figure 12-1, to much more ornate. Style incorporates principles of design and construction. Let's list several:

1. The center panel in each section should be wider than the others.
2. The side panels should be equal in width and narrower than the center one.
3. The panels must never touch the porch floor.
4. The screen wire is always on the outside of the screen panels.
5. Screen wire is never nailed to 2 × 4s spaced 24 in. apart or wider.
6. Lattice is used along the floor and prepared to let rain or other water escape.
7. Panels are held in place with nails, and gaps are finished with quarter round.
8. Panels are primed with paint before the screen wire is applied.

For the generic porch project, we use the doweling technique of joining the stiles of the panels to the rails. Other methods include the mortise and tenon

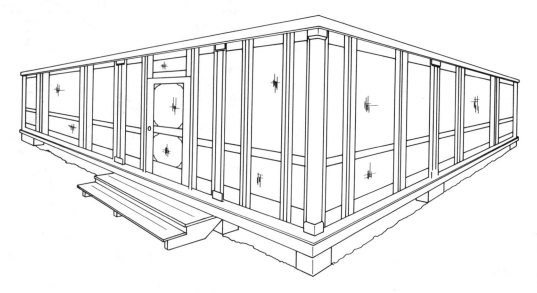

Figure 12-1 Perspective view of the screened porch.

technique, which is much more difficult to accomplish and requires different machines. The butt joint fastened with corrugated nails is never used. Glued butt joints even with exterior types of glue are not suitable due to the pulling effects of the sun and the expansion effects due to moisture.

We start with the specifications.

SPECIFICATIONS

For the generic project of screening a porch, we use the generic porch project from the past few chapters. This translates to the following requirements: The screen door will be centered in the front of the porch, and the areas between the posts will be enclosed with panels of screen wire. There are four 10-ft sections, two on each end, and three 7-ft sections on the front. To make the design attractive and construction simple, 2 × 3 dividers will be installed to separate the panels. Table 12.1 lists the specifications in detail.

TABLE 12.1 Specification Listing
PROJECT: *Screening the Porch*   **DATE:** _____

General Description

Two ends and the front side of the porch will be screened. There will be three sections of screen (panels) between columns and house walls. The center panel will be wider than the side panels. All will have the same rails and stile dimensions. The screen door will replace the center section on the front side of the porch. A small screen section will be built and installed above the screen door. The screen door will open into the porch, since no landing is built on the outside. Priming of all wood will be done before screen wire is installed. All panels will not touch the porch floor, and provisions for escape will be incorporated into the design.

Specifications

Item	Specifications
Panel design	Stiles $\frac{5}{4}$ × $2\frac{3}{4}$ in. wide full length, top rail $5\frac{1}{2}$ in. wide, mid rail $3\frac{1}{2}$ in. wide, bottom rail $7\frac{1}{4}$ in. wide. All joints doweled (2 per joint). Exterior glue bond
Panel length	Total height from header to floor less $\frac{1}{2}$ in.
Panel spacers	2 × 3 No. 2 common KD or better
Screen wire	Nylon or aluminum
Screen door	3 ft by 6 ft 8 in. wood, hung with mortise or screen door hinges
Panels encased	$\frac{1}{4}$ round on both sides and top bottom—$\frac{1}{4}$ × $1\frac{5}{8}$-in. lattice
Glue	Exterior waterproof type
Screen moldings	Screen wire edges and staples covered with molding

MATERIALS ASSESSMENT

As we have done in other chapters, we shall make an assessment of the variety of direct, indirect, and support materials needed for the generic screen porch. These are listed in Table 12.2.

PANEL DESIGN AND CONSTRUCTION

Predesign and Construction Work

Before we can design and build the frames, we must do one task. We must cut and install vertical 2 × 3s as dividers. Using Figure 12-1 as a reference as well as the specifications, we know that there must be three panels per section and that the center panel will be wider than the side panels. For our generic project, each of the four side sections will have a 4-ft-wide center panel. Each front section will have a 3-ft-wide center panel.

Further, these 2 × 3s must be dressed and may be routed with a cove bit to add style. They will be toenailed to the header flush with the inside of the outside one. Each will be toenailed to the floor. All will be plumb.

The tasks are

1. Rip 2 × 6 No. 2 common KD pine or fir and dress the edge.
2. Lay out the position of each vertical separator on the header and floor.
3. Cut each for fit and toenail in place.

Panel Design and Construction Work

We use one drawing, Figure 12-2, to describe the tasks associated with constructing the panels. With it we define the characteristics of each panel, and decide how best to cut the materials and how to assemble them. Then we briefly discuss the screening and screen molding tasks, since these are fairly straightforward.

A review of Figure 12-2 shows that the stiles will reach full length; that is, they will fit tightly under the headers and will extend to $\frac{1}{2}$ in. above the floor. The rails will butt to the stiles and the joint will be secured with dowels and exterior glue. The total width of the panel will be $\frac{1}{2}$ in. less than the width between post and divider or divider and divider.

Standard stock materials can be used in building the frames, so considerable cost in materials can be saved. A $\frac{5}{4}$ × 6 ripped in two creates a pair of stiles. Head rails are made from $\frac{5}{4}$ × 6, which is actually 1 × 5$\frac{1}{2}$ in. The center rails are made from stock $\frac{5}{4}$ × 4, which is actually 1 × 3$\frac{1}{2}$ in. and the bottom rails are made from $\frac{5}{4}$ × 8, which is actually 1 × 7$\frac{1}{4}$ in. Standard lattice is used across the bottom to cover the gap between the screen panel and porch floor. Quarter-round mold-

TABLE 12.2 Materials Assessment
PROJECT: *Screening the Porch*   **DATE:** _____

Direct Materials

Type or Description	*Use or Purpose*
$\frac{5}{4}$-in. stock lumber	Framing rails and stiles
Screen wire	Wire stapled to frames
Staples	Used to install wire
Exterior glue	Aids in joint construction
$\frac{3}{8}$-in. dowels	Aids in joint construction
Screen door	Access to yard and porch
3-in. mortise hinges	Hang the door
Screen door lock	Secure the door
Screen door spring	Aids in closing the door
Quarter round molding	Fills spaces between the frame and post or spacer
Lattice	Completes the base and permits water runoff
Nails	Install panels and moldings
Screen molding	Cover staples and screen edges
Primer and paint	Paint all wood

Indirect Materials

Type or Description	*Use or Purpose*
Paint brushes and pads	Apply paint products
Drop cloths	Keep paint off the porch floor
Masking tape	Keep paint off the columns
Scrap $\frac{5}{4}$ stock	Test pieces for making joints

Support Materials

Type or Description	*Use or Purpose*
Sawhorses and planks	Workbench
Table saw and combination blade	Improves accuracy in making joints and ripping lumber
Carpentry tools	Construction
Dowel centering tool	Provides accuracy in doweling
Power drill and drill bit	Creates dowel holes
Power joiner	Smooths the ripped edges of lumber
Electrical extension cords	Connect power machines
5-ft bar clamp	Pull stiles to rails at joints
Staple gun (manual or electric)	Install screen wire

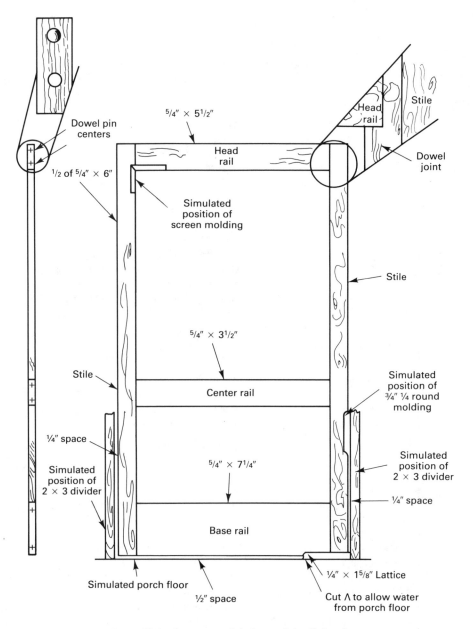

Figure 12-2 Screen panel design and detail drawing.

ing finishes the installation by covering the gaps along the stiles and across the header inside and outside.

Now let's list the tasks that must be done:

1. Rip 20 $\frac{5}{4}$ × 6s into 40 stiles, smooth edges, and drill holes for dowels.
2. Cut the head rails, center rails, and base rails for each panel, and drill, matching the holes for the dowels.
4. Apply glue to the joints and insert dowels.
5. Clamp the stiles to the rails.
6. Prime panels with an exterior paint primer.
7. Install screen wire with staples.
8. Install screen molding.

The simple way to build the panels is to mass-cut as many pieces as possible with one setting of a machine or doing one task. That is why all stiles should be cut and dressed at the same time.

Since there are four 4-ft panels on the sides, we should cut the rails in mass for these; 48 in. − (5$\frac{1}{2}$ in. + $\frac{1}{2}$-in. space) = 42 in. Mark these, cut and stack them aside. Repeat the process for the remaining panels. Doing this precludes making individual measurements and lessens chances for misfits.

Next, lay out the position of the rails on the stiles, the head at the top, the center rail at 32 in. up from the bottom, and the bottom rail even with the bottom. As shown on the left of Figure 12-2, dowel holes are equally distributed between extremes. When the six dowel positions are located, a dowel-centering tool is used to guide the drill bit in boring the holes. Figure 12-3 shows such a tool. Notice the clamp on the drill bit. This is set for the depth. We use 1$\frac{3}{4}$-in.-long by $\frac{3}{8}$-in.-diameter dowels. Half of the dowel, or $\frac{7}{8}$ in., is inserted into the stile, and the other $\frac{7}{8}$ in. is inserted into the rail. We should drill the holes 1 in. deep to allow for air and sawdust.

Once the holes are drilled into the stile the head piece can be set against the stile, but first insert the dowel-centering pin. Its point will show the exact position of the corresponding hole. Using the impression in the end of the rail, position the dowel-centering tool over it and drill the hole 1 in. deep.

After all holes in a panel set are drilled, squirt or force a bit of exterior wood glue into each hole and along the surfaces to be bonded. Tap the six dowels in each stile. Then position the rails in place and use the clamps to pull the parts together. Finally, wipe away any excess glue and use the framing square to make sure that each frame is perfectly square. If a panel is not square, rack it until it is square. Set the panel aside to dry and construct another one.

A small panel must be made to fit over the door. We know that it will be 36 in. wide, since the door is 36 in. wide. In real terms we measure up from the floor

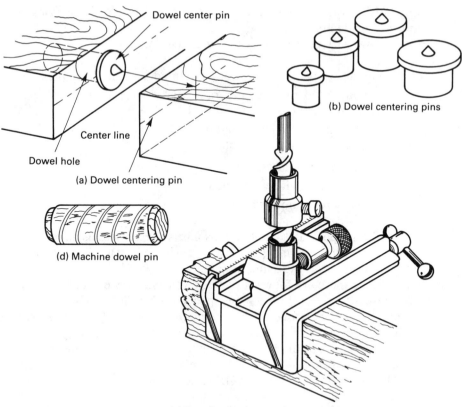

Figure 12-3 Dowel centering and drilling tool with dowel centering pins.

the height of the screen door and add allowances for space under the door ($\frac{1}{4}$ in.) and at the head ($\frac{1}{4}$ in.). This measurement is the bottom of this panel. Then we simply measure from the pencil mark to the porch header to determine the exact height of the small panel. Once the height is known, we build it.

Screening the Panels

Screen wire is bought in widths incrementing 2 in. at a time up to 40 in. and in 4-in. increments after that. For the 4-ft panels we use 44- or 48-in. wire. For the 3-ft panels we use 34- or 36-in. wire, and so on.

Screen wire is installed as follows and is numbered in Figure 12-4. Any other method causes problems.

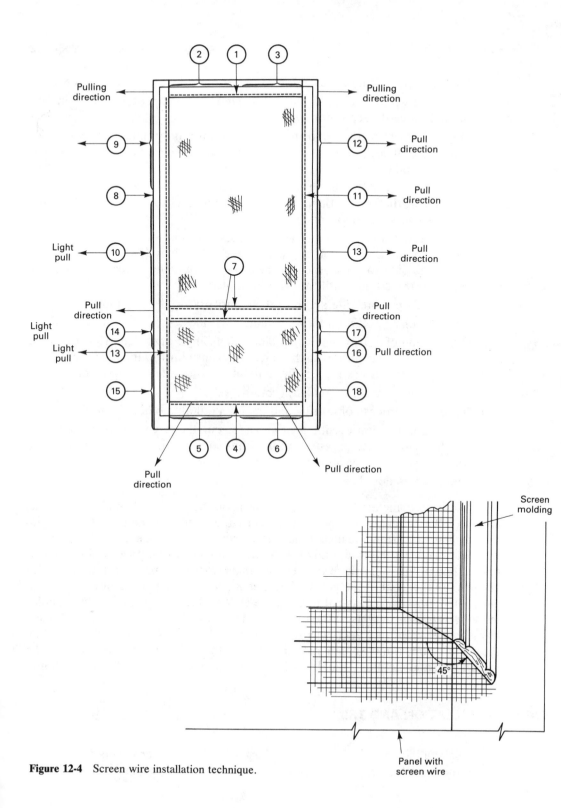

Figure 12-4 Screen wire installation technique.

1. Lay the wire so that at least 2 in. extends over the areas to be screened.
2. Staple the wire to the head rail end, beginning in the center of the wire and stapling toward each outer edge.
3. Staple the wire to the opposite end or bottom rail by pulling the wire tight with the front edge of the stapler and squeezing off a staple. Work your way out to the edges.
4. Staple the wire to the center rail, making sure to put all staples within $\frac{1}{2}$ in. of the edge of the wood. Begin at the center and pull the wire from the outer edge as you squeeze off each staple.
5. Start at the center of any of the four edges yet to be stapled and gently pull the wire tight. Squeeze off a staple. Move left or right 2 to 3 in. at a time and staple the side to the corner. Repeat the process the other way from the center to the corner until the wire is stapled.
6. Go to the opposite side and repeat the process—pull and staple.
7. Repeat steps 5 and 6 on the remaining two sides.
8. Cut one end of a strip of screen molding at an angle of 45 deg. Lay it in place so that the inner corner of the miter is even with the inner corner of the screened area. Mark for length, and cut the opposite 45-degree miter.
9. Nail the piece in place with $\frac{3}{4}$-in. brads.
10. Repeat the process of cutting and nailing until all molding is in place.
11. Using a utility knife with a new blade, cut the excess wire next to the molding. Moderate pressure on the knife and a lifting of the wire into the knife does the job easily.
12. The panel is done!

We have completed the job of preparing all the panels when all of the tasks are done. Let's recap! We needed to define the widths of the panels, but to do that we first had to cut and install the vertical separators. Once the task was done, we could mass-cut the stiles and drill all the dowel holes. Next we could mass-cut quite a few of the rails, since the center panels were the same width on the sides and also on the front of the porch. We then made the side panels for each section and, where possible, mass-cut these as well. Recall that we made matching holes in the rails for the dowels. When we were done, we glued and clamped the panel frames. We made sure each was square and let the glue set. Then we primed all the panel frames and screen molding. When the paint dried, we installed the screen wire and molding. Finally, we trimmed the excess wire with a utility knife.

PANEL INSTALLATION AND TRIM

Let's make a big splash for the folks. We'll install the center panels first, except where the door fits. These panels will fit right into the openings without further preparation. All we need to do is install the quarter round outside, nail the panel in place, install the molding on the inside, and then cut and install the lattice along the bottom inside and outside. The side panels will need further cutting to fit around the base and crown moldings. The tasks are as follows:

1. Cut and install the quarter round flush with the outside of the vertical separators, as shown in the top view in Figure 12-5. Miter the top piece to the side pieces. Nail each in place with 4d galvanized finish nails.
2. Install the panel against the quarter round, raise it up tightly to the headers, and toenail the panel into the vertical members.
3. Install the quarter round on the inside top and sides.
4. Measure and cut two lattice pieces to fit against the base rail and between the quarter round. Before nailing each in place, make one or two inverted Vs (^) to allow for water to escape.

On the columns, install the quarter round between base and crown moldings and nail it to the post. If you do not do a first-class job in cutting the panel around the posts, you must add quarter round molding up the base and up the crown. This means quite a few small pieces, each with 2 miters, making those returns.

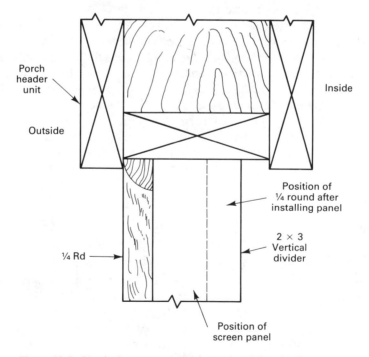

Figure 12-5 Vertical separators and $\frac{1}{4}$ round molding detail drawings.

Most of the side panels must be trimmed to fit around the crown and base moldings. Always work from the header and head rail down when marking the panel stile for trimming. Keep the cuts as accurate as possible for a quality job. When the panel is fitted properly, install it and put the quarter round on the inside.

Now, what's left to do? Well, the panels that almost touch the house must be installed and finished. That is, we need to make sure that the space between the panel and the house is trimmed. If the house is sided with reverse board and batten as in our example, there is no problem in nailing the quarter round to it. But if the siding is lap-siding, then quarter round will leave gaps for bugs to enter. If the siding is brick, the gap will be irregular. Both of these problems are solved with form-fitting a piece of 1×2 instead of the quarter round. Each piece of 1×2 is placed against the wall/panel and tacked in place. Then a scribe is used to make a mark on the 1×2 parallel to the irregular wall surface. Finally, we cut the board along the pencil line and then apply a bead of caulking to the freshly cut piece and install it or them.

DOOR AND HEADER INSTALLATION

Now we come to the installation of the door and the header panel over the door. The door should fit into the opening without cutting, but try it to be sure. Next install the mortise hinges. *Note*: If you are unskilled in the installation of this type of hinge, buy surface mount hinges and install one about $6\frac{1}{2}$ in. down from the top and the other $8\frac{1}{2}$ in. up from the bottom. Place the door into the frame flush with the inside of the vertical separators. Screw the hinge to the 2×3. Install the door stops, making the front edge of the door flush with the 2×3 separator. Next follow the instructions that accompanied the lockset and install the lock and pull unit. Finally, install the screen door spring or closure unit.

Last build the header screen assembly and install it over the door. A piece of door stop must be nailed to the front side of this unit to act as a head door stop.

The construction job is done.

PAINTING

Before any serious painting can begin, we must clean the entire porch area of sawdust, chips, tools, and extra wood. Let's have a flat, safe area to place the drop cloths on and avoid the chance of an accident.

We have already primed the panel frames and screen molding. But the quarter round, lattice, door, and stops may not have been primed. If not, complete the priming. Then use a good-quality exterior latex semi-gloss paint to complete the painting project. If there are knots in the lumber, a precoat of

TABLE 12.3 Materials Invoice
PROJECT: *Screening the Porch*   **DATE:** _____

Quantity	Type	Total
7 ea.	8 ft 2 × 6 No. 2 common KD fir or southern pine	10 ea.
22 ea.	8 ft $\frac{5}{4}$ × 6 clear pine or cypress	88 bd ft
60 lin ft	$\frac{5}{4}$ × 6 clear pine or cypress	30 bd ft
60 lin ft	$\frac{5}{4}$ × 4 clear pine or cypress	20 bd ft
60 lin ft	$\frac{5}{4}$ × 8 clear pine or cypress	40 bd ft
644 lin ft	$\frac{3}{4}$ in. $\frac{1}{4}$ round	644 lin ft
1 ea.	3'0'' × 6'8'' wood screen door	1 ea.
1 pair	Mortise or screen door hinges	1 pair
1 ea.	Screen door lock set	1 ea.
1 ea.	Screen door closure	1 ea.
64 lin ft	$\frac{1}{4}$ × $1\frac{5}{8}$ in. lattice	64 lin ft
18 lin ft	$1\frac{1}{4}$-in. door stop	18 lin ft
258 ea.	$\frac{3}{8}$ × $1\frac{5}{8}$-in. dowels	258 ea.
1 qt	Exterior wood glue	1 qt
5 lb	4d fin galv nails	5 lb
5 lb	$\frac{3}{4}$ in. brads	5 lb
32 lin ft	44- or 48-in. wide screen wire	32 lin ft
86 lin ft	34- or 36-in. wide screen wire	86 lin ft
48 lin ft	24- or 26-in. wide screen wire	48 lin ft
$1\frac{1}{2}$ gal	Exterior primer paint	$1\frac{1}{2}$ gal
2 gal	Exterior semi-gloss paint	2 gal
1 ea.	3-in. paint brush	1 ea.
1 ea.	Paint pad	1 ea.
1 ea.	Miter box	1 ea.
1 box	Staples	1 box
1 package	Utility blades	1 package
1 ea.	Combination saw blade for table saw	1 ea.
2 ea.	Drop cloths min 9' × 12'	2 ea.
1 roll	1 to $1\frac{1}{2}$-in. masking tape	1 roll

Rental Equipment	*Duration of Rental*
Table saw	Three days
5-ft bar clamps	Three to four days
Power drill	Three days
Staple gun (manual or electric)	Three days
6-in. joiner	Three days

shellac or varnish covers these very well, and they will not show when the final coats of paint are applied.

Clean up tools as soon as the painting is completed.

MATERIALS LISTING

Our generic project is completed except for making the materials invoice that shows the exact materials necessary to complete the job. These are shown in Table 12.3 on page 179.

13

Finishing Techniques for Porches

OBJECTIVES

- Plan for the addition of trim, lattice, railings, spindles, and other types of materials to a porch.
- Maintain architectural integrity of the house design.
- Plan for a painting or other finishing scheme for the porch and trim.

MAINTAIN ARCHITECTURAL STYLE

Homes today generally fall into six different styles—southern colonial, colonial, cape cod, ranch, modern, and ultramodern. Some of these styles are much more prominent in local areas, such as the cape cod, while others are widely used around the country. Even within local areas the predominance of modern or ranch styles in heavily wooded areas or on larger parcels of property is frequently seen.

What we need to understand is that the style of the house must be maintained when finishing techniques are added to the porch. We list some rules and guidelines that will help keep us on track.

1. The cape cod house design is one that can incorporate *gingerbread* in its cornice design. This means that curved add-ons to the peaks of the gable ends look good. Extensions of the picket fence theme are appropriate as well. Several of these and other appropriate designs are provided in the next section.

2. Southern and southern colonial, as they are frequently called, have large columns on the porch as a rule. These columns are usually round, but not always. Since mass is bold as a rule, the finishing touches in making the porch blend with the house must include the sensation or feeling of boldness and mass. That is why we often see turned spindles in the porch railing assembly; these are frequently 2 in. in diameter. Further, they are spaced closely to increase the mass effect. Scroll types of gingerbread also apply as adornments around the crowns of the columns.

3. Ranch-style homes were originally designed for the southwestern part of the country. They were designed low to the ground and had extensive porches and overhang. The low profile gave tolerance for the winds and weather; the porches and large overhangs likewise helped to keep the interiors cool. These homes frequently used exposed wood and let it age naturally. Paint was not normally employed. Not many curved pieces were used in adding finishing touches. Rather, plain, straight wood members were used in railings and as braces between the columns and headers. Exposed beam construction also permitted the finishing techniques to employ ends of stock open to the weather.

4. Modern, the catch-all of design. The modern house is a mixture of modern materials and early building materials. These are used in thousands of combinations such as brick (old) and prefinished aluminum siding (new). This set of conditions makes the job of adding the finishing touches to a porch more difficult rather than easier. There is no one clear-cut solution to the problem. The simplest and often the best solution is to carry the most predominant characteristic of the house trim or style into the porch. We know enough to make the cornice the same and finish it in the same way as the main house. Added gingerbread and railing assemblies must either match the house or complement the style. Some curves are permitted. Spindles are permitted, but not usually as massive as those used in colonial-style homes. Patterns associated with Doric column crowns are more attractive than other, much more ornate designs.

5. Ultramodern, a really unique design, must be maintained. In almost every situation the wood applied to the house is a special characteristic of the house. Porch columns, railings, and other finishing touches must follow the exact design. If, for example, the siding is almost vertical—say, 10 degrees to the right of straight up, the porch should have a closed railing with siding at the same angle. Further, the material selected must be the same kind and finished in the same way. Here contrast is not an acceptable alternative as a finishing technique.

BUILDING MATERIALS

In this section we identify a variety of railing assemblies, gingerbread and like trims, common moldings, posts, lattice designs, and oversized lumber shaped for specific style. These are shown in Figures 13-1 through 13-6, and the captions provide a name or house style where appropriate.

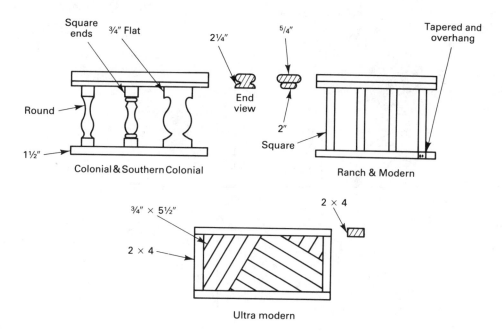

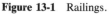

Figure 13-1 Railings.

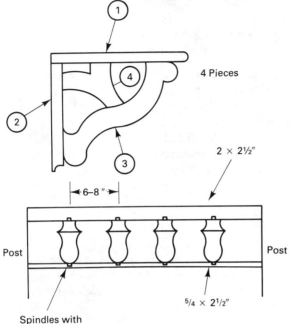

4 Pieces

$2 \times 2\frac{1}{2}''$

6–8"

Post   Post

Spindles with
dowel ends

$^{5}/_{4} \times 2^{1}/_{2}''$

Modern, colonial

Figure 13-2 Gingerbread and spindles.

¼ Rd   Cove   Bed molding

Cove

Frieze
molding
(chair rail)

Figure 13-3 Common moldings.

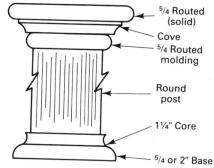
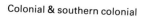

5/4 Routed (solid)

Cove

5/4 Routed molding

Round post

1¼" Core

5/4 or 2" Base

Colonial & southern colonial

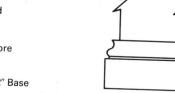

Cove

1" × 5"

Square post

Bed

1" × 6"

Modern   Ultra Modern

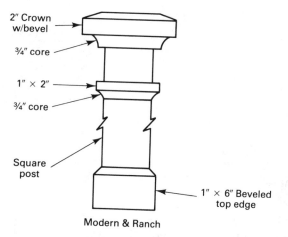

2" Crown w/bevel

¾" core

1" × 2"

¾" core

Square post

1" × 6" Beveled top edge

Modern & Ranch

Figure 13-4 Posts with moldings.

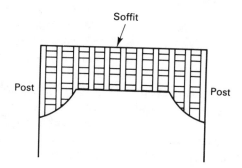

Soffit

Post   Post

Figure 13-5 Lattice, near the soffits.

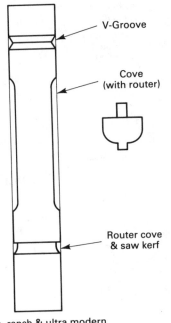

V-Groove

Cove
(with router)

Router cove
& saw kerf

Modern, ranch & ultra modern

Figure 13-6 Oversized lumber shaped into posts and columns.

PAINTS AND OTHER FINISHES

There are numerous methods that can be used to create a final finish to the porch with paints, stains, and other coatings. For the most part, porches are constructed with lumber that is not treated. This makes most finishing techniques easier. We examine the various types of materials and their application in the next few paragraphs. We also use earlier techniques of listing the tasks associated with specific combinations of materials.

Major manufacturers of paints and coating systems establish standards that are basic specifications. These are usually placed in instruction sheets and on cans, and they include such items as cleaning requirements for tools, surface preparation for unfinished materials, and other instructions for preparation for previously finished materials. We use some of these specifications later.

In addition, directions for the DFT (dry-film thickness) are provided in a unique way. It is impossible for the average person to measure the thickness of each coat of covering; however, the average DFT of a finished job for most paints and final coats of films should be 5 mils. Further, one coat properly applied provides only an average 1½- to a maximum 2½-mil thickness. That is why most instructions recommend two applications. The reasons are stated in Sherwin Williams' *Painting and Coating Systems for Specifiers and Applicators*, as follows:

Don't skip this thickness to reduce costs and expect a good paint job. At least two coats are needed to arrive at a total DFT of 5 mils. A single coat that produces 5 mils DFT will seldom result in perfect continuity. "Misses," inclusions of foreign materials such as lint, and "fallout" will cause the formation of "wicks" or channels, which draw in moisture and chemicals. These act as focal points for premature film failure. Remember, multiple thin coats are better than a single thick coat. The film thickness of the total paint system is the important fact and not the film thickness per coat.[1]

The paragraph you just read addresses one of the most important issues facing everyone finishing some materials. For our purposes in this chapter we are most concerned with finishing wood. Most of it is new, unfinished wood. The tasks are

1. Prepare the wood for painting or staining.
2. Meet the specifications for finishing exterior-exposed wood.
3. Apply the base or prime coat, whether paint or stain.
4. Apply the top coats.
5. Clean up tools and equipment.
6. Use safety precautions.

For task 1 the range of preparations includes removal of all dirt that may have been picked up and deposited on the lumber during construction. Dirt has chemicals and silicon (sand) granules, which prevent a complete covering. If the wood lay uncovered and absorbed rain or other moisture, it needs to dry for several days. If any shows any sign of mold or mildew, this must be removed with household bleach and water; then this wood must be allowed to dry. In fact, all wood must be dry for the best painting or staining systems to be done properly.

In meeting task 2 requirements we could follow Sherwin Williams S-W 23 Wood—Exterior specifications for its users. This specification, besides recommending that wood be clean and dry, also recommends the following:

1. Never paint right after a rain or in foggy weather.
2. No painting below 50°F.
3. Knots and pitch streaks shall be scraped, sanded, and spot primed before full priming coat is applied.
4. All nail holes or small openings shall be caulked after priming coat is applied.[2]

[1] *Painting and Coating Systems for Specifiers and Applicators,* Sherwin Williams Co., Cleveland, Ohio, p. 4.
[2] Ibid., p. 5.

Exterior Painting
and Staining Systems

We shall examine several different painting and staining systems that will add
character and long life to our porch project. The explanations could get very
technical, but we'll keep them simple. If you want full details, your local paint
distributors can provide the information free for the asking.

Porch floors.   A gloss, alkyd paint system will do an excellent job. Both
primer and finish coats should be the same types. Each coat should be about 2.0
mils DFT/coat. An alkyd paint is one that contains oil soya alkyd resin. This
product is abrasion resistant and dirt resistant, has a high gloss, and has high
durability. Volume solids range around 44 percent per gallon, so expected coverage is about 350 sq ft. Most of these paints are ready for a second coat in 8 hours,
and will dry to the touch in one to two hours.

Plywood.   Several systems work well with plywood. In our porch project
we used plywood under the overhang and on the ceiling. We could stain the
plywood with one of two systems, or we could paint it in one of three ways. Let's
examine the stain systems first, and then the painting systems.

1. An oil-modified, alkyd, flat stain system can be used with a semitransparent wood preservative stain. The prime and finish coats should be of the same
materials. Since semitransparent stains penetrate the wood, no DFT is applicable. The manufacturer's instructions must be followed, and preparation requires
extreme care to avoid discolorations. Stains containing preservatives provide
protection against water damage, rot, mildew, and deterioration. Repeat coats
should be applied after a 24-hour waiting period. The average coverage is quite
varied and depends upon the porosity of the wood and the rate of absorption. A
gallon can cover up to 200 sq ft on very smooth wood, such as sanded plywood.
In contrast the coverage could be as little as 100 sq ft per gallon on unsanded or
rough-cut wood and plywood.

2. An oil-modified, alkyd flat stain can be used with a solid-color stain
system. These stains employ light-fast, nonbleeding pigments. Whereas the
semitransparent stains allow the grain to be fully exposed, the solid-color systems
have full hiding, deep-color capacity. They, too, provide resistance to mold and
rot, and in addition, they resist peeling and cracking. Because there are more
solids per gallon, the coverage can cover 200 to 350 sq ft. This, of course, depends on the porosity of the wood. Some practice is required to apply this stain
correctly. The working edge must remain wet to avoid double coating and an
uneven application.

3. A vinyl acrylic flat stain is another system for finishing plywood. This
system requires that the primer be a pigmented acrylic emulsion, which helps

prevent cracking of the wood. Simply stated, use a wood protector as a primer. Then apply two coats of exterior latex solid-color stain. This system produces a finish resistant to chalk staining, blistering, color fading, and peeling. It also has good hiding quality and may be touched up easily. The second finish coat must be applied no sooner than 16 hours and no later than seven days after the first for proper bonding. Interestingly, this paint must cure for about 10 days to reach maximum protection.

Rough-sawn lumber. Three systems apply to finishing rough-sawn lumber, and we shall briefly examine each.

1. A flat, acrylic latex system requires an exterior alkyd, wood primer to seal unfinished wood and provide a substrata for the finish coats. This paint penetrates very well into the rough lumber. The finish coats should be a flat acrylic latex. Its DFT would be thinner than the primer, or about 1.3 mils thick. One gallon could cover up to 400 sq ft.

2. A flat, alkyd system uses alkyd primer and finish paints. The alkyd primer penetrates the raw wood and becomes the substrata for the finish paint. The finish coats of alkyd paint contain resins that provide good hiding and brushing qualities. They also provide long-term durability, resistance to mildew, and extended fume resistance. The finish paint covers an average 400 sq ft per gallon at 2 mils DFT.

3. Flat stain systems described above for plywood would work on rough-sawn wood. The same application sequence must be used.

Finished lumber, trims, railing assemblies, and such. There are six different systems that can be used to finish these kinds of materials. Those that already have been covered in the paragraphs above are

1. Gloss, alkyd
2. Semi-gloss, satin, and flat acrylic latex
3. Flat alkyd
4. Flat stain alkyd
5. Flat stain vinyl acrylic

The one not covered earlier is the *gloss clear alkyd*. For this system exterior varnish is used as the primer and two finish coats. It protects against the effects of direct sunlight, salt and fresh water, and temperature extremes. The grain of the wood is seen through the material. This material can be recoated after 18 hours. Delay walking on the surface for a minimum of three days. Average coverage is 450 sq ft per gallon (range: 350 to 550 sq ft). Manufacturer's directions must be

TABLE 13.1 Equipment Selection for Painting Systems (Courtesy Sherwin Williams Co.)[1]

System	Brush	Airless Sprayer	Roller	Conventional Sprayer	Cleaner
Alkyd, general	Yes	Yes	Yes	Yes	Mineral spirits
Acrylic primer	Yes	Yes	Yes	Yes	Water
Acrylic latex	Yes	Yes	No	No	Detergent and water
Latex solid color stain	Yes	Yes	Yes	Yes	Soap and water
Exterior varnish	No	Yes	No	Yes	Mineral spirits
Alkyd resin enamel	Yes	Yes	Yes	Yes	Mineral spirits
Semi-transparent wood preservative stain	Yes	No	Yes	No	Mineral spirits
Alkyd, solid color exterior stain*	Yes	Yes	Yes	Yes	Naphtha

* Wood may also be *dipped* in the stain as a means of application.
[1] Information assembled from *Painting And Coating Systems For Specifiers and Applicators, 1988.*

followed, but the prime coat should be thinned by one pint of paint thinner per gallon of varnish. The final finish coats should be applied full strength.[3]

Equipment and Equipment Maintenance

A wide variety of equipment may be used to apply one or more of the systems described earlier. For example, alkyd paints may be applied with brush, roller, airless spray, and conventional spray equipment. These items of equipment are then cleaned with mineral spirits or a manufacturer's recommended cleaner. When buying the paint system and materials, you should ask the salesperson for specific instructions for each type of applicator. For example, if an airless spray equipment is selected, it should operate at 2000 psi, require a 60 mesh filter, and have a 0.019 × 40-deg tip; you would not use a reducer in the paint.[4]

Table 13.1 provides a simple cross reference listing for the types of equipment best used with different painting and staining systems.

[3] Most of the technical data contained in this discussion were provided by Sherwin Williams in their *Painting and Coating Systems for Specifiers and Applicators,* 1988. I have used the data in a more narrative form for readability.
[4] Ibid., p. 17.

14

Gazebos:
Styles and Uses

OBJECTIVES

- Understand some of the styles used in gazebos.
- List some of the uses for a gazebo.

STYLING THE GAZEBO

Gazebos are made in every possible shape and from almost every building material. The foundation for a gazebo can be wooden posts, brick with wood, brick, block, or a concrete slab. They all work well. Several factors should be considered in making a selection. The style and the cost are the two most important considerations. The "walls," so to speak, are seldom solid, since the idea is to provide for 360-deg vision. Some walls are just posts. Many contain some sort of lattice paneling to filter the sunlight. The walls generally contain some railing assemblies to give a sense of dimension. It is also possible to screen the gazebo. Screening the gazebo could be done by using the guidelines in Chapter 11. The roof may be flat, as shown in Figure 14-1. Actually, it is not perfectly flat, since there is a small rise toward the center. The number of roof surfaces varies in accordance with the number of sides or walls. A six-sided—hexagon-shaped—gazebo has six sloped areas to its roof. The coverings for the roof can vary from filtered slats, as shown in Figure 14-1, to a shingled roof. Cornices can be formal or open rafter end.

By combining the fundamental characteristics mentioned above, a wide variety of styles of gazebos can be achieved. For example, an octagonal gazebo with an open, slated, pagoda-style roof would certainly decorate a garden where Japanese or Chinese is the theme. Or a square gazebo that is basically open could be

Figure 14-1 Gazebo in a garden setting.

decorated with just enough lattice panels to filter the sun. The flat roof with open lattice work is easy to construct, and would permit maximum airflow, thus avoiding the hot pockets often found under a solid roof. A hexagonal gazebo with rails and latticework is very common and beautiful. One made in rectangular form with a pitched roof is easy to build and could nicely fit into a geometric garden setting.

Most gazebos have one entrance, but there can be several if there is a need. For example, entrances on opposite sides make it possible for the gazebo to permit access from a traffic area into a garden or pool area.

Methods of Incorporating the Gazebo into the Surroundings

One of the most important considerations before building a gazebo is to define how to incorporate it into the garden or other surroundings. This thinking task will ultimately contribute to the final style selected. Let's explore several concepts in the next paragraphs with the hope of stimulating ideas.

A gazebo can make a big difference in a backyard, beside a house, near a pool, or even in front of a house.

Suppose you have a swimming pool but do not have a shaded place to rest after swimming. Wouldn't a gazebo be a very useful addition to the pool area? You could get out of the pool, step up into your gazebo, and sit and relax until you wanted to go back into the pool. It's even possible to have a wet bar in a gazebo, where any type of refreshment could be very handy.

Picture a beautiful wedding. The setting is the gazebo, which may be decorated with flowers, or the garden itself may provide natural decoration. The sun is shining, and the mixture of the floral motif with filtered sunlight sets a superb scene.

Or suppose your property is situated on a lake. The gazebo could be incorporated into the lawn area to provide a sitting area while you enjoy the sunrise or sunset. Indeed, think about sitting there any time of the day you have a few minutes.

A gazebo can be the focal point in your landscaping. You can build the gardens and lawn around the gazebo, and then sit back and enjoy all of the scenery as the seasons and colors change.

Imagine a gazebo around a tree with the tree being the focal point, as shown in Figure 14-2. For this type of application we would need a tree that had a wide canopy of branches. The gazebo probably would not have a man-made roof.

These ideas are the usual ones. There may be many more that suit a mountain home, a home in the desert, a home next to a golf course, and so on. No matter where you eventually place a gazebo or what design you use, try to incorporate it into the property in a way that does not make it stand out like a sore thumb.

Figure 14-2 Gazebo with tree for a natural canopy.

Style by design.   We know that a gazebo with a multisided design permits
an all-around view. Since you should be able to see the garden from all sides of
the gazebo and be able to sit just about anywhere you want to have an excellent
view, the railings in this designed gazebo would normally be low enough to permit
excellent viewing of the area.

To create a cooler area to actively enjoy the surroundings, you can use
decorations, fretwork, spandrels, or brackets around the very top of the gazebo to
filter sunlight and block direct sunlight, thus providing shade. For added comfort,
and with the addition of electricity, a ceiling fan can provide a mild breeze for
those times when natural wind is not blowing. The fan really helps in the middle
of the summer day when air currents are minimal.

Focal point.   Integrating the gazebo with its surroundings creates a focal
point. Gardens can be placed immediately around the gazebo. The flower and
shrub arrangements should be designed to show masses of color as viewed when
approaching the gazebo. Their full height should never be more than chair rail
height. From the opposite viewpoint, walkways woven through the gardens
should lead to the gazebo. Another way to create a focal point is to use a small or
narrow walkway around the gazebo, and then extend gardens outward from these.

If you are fortunate enough to have a waterfront property, the focal point
would probably be toward the water. The design selected should lend protection

from the natural rain and sun and yet allow the wind from the water to pass cleanly through the gazebo.

Finally, we should consider the inclusion of perimeter seating within the gazebo. This would be ideal but not essential to create ways to view the surroundings.

Accents and Extensions of Wood Decks

When the gazebo is made as the extension of a deck, several design principles must be followed. We shall examine several ideas:

1. Carry the central theme of the deck into the design of the gazebo.
2. Use the same materials and finishing techniques in both deck and gazebo.
3. Plan for the floor height to be level or one step up or down, and let the terrain play a role in the decision.
4. Plan for the gazebo to blend in with the railing and seating style of the deck.
5. Painting, sealing, or staining systems should be the same for deck and gazebo.
6. Trim around the top of the gazebo should carry the theme of the main house.
7. The roof style should match the main house in some way.

These seven principles are the fundamentals for any gazebo design where there is an opportunity to have the deck extend into the gazebo. In principle 1, perimeter seating on the deck should be carried over into the gazebo. If railing assemblies are used on the decking, use the same style on the gazebo. If $\frac{5}{4} \times 6$ decking is used on the deck, use it in the gazebo, and so on.

Usually treated lumber and some sort of wood protector is used for constructing decks. Use the same material types in the construction of the gazebo; further, use materials of the same proportions.

Principle 3 suggests that the floor of the gazebo be level with the deck floor, below it, or above it. Where the natural terrain falls away, the design should be to step down one or more steps. Where the terrain rises, use stairs going up to reach the floor of the gazebo.

Principles 4, 5, and 6 require very little explanation.

Principle 7 states that the roof design should match the main house *in some way*. The exception is where the roof design on the main house is gable-ended. This design does not usually work well for a gazebo roof style.

The pitch of the gazebo roof could be different, and there would still not be a problem. Another aspect of the main roof should be selected, for example, the same style and color of shingles, or the same type of overhang and cornice.

Style of the Roof

Several styles of roof are customarily used on gazebos. One type is the solid roof made from rafters, sheathing, and shingles. The roof will have as many slopes as there are sides. This translates to complex roof rafter design and cutting, as a rule. Even though the rafters can be 2 × 4s or at most 2 × 6s, the compound miter cuts made on each rafter is a task reserved for someone with more experience than a beginning novice.

Let's continue. The selection of the pitch of the roof will create many different characteristics. A 3-in-12, low-pitch roof will be very nondescript, so another characteristic about the gazebo will be the dominant one. In contrast, a 12-in-12 or steeper-pitch roof will be a dominant characteristic.

The type of roof covering makes a difference. If strip shingles are used, not much more character is added than would be on the main house. But if decorator shingles or wood shakes are used, considerable character is added. Another roof covering is metal. Copper is one possibility; it is expensive, but no one will dispute its beauty and lasting quality. Another is the anodized aluminum roof. It is most often used commercially, but looks really good on a steep-pitched roof.

Not all gazebos have solid roofs. The one shown in Figure 14-1 has a slatted roof. For this roof, I ripped treated 2 × 4s into thirds and spaced them $\frac{3}{4}$ in. apart over a 2 × 4 frame. The effect is perfect—maximum filtered sun, no possibility of buildup of heat under the roof, and every opportunity for breeze from any direction. It's not easy to see in the figure, but I raised the center 4 square feet and installed a finial to add room for a fan and light, which added character. It's great for nice weather, but fairly wet in the rain.

Many opportunities exist for styling the roof. Be sure to select a style that either matches the main house or accents the main house, garden or pool area, or other prominent portion of the property.

Style of Trim—Gingerbread

Lattice is the most common and practical material used to decorate the gazebo. It can be made to look very different, as Figure 14-3 shows. It can be made in perfect squares; each hole is a perfect square. This is even possible when the square sides are equal to twice the width of the lattice pieces. Another design made with lattice is to rotate the panel 45 degrees. But the squares are still square. However, the holes do not need to be square. A not-so-common design, also shown in Figure 14-3, is the diamond-shaped hole. This pattern is not easy to build, but can be attractive. Note that the proportions of each hole are three units up and down by two units left and right.

Lattice is usually $\frac{1}{4}$ in. thick and ranges from $1\frac{1}{4}$ in. to $1\frac{3}{4}$ in. wide. Yet lattice looks even more bold if the lattice pieces are made from $\frac{3}{8}$-in. or $\frac{1}{2}$-in.-thick stock.

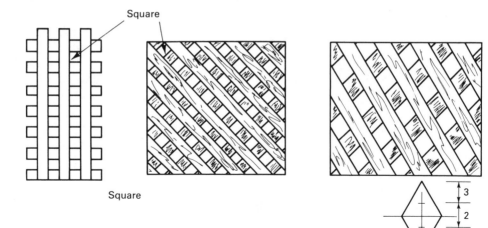

Figure 14-3 Lattice works.

Airy panels made from lattice surrounded by either $\frac{5}{4}$- or 2-in. stock can be placed as desired. They can be placed vertically or horizontally. They can be narrow or wide. Everywhere they are used, they filter sun and permit breeze passage.

Where *scrollwork* or *gingerbread* (designed, cut, and installed, or purchased from specialty shops) is used, it adds character to the gazebo and sometimes adds strength. Handmade scrollwork should be made from $\frac{5}{4}$-in. to 3-in. thick, clear stock. French curves are used most often. These can be made with the use of an illustrator's French curve tool (plastic), which is sold in various sizes. Figure 14-4 shows two French curve drawing tools.

Scrollwork is usually added to corners. When designed well, it looks very nice; often the proportions are a function of the "golden mean rectangle" which is also shown in Figure 14-5. For example, if one side of the rectangle is 1 ft long, the other, longer side should be 1 ft $6\frac{1}{8}$ in. long. This ratio is used in many places and works very well for custom-designed scrollwork.

Other dimensions such as the square work well, too. Several brackets are shown in Figure 14-6. In addition to the brackets, spandrels can be purchased to meet custom measurements. The brackets and spandrels shown in Figure 14-6 are available from Vintage Wood Works. (See the reference list for the address.)

Figure 14-4   French curves.

Styling the Railing Assemblies

We could repeat the various railing styles shown in Chapter 13. But the fact is
that they are all possible solutions when railings are used in the design of the
gazebo.

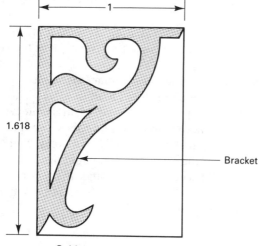

Golden mean rectangle

Figure 14-5 Golden mean rectangle.

Figure 14-6 Spandrels and brackets. (*Courtesy of Vintage Wood Works, 513 S. Adams, #1136, Fredericksburg, Texas 78624.*)

Where railings are to be used, they should be kept low to avoid obstructing the view. This is crucial.

Where railings are part of the perimeter seating arrangement, they should be kept as low as possible, but we need to recognize that the back of the seat must be high enough for comfort.

When comparing the spindle or balustrade placement on a porch railing system to those used on a gazebo, we can select an alternative. The spindles on the porch should be closely spaced to preclude a small child's squeezing through. Porches are frequently several feet above ground, and this safety precaution is a key design issue. In contrast, a gazebo is usually not very high above the ground. When this situation exists, the spacing of the spindles farther apart is a viable option, because a small child who crawls through them is not likely to be injured. Let the height of the gazebo floor be a consideration when you plan spacing of the spindles in a railing assembly and design.

Styling the Cornice

A great many possibilities exist when it comes to styling the cornice. Simple open-end rafter ends are one end of the spectrum. The closed-box cornice is the most complicated and represents the other end of the spectrum.

A safe way to design the cornice is to copy the one on the main house. You can downsize it to fit the size of rafters used in the gazebo.

Another technique is to shape each rafter end by cutting it on a bandsaw. The ends can look like those shown in Figure 14-7.

Still another technique is to use oversized building timber and let it remain unfinished, but stained and sealed.

Finally, a Chinese or Japanese flavor can be used. This technique may require the joining of several pieces in order to complete the flare and curved, extended, and exposed rafter ends.

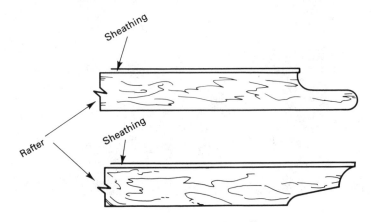

Figure 14-7   Shaped rafter tails.

USES FOR GAZEBOS

At the beginning of the section on styling the gazebo, we identified the possible settings around the swimming pool, as a backyard enclosed patio, overlooking the lake or river, as a centerpiece of a garden, and around a large tree with widespread branches.

With these settings we can identify several uses for the gazebo.

Pleasure

A fundamental reason for having a gazebo is the personal pleasure it provides for members of your family, friends who visit, and you. For some, having an outdoor "room" to watch a football game on TV is reason enough to build a gazebo. For some, a pending wedding or periodic parties with friends would be reason for having one built. Reasons can be as varied as the different cultures and subcultures in the community.

Work Station

Here is a use that you may have seen in more than one movie. Yet using the gazebo as a work station is very viable. It could easily become a setting for me to write this book. Of course, I would have to transport my computer there. That would not be so difficult if I had a lap-top computer. I would not even need power. But power in the gazebo is desirable for many reasons, among them being the possibility of installing lights and a circulating 60-cycle fan to gently move the air.

Writers are not the only ones who can use the gazebo as a work station. People who create craft-type items could easily do so in the gazebo. These might include sewing, decoupage, and making collages; even some types of artistic painting can be done there.

Outdoor Eating Area

For eating a simple breakfast or lunch, the gazebo can be ideal. Either can be carried out there on a tray. For having drinks in the afternoon such as tea or coffee, the same approach can be used. It is also a pleasant place for evening cocktails and dinner.

If you plan to serve a dinner for four or more people in your gazebo, be sure that you build one with adequate room for a table, chairs, and a serving tray. Also, to serve dinner in the gazebo, power should be available. It is likely that darkness will descend before the dinner is completed.

SUMMARY

We have explored quite a few styles and uses for a gazebo. Its style should follow the main house design and blend with the deck if attached. A gazebo should have a distinctive style of its own or add an accenting feature to the surroundings. Its uses are many, but the central one is *for personal pleasure*.

15

Design and Construction Techniques for the Gazebo

OBJECTIVES

- Plan for the construction of the gazebo.
- Plan the specifications and materials assessment.
- Establish the basic floor plan for the hexagon shape.
- Determine the foundation requirements.
- Understand the method of defining cutting angles for gazebos with more than four sides.
- Determine the sequence of construction of the floor assembly.
- Define the walls/columns that will support the roof.
- Establish the basic sequence for construction of the roof frame.
- Select the type of roofing and cornice or rafter tail finish.

BACKGROUND

The job we face is to build a hexagon-shaped gazebo. It is a complex series of tasks from the ground up. There are many angles to contend with, and we need to use a variety of tools to cut and assemble members that connect together.

Our generic design uses blocks for the foundation. However, an alternative system would use treated posts as the basis rather than the block foundation. The reason for selecting the block foundation is to provide more training and understanding of the way materials are customarily used.

This project is physically intensive. There are blocks to cut and lay, mortar to mix, and flooring framing members to fit, cut, and nail in place. Wall panels are manufactured and raised in place. Then headers are cut and installed. All roof members require physical effort to cut, fit, and install. Sheathing and shingling tasks are also strenuous. Some climbing is required.

We make good use of the framing square and bevel square. We may even use a protractor to set angles on the bevel square. The power saw must be set for compound miter cuts in some cases.

As usual, we use the standard chapter organization beginning with specifications, continuing with material assessments, describing the numerous tasks, and finishing up with the material invoice.

If you build a gazebo using the principles of construction, design, and estimating in this chapter, it could be a very significant accomplishment. But let me assure you that it will cost a lot of money. Materials are not cheap, and as you will see many are used.

Now let's begin with the specifications.

SPECIFICATIONS

Table 15.1 lists the specifications for the generic gazebo. Before we study them, a few comments are necessary. The size of a gazebo is an optional consideration. The one we are going to build will accommodate patio furniture, which means that it will be about 10 ft across. If the need is for a smaller one, some scaling of the dimensions is required and adjustments to all material quantities and sizes is also required.

MATERIALS ASSESSMENT

Table 15.2 (page 206) provides a very good picture of the variety of materials needed for the generic gazebo. You should recognize many of the names if you have studied or used other chapters.

TABLE 15.1 Specification Listing
PROJECT: *Constructing a Gazebo*   **DATE:** _____

General Description

A hexagon-shaped gazebo will be constructed with a cement block foundation, wood-framed and -covered floor, wall panels with railings, gingerbread braces, and spandrel panels of lattice. The roof design will be hip style, shingled with strip shingles, and incorporate shaped open rafter tails. All wood will be coated with protective coatings such as sealers and paint. The ceiling will be made from plywood and painted as well. Lighting and other accessory conveniences may be added.

Specifications

Item	*Specifications*
Dimensions of hexagon	Diameter = 10 ft, Header height = 7 ft 9 in. from finished floor.
Foundation	Concrete footings, 2 courses of block with joints struck, termite shield installed, and anchor bolts.
Floor assembly	Partial L-type sill, joists on 2-ft centers, T&G flooring.
Wall assemblies	Five identical panels with railings and gingerbread, height 7 ft 9 in. One panel will be access with gingerbread. All panels will have spandrel assemblies of lattice.
Roof pitch and design	4 in 12 hip roof, strip shingles; includes a finial at the peak
Roof framing	2 × 4 rafters, $\frac{7}{16}$-in. plywood sheathing
Rafter tails (ends)	Open design sculptured, extending 16 in. past the header
Painting system	Wood protective followed by prime and finish coats

GROUND PREPARATION AND MASONRY TASKS

In this segment of the construction project, we must complete the tasks pertaining to the foundation. Many of these have been covered before; therefore, a short refresher description will be used. The tasks are

1. Clear an area about 15 feet in diameter.
2. Set the batter boards.

TABLE 15.2 Materials Assessment
PROJECT: *Constructing the Gazebo*

Direct Materials

Type or Description	*Use or Purpose*
Concrete	Footings
Rebars	Reinforcement of footings
Mortar mix and sand	Cement blocks in place
Cement blocks	Foundation
2-in. lumber	Sills, headers, joists, rafters, and wall vertical members
T&G flooring	Gazebo floor
Railings	Assemblies of rails and balusters
Plywood	Sheathing and ceiling
Tarpaper and shingles	Roof covering
Gingerbread and spandrels	Decorations
Nails and bolts	Fasteners

Indirect Materials

Type or Description	*Use or Purpose*
Batter boards	Reference lines and heights
Forms and stakes	Footing forms and wall braces
Mason line	
Mortar board	Hold mortar; eases work

Support Materials

Type or Description	*Use or Purpose*
Scaffolds and planks	Work surface
Ladder	Access off-ground work
Sawhorses and planks	Work station
Portable power tools	Ease cutting masonry and wood
Carpentry tools	Construction
Mason tools	Construction
Mortar box	Mix concrete and mortar

3. Excavate the ground for the footings.
4. Pour the footings.
5. Lay the two courses of cement block.
6. Set the J-bolts in place.
7. Cut and lay the termite shield over the top course of block.

We need a clean, clear area to have adequate space to perform the variety of tasks in this section and later ones. If there is vegetation, it should be removed during the clearing action.

Task 2 requires us to set the batter boards. Even though the gazebo is a hexagon, we need only four corners of batter boards. The four sets of batter boards should be placed as shown in Figure 15-1. Notice that these are set about 2 ft wider than the 10-ft diameter of the gazebo. Two additional boards can be placed at the point of the intersection labeled A and B. These aid in defining the exact two points. Further, the final height of the finished floor is 16 in. above the lowest point on the ground. For full instruction on installing batter boards, refer to Chapter 1.

To draw a hexagon on paper is not too difficult. One merely draws a circle and marks off six equally spaced points on the circle 60 degrees apart, as shown in

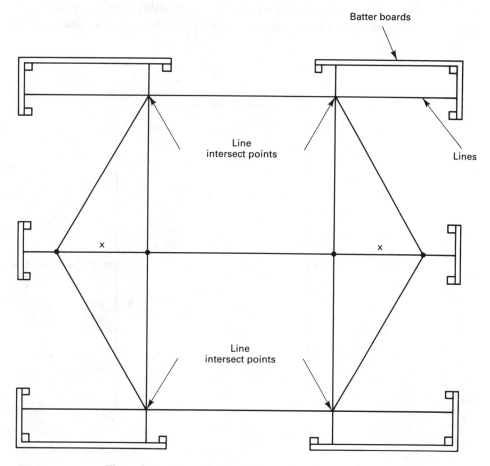

Figure 15-1 Gazebo basic design and batter board layout.

Figure 15-2. Then the points are connected with straight lines. Notice that there are three sets of parallel lines—sides 1–4, 2–5, and 3–6. Further, each side is the same length. Next, we connect points a–e or b–d with a line. Last we measure the distance x from points f–g. With this length we can define the ratio of a–e to g–f and use this in the actual layout. Or better yet, we can establish a scale for the paper drawing and use actual dimensions.

Let's skip between Figures 15-1 and 15-2 to understand setting perimeter lines on the batter boards. We should begin with setting lines for a–b and d–e, and then a–e and b–d. Last, stretch a line for points c–f, centered midway between points a–e and b–d. From the intersect points g and h measure outward distance x. This is the exact vertical point of the footing, foundation, and floor frame.

In accomplishing task 3 we should attempt to use the natural earth as a form. (See Figure 15-3.) Barring this, our materials assessment provided for forms. Due to the limited weight of the structure, we can plan for a 6-in.-thick footing. To be sure that the footing is within local codes, you might discuss this

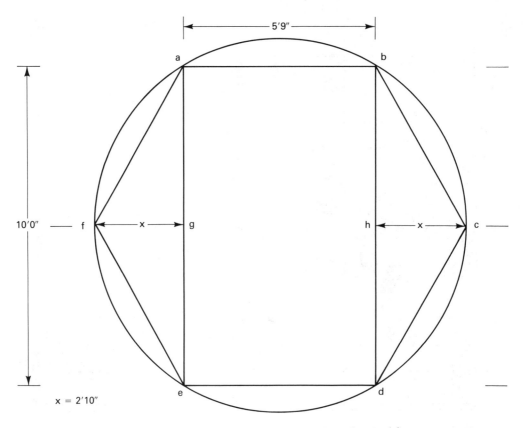

Figure 15-2 Gazebo basic dimensions and form.

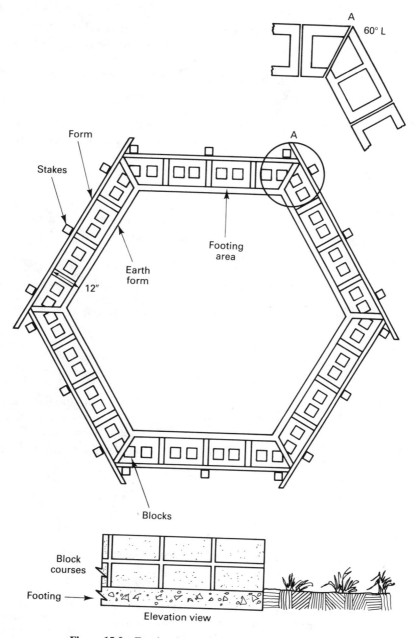

Figure 15-3 Footing forms, footings, and block layout.

aspect with the local building inspector or city engineer. The footing needs to be 12 in. wide with the extra width toward the inside. Later the blocks will be set flush with the outside of the footing. The formed area should look like the one in Figure 15-3.

The footing width should be formed as close to 12 in. wide as possible to avoid the expense of excessive concrete. The amount of concrete should be about 18 cubic feet, or $\frac{2}{3}$ cubic yards. Pour and screed it off flush with the form top.

After the concrete sets, the blocks should be cut and laid. The details in Figure 15-3 show several requirements. One is the angle that must be cut into the blocks at the six corners. Each angle is 60 deg. Further, the courses of block are laid flush with the outside of the footing. Last, the courses are *stacked*, not offset. This creates a pleasing pattern. (If necessary, see Chapter 2 for mixing mortar and block laying.)

Several other tasks must be done with the blocks. The joints must be struck before the mortar sets hard. Four J-bolts must be installed to secure the plate part of the L-sill. Two sills are to be installed.

When the cement work and masonry work is done, the forms should be removed and cleaned. The ground should be leveled, and excess dirt should be removed for safety reasons. All mason tools must be cleaned immediately after use. This includes the mortar box and mortar board.

FLOOR ASSEMBLY

In this section we examine the tasks needed to complete the construction of the floor assembly. These tasks will have us build the floor joist and header assembly, install one set of bridging, install the tongue-and-groove flooring, and install the perimeter trimmer board and cove molding under the overlap of the flooring. The tasks are

1. Install the termite shields, sills, and headers.
2. Cut, fit, and install the joists.
3. Install the one row of X-bridging.
4. Install the perimeter 1 × 8 trimmer board and $\frac{3}{4}$-in. cove molding.
5. Install the tongue-and-groove flooring and trim it off.

We use Figure 15-4 as a visual aid along with the discussion. Two 2 × 6 treated sills must be installed opposite each other. For our generic project we install them on surfaces *a–b* and *d–e* (Figure 15-2). The J-bolts are already there. We need to set the sill so that its outer edge and ends are $1\frac{1}{2}$ in. back from the edge of the block's outer surface (see the detail in Figure 15-4). Let's use a short piece of 2 × 4 for this. Position the 2 × 6 and mark the places where the bolt holes will be drilled. A framing square is the tool to use for alignment. Measure

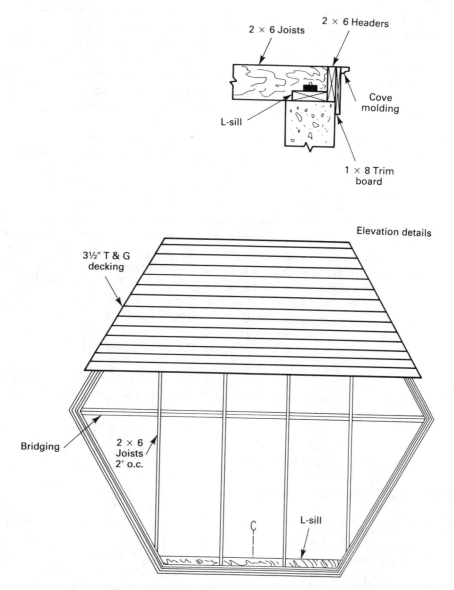

Figure 15-4 Floor framing and finishing details.

the distance back with a ruler. Slide the sill over the bolts and verify that the 2 × 4 will fit correctly. Ensure that the mitered ends are cut accurately. They may be a slight bit shorter than needed, but they must not be longer.

Next we cut and install the 2 × 6 floor headers. Then we bevel the ends of all six pieces 60 degrees. We can accomplish this by setting the portable power saw at 30 degrees. Measure, mark, and cut a piece. Nail the first two to the L-sills. Then nail the remaining four pieces at the corners.

Next we need to lay out the position of the joists, also shown in Figure 15-4. We place these on 2-ft centers. Let's begin at the center of the headers with the L-sills behind them. Mark off a point 12 in. on each side of the center. Then we can mark off the next two joists at 2 ft o.c. Finally, we simply cut each to fit in place. *Note:* An offset must be cut to fit over the sill. Nail each in place with two 16d common nails per joist end.

Finally, cut and install the X-bridging across the middle of the 10-ft span.

Now let's begin the finishing phase of the assembly. According to the task list, the 1 × 8 trimmer boards should be cut and installed. Each piece must be measured and have a miter cut on each end before it can be nailed in place. The bevel is the same as the one on the headers. Each 1 × 8 must be nailed over the header and held flush with the top edge of the header. All miter joints must fit exactly. Nail the pieces in place with 8d galvanized finish or casing nails.

After all six pieces are in place, cut and install the six pieces of $\frac{3}{4}$-in. cove. It, too, must be flush with the top of the header edges (or 1 × 8). Use a miter box to make the miter cuts. Use 4d galvanized finish nails for the nailing job.

The last task is to install the tongue-and-groove flooring and trim it off. Since we want it to extend over the cove molding by 1 in., we should begin with setting the first board about $1\frac{1}{2}$ in. beyond the cove. Then later we can trim it to 1 in. with the power saw. The ends on the other angles should be trimmed after all floor boards are nailed in place as well.

To trim the boards we should use a chalkline. Then with a sharp crosscut blade in the power saw, we simply follow the chalkline. Finally, we use a block plane to smooth off the sawn edges of the flooring just cut.

WALL (COLUMN) CONSTRUCTION

Wall Panel Construction

We know that the gazebo has six sides. Five require walls or columns, and the last one must be open to provide access to the gazebo. For our generic project five panels, as shown in Figure 15-5 must be made and installed. Later the final access panel will be built. For a beginning, observe that the panel provides several characteristics commonly used on gazebos. The main supports are 2 × 4s. These are cut 7 ft 9 in. long. The lower rail is a $\frac{5}{4}$ × 6 piece sculptured as shown to permit maximum rain runoff and style. The chair rail is a 2 × 4 routed along the top edge for style. The spindles are plain but can be changed to a more elaborate style. These are nailed to the bottom rail and toenailed under the hand rail. The upper lattice panel is prefabricated from 2 in. stock $2\frac{1}{4}$ in. wide. A groove must be made in the center of the $\frac{5}{4}$ width to accommodate the lattice. In addition, brackets are made or purchased and installed under the lattice panel and in the panel.

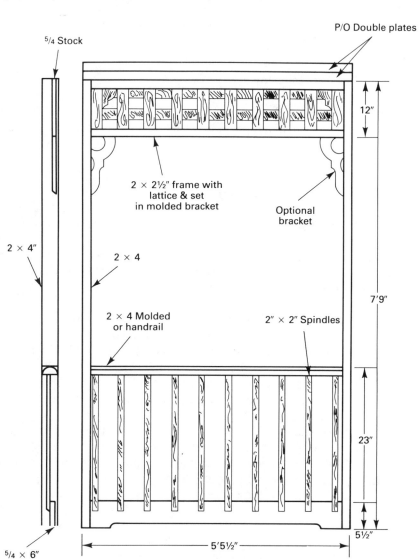

Figure 15-5 Wall/panel design and details.

You should notice that the overall width of the wall panel is 5 ft, 5½ in., yet the perimeter of the headers measure 5 ft, 9 in. on any one side. The reason is shown in the inset in Figure 15-5. We must plan for the panels to meet on the inside corner on the floor. Since all angles on the wall panel are 90 degrees versus 60 degrees, we must make allowances. Later we will place a tapered board into the gap and finish the column.

Where nails will show, use casing nails. Where they do not show, use common nails or screw nails.

Wall Panel Installation

Let's assume that the five panels are made and even primed. Now we can proceed with their installation. The tasks needed to complete are relatively easy:

1. Install the five panels.
2. Install the double wall plates.
3. Complete the access wall segment.

To complete the installation of the wall panels, we need to set the combination square to a depth equal to the distance from the trimmed flooring to the headers. This should be about $2\frac{1}{4}$ in. ($\frac{3}{4}$ in. overhang + $\frac{3}{4}$ in. cove + $\frac{3}{4}$ in. trimmer board). Make a pencil mark around the six sides by using the square and a pencil. Next, set a bevel square for 60 degrees and make a mark at each corner through the other lines at least 4 inches.

With the aid of Figure 15-6, let's assume we position panel 1 such that the inside corner of the 2×4 stiles touch the 60-deg lines and $2\frac{1}{4}$-in. lines. Once located, toenail through the 2×4s into the flooring with 12d common nails or nail screws. Four fasteners should be enough.

Repeat the process four more times.

To tie the five wall panels together, we install a double row of wall plates. But rather than cut inside miters at the corners, we gain a considerable amount of strength by using outside miters. See the details in Figure 15-6. The bevel square should be used to mark each piece. Install one row from right to left and the next from left to right. Be sure to use nails that do *not* penetrate through the first 2×4 when nailing the second row of plates.

Last, complete the access entranceway. This is done by first installing a 2×4 stile on each side. Then install the lattice panel and brackets flush against the plates.

Finally, prepare six inserts, as shown in the detail in Figure 15-6. These are cut from 1-in. clear stock. They must be cut full. The fullness makes it possible to keep the outer corner of the 2×4 and 1-in. stock flush, thereby making a perfect finished corner.

ROOF CONSTRUCTION

The roof design for the generic project is a hip roof. Therefore, we have a complex job on our hands. We complicate the construction slightly with the inclusion of a finial at the peak. The types of rafters we need are the hip and the hip-jack.

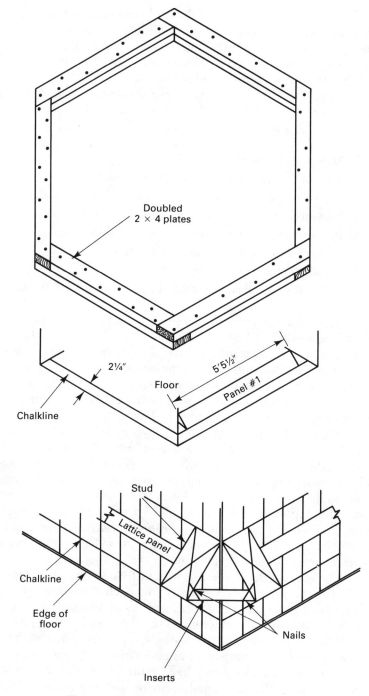

Figure 15-6 Wall placement and double top plates.

Figure 15-7 shows a picture of the roof framing, and the details show some of the cuts we need to understand. In addition, we plan to use the open rafter tail construction with sculptured ends. The cuts in each rafter will be bird's mouth at the plate, rafter tail cuts, and ridge cuts. An additional cut called a *backing cut* will be made into each hip rafter.

After the rafters are in place, the sheathing is installed. Then the 15# felt is applied and finally the strip shingles are installed.

Let's take the tasks one at a time:

1. Make a ridge hexagon block.
2. Measure, cut, and install the six hip rafters.
3. Measure, cut, and install the 12 jack rafters—six left cut and six right cut.
4. Measure, cut, and install the six pieces of plywood.
5. Install the metal edge around the plywood edge.
6. Prepare and install the finial at the peak.
7. Tarpaper the roof.
8. Install the shingles, and then the flashing around the finial.

There are numerous ways to construct the hip roof. This is one of them: From Figure 15-7 we have a bird's-eye view of the rafter. All six hip rafters join at the ridge/peak. We prepare a block of wood in the shape of a hexagon about 8 in. long. Each surface must have a minimum $1\frac{1}{2}$-in. surface for contact with the hip rafter. This technique makes cutting and fitting the hip rafters much easier, because the ridge cut will have only a plumb cut versus a compound miter cut. The details for the block are included in Figure 15-7.

We use the on-site method of laying out the rafters. First the rafters must rise 3 in. for each 12 in. of common span. This gives us the 3-in-12 rise the specifications called for. But when we lay out the hip rafters, we must use a 3-in-17 rise, since the distance from the corner to the center is longer per foot of rise than on the common rafters. I know that this is very complicated, but it is accurate information. If you need a full in-depth study of the principles of roof construction, please read *Carpentry Framing and Finishing,* 2nd ed., Byron W. Maguire (Prentice Hall, Englewood Cliffs, New Jersey). In this chapter we do the work without all the explanations.

On-site layout of the hip rafters follows the sketches included in Figure 15-7. On the ground or driveway, snap chalklines at 90 degrees. Follow the guidelines by marking off five increments at 17 in. along one line and five increments of 3 in. along the other line. These represent the points of the hip rafter that touch the outside edge of the plates and the underside of the ridge point. Lay a 2 × 6 so that the member touches both points. Overlay the square on the vertical (ridge) line and make a pencil line on the 2 × 6 in. line with the chalkline. Next make a line on the horizontal segment with the square. Then make the bird's mouth marks, as shown in the figure. Last, measure and mark a point $25\frac{1}{2}$ in.

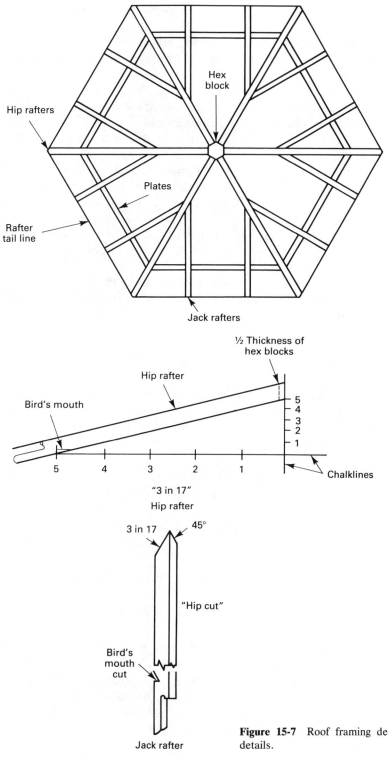

Figure 15-7 Roof framing design and details.

beyond the intersect point on the horizontal line and then square down to the rafter. This last line should be vertical; it represents the overhang or rafter tail of the rafter.

Make the ridge plumb cut and the bird's mouth cut and trim the rafter for the overhang. Next, lay out the sculpture of the rafter tail. Finally, trim the ridge cut by half the thickness of the ridge block.

Repeat the process just described five more times for a total of six hip rafters.

Now we need some help to install these. First nail one ridge cut end to the hexagon block, keeping the block even with the top of the rafter. Then nail the opposite rafter to the hexagon block. Raise the assembly to the plates and try for fit. The heel of the bird's mouth should touch the outer edge of the plate, and the other surface of the bird's mouth should rest evenly on top of the plate. If all is well, nail these in place with half of the rafter thickness on each side of the corner in the plate.

If some trimming must be done, make the necessary adjustments and then nail the assembly in place. Make the same adjustments to each of the remaining four rafters.

Place rafters 3 and 4 opposite each other and nail at the plate. Then place rafters 5 and 6 opposite each other and nail these at the plate. Finally, nail all four at the ridge while maintaining the accuracy of the rafter top even with the hexagon block.

Let's move on to task 3, where we need to cut and install 12 jack rafters. Using information from Figure 15-7, we see that these rafters are spaced about 2 ft apart. Once we have one that fits, we will use it for a pattern to make the rest. Again we use the on-site method.

1. Find the center along one side. It should be about one-half of 5 ft, 9 in. Then measure and make a mark 12 in. left and right. This is the position of each jack rafter.

2. Take a piece of scrap 1 × 2 or 1 × 4 and lay it onto the hip and plate so that a 90-deg corner is made by using a framing square along the plate. Mark the point on the hip rafter.

3. Stretch a chalkline or mason's line between the lower, top corners of the hip rafters.

4. Lay out the hip-jack rafter cut as shown in Figure 15-7. The framing square shows 3 and 17 as the points.

5. Make this cut by setting the power saw at 45 deg and follow the line. This makes a compound miter that fits perfectly.

6. Tack the jack in place with the top edge above the hip about ¾ in. and in line with the pencil mark. Now use the folding ruler to mark the bird's mouth. The depth should be the same as the one on the hip. *Note:* If we were using a much steeper pitch, we would need to make a backing cut on the hip or a

drop cut in the hip's bird mouth, but since the pitch is shallow, we can skip this requirement.

7. Remove the rafter and make the bird's mouth cut. Then try the jack for final fit. If it is okay, mark the rafter tail where the mason line touches it and use the level to make a plumb line.
8. Trim the rafter tail, lay out the sculpture, and cut it.
9. Make five more identical jacks.
10. Make six jacks with the opposite compound miter cuts.
11. Install all 12 pieces.

Task 4 requires the layout, cutting, and installing of the sheathing. We should use CD grade $\frac{7}{16}$-in. plywood sheathing or equivalent. The simple way to do this is to place a full sheet on one of the slopes so that the lower edge extends over the sculpture by $\frac{3}{4}$ in. Tack-nail it in place. Then use a chalkline to snap two lines, one at the midpoint along each hip rafter. Then remove the sheet and place it on the workbench. Next tilt the saw blade or base of the saw at 15 deg and undercut each chalkline mark. Try the piece for fit on the first slope and then the others. If it fits everywhere, make five more just like it.

Install the plywood by nailing it with 6d common nails at 6-in. spacing.

Since the rafter is longer than the width of one sheet, we must fit and cut the smaller remaining six pieces. Before this it is a good idea to cut and install the finial.

Figure 15-8 shows one suggestion for a finial. This one is made from a piece of 6 × 6 material, but it could be built up. Notice that there is a cut/score on each surface that slants up slightly. This is used for the flashing, and later will be filled with caulking. Once it is cut, nail it in place before the final plywood pieces are fit and nailed in place.

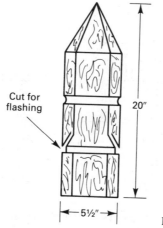

Figure 15-8 Roof peak finial.

Then complete the remainder of the roof by placing the metal roof edging in place and nailing it. Install the tar paper and shingles. Finally, cut, fit, and install six pieces of aluminum flashing into the finial and onto the roof. See Figure 15-8 again.

STEP CONSTRUCTION

We know that the finished floor height of the generic project is 16 in. above ground level. Therefore, we need a step to make it easy to step up into the gazebo and step down from it. Since the opening is about 5 ft, 9 in. wide, the step should reach all the way across.

For our project we use a combination of materials. The step itself is made from 2-in. treated lumber. The supports are made from decorator-styled cement blocks set in a bed of concrete. The tasks to perform are

1. Dig out a rectangular area about 4 in. deep by 2 ft wide by 60 in. long, as shown in Figure 15-9.
2. Mix concrete relatively dry and fill the area flush with the bottom of the first course of foundation block.
3. Mortar decorator and 4-in. solid blocks onto the concrete and against the lower course of the foundation.
4. Install a 1 × 4 oak or treated piece of lumber on the top of each block with bolts.
5. Cut and install the step treads onto the 1 × 4 stock.

Figure 15-9 shows most of the tasks to be done. Overall the job is simple in design, but it requires some physical effort to accomplish. The amount of con-

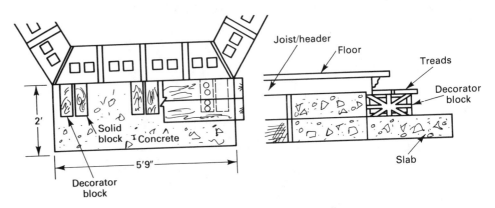

Figure 15-9 Step design and details.

crete is so small that ready-mix is not the answer. We would buy bags of pre-mixed concrete and mix the water in a wheelbarrow. We have about 4 cu ft of concrete to mix—about 8 bags @ 0.5 cu ft per bag.

The decorator blocks are not the strongest in the world, but if care is used they can do the job. However, the solid blocks will support impact force, and this is where we shall embed the anchors for the bolts.

There should be two anchors per block. Once in place, the treads made from two 2 × 10s can be installed by screwing them to the 1 × 4. *Note*: One of these must be trimmed so that the overhang is limited to $1\frac{1}{2}$ in.

Predrill six screw holes in each tread wide enough to pass the body of a No. 12 flat head wood screw through. Taper the top of the hole so that the screw head fits snugly into it and is about $\frac{1}{4}$ in. below the surface of the tread. After installing the screw, fill the area with wood filler.

A finishing touch to these steps is needed. After prefitting the treads and before fastening them in place, bevel the ends and the front top lip with either a block plane or a router.

FINISHING TOUCHES

Adding the finishing touches may include many things. Several that we shall add to the generic gazebo are lighting, sealing the raw wood, and deciding on the final finish.

Adding Electrical Service

The need for electricity in the gazebo is, of course, optional. But for our generic project we shall install it. The plan is to have a double receptacle and power for a ceiling fan and lights. A power box should be installed as a junction for the underground cable from the main house service to the gazebo. A fused circuit should be established for the fan, lights, and the receptacle outlets. All installation must meet weatherproof standards. To be sure of an approved installation we will employ a licensed electrician.

Adding a Ceiling Between the Rafters

We recognize that the nails from the shingles came through the sheathing, and these detract from the overall great appearance. So let's install $\frac{1}{4}$-in. plywood pieces between the rafters. Cut a piece of 1 × 1 stock and nail it along the lower edge of the sheathing, reaching from rafter to rafter. Then cut and install 1 × 1 strips of wood next to the sheathing and nail these into the rafters. Have each reach to the lower end of the sheathing where the end 1 × 1s are. Then cut and fit a piece of plywood in each space. Next use quarter round and cover the edge of the plywood where it meets the rafter. No molding goes across the lower end.

Designing the Painting System

We must select a system of painting that meets several requirements. Some of the wood must withstand the direct sun, rain, ice, and snow, as well as very hot weather. Some, such as the floor, needs a durable paint that resists abrasion and weathers well, too. Finally, most of the wood probably contains knots that can bleed through the paint unless special measures are taken. In addition, we may want to cover the exposed block foundation and step supports with paint.

Painting the concrete.   Let's assume that the block-laying job has been done very well and that there is no overspray of mortar on the surface. Further, the joints have all been struck and smoothed.

1. Prime-coat the raw surface with a *heavy duty block filler*[1] such as that which Sherwin-Williams produces.
2. Finish coats should be acrylic latex; they can be flat, satin, or semi-gloss.[2]
3. All products should be applied with paint brush.
4. Delay painting for 30 days.

Painting the floor and step treads.   The wood flooring must be protected with an excellent system. One recommended method is to apply an alkyd-base paint, preferably a gloss. Good-quality paints of this variety are abrasion resistant, have long-lasting durability, and remain glossy because they do not chip and flake readily. The two-step system is

1. Apply a prime coat of gloss alkyd (resin) coating.
2. Apply two finish coats of the same paint.
3. Clean up with paint thinner or mineral spirits.

Painting the exposed wood, other than the floor.   Since all the wood we used to build the gazebo was dressed, we should select a painting system made for smoothed lumber. First, we must neutralize the knots.

1. Apply a single coat of varnish over the knots and let it dry for 24 hours.

---

[1] This product is a pure acrylic resin block filler. Source: *Painting and Coating Systems for Specifiers and Applicators,* 1988, pp. 6 and 29.
[2] Ibid., p. 6.

2. Apply alkyd primer and clean up with mineral spirits.

3. Fill the nail holes with carpenter's putty and sand them smooth in 24 hours.

4. Apply two coats of finish latex house and trim paint in gloss, satin, or flat.

5. Clean up with detergent and water.

SAFETY AND CLEANUP

Let's revisit the project we just studied from the safety angle. Every time some building material is lifted, back strain can occur, so we must lift with our legs and arms, not with our backs. Mixing concrete is heavy work. Using the hoe in a mortar box requires considerable strength. An alternative that reduces part of the labor is to rent a power mixer. Laying the blocks, which weigh from 40 to 80 lb each, is strenuous.

Building the floor assembly is somewhat strenuous but not all that bad. Still, back strains can happen. Further, sooner or later you are likely to bash a finger with the hammer.

Building the walls and framing the roof are not such heavy tasks, but you must work off the ground. Care while working on the ladder and scaffold is paramount. Nailing plywood is easy on this small job, but you probably will need to climb onto the roof to complete the job. Do not fall off. The same goes for shingling and flashing around the finial. Don't fall off.

Strains can also happen while painting. This is especially so because much of the painting is done overhead and from ladders.

Cleanup of the grounds should be a constant practice. When excavation of the ground is done and the foundation is built, level the ground and remove the batter boards. Pick up scrap ends of joists, flooring, and other lumber as they begin to accumulate. Do not let any lumber lie around with nails showing. Finally, pick up nails to prevent their getting into grassed areas and perhaps become projectiles when the grass is mowed.

Clean up all painting tools immediately after use and store them for other projects.

When all building is complete, make the final cleanup with rakes and broom. Then landscape as designed.

MATERIALS LISTING

We finish the chapter with a materials invoice. Table 15.3 provides a listing of materials used in this project. In it you will see listings for direct and indirect materials as well as recommended rental tools.

TABLE 15.3   Materials Invoice
PROJECT: *Constructing the Gazebo*   **DATE:** _____

Quantity	Type	Total
18 cu ft	Concrete (footings)	$\frac{2}{3}$ cu yd
30 ea.	8 × 8 × 16 cement blocks	30 ea.
1 bag	Mortar mix	1 bag
$\frac{1}{4}$ yd	Washed sand	$\frac{1}{4}$ yd
50 lin ft	Aluminum flashing 16″ wide	1 roll
3 ea.	Decorator blocks 8 × 4 × 16	3 ea.
3 ea.	Blocks 4 × 8 × 16 Solid	3 ea.
8 bags	Concrete mix	8 bags
1 ea.	2 × 6 12 ft (sills)	12 lin ft
3 ea.	2 × 6 12 ft (headers)	36 lin ft
4 ea.	2 × 6 10 ft (joists)	40 lin ft
3 ea.	1 × 3 12-ft spruce, (X-bridging)	36 lin ft
100 sq ft	1 × 3 T&G flooring (fir)	100 sq ft
3 ea.	1 × 8 treated pine (trimmer)	36 lin ft
36 lin ft	$\frac{3}{4}$-in. cove molding	36 lin ft
3 ea.	1 × 6 pine (footing forms)	36 lin ft
6 ea.	2 × 4 8-ft pine (batter board posts)	48 lin ft
3 ea.	1 × 4 12-ft pine (batter boards)	36 lin ft
12 ea.	2 × 4 8-ft pine studs	96 lin ft
3 ea.	$\frac{5}{4}$ × 8 12-ft pine (panel rails)	36 lin ft
6 ea.	2 × 3 14-ft pine (spandrels)	84 lin ft
12 ea.	Brackets	12 ea.
200 lin ft	$\frac{1}{4}$ × $1\frac{5}{8}$ lattice	200 lin ft
3 ea.	2 × 4 12 ft (rails)	36 lin ft
60 ea.	Spindles @ 24 in. long	60 ea.
72 lin ft	2 × 4 (top plates) pine	72 lin ft
6 ea.	2 × 6 8-ft pine (hip rafters)	48 lin ft
6 ea.	2 × 6 10-ft pine (hip jack rafters)	60 lin ft
9 sheets	$\frac{7}{16}$-in. CD sheathing plywood 4 × 8	9 sheets
9 sheets	$\frac{1}{4}$ AC exterior plywood (ceiling)	9 sheets
1 roll	No. 15 felt	1 roll
5 sq	Strip shingles (color optional)	5 sq
36 lin ft	Roof metal edging	36 lin ft
1 ea.	2 × 10 12-ft treated pine (treads)	24 lin ft
4 ea.	6-in. J-bolts	4 ea
5 lb	16d galv common nails	5 lb
3 lb	8d galv casing nails	3 lb
10 lb	8d flooring nails	10 lb
8 lb	1-in. roofing nails	8 lb
3 lb	6d fin galv nails	3 lb
2 lb	4d galv fin nails	2 lb
4 lb	10d galv casing nails	4 lb

TABLE 15.3   (Continued)

Quantity	Type	Total
18 ea.	No. 12 1½-in. galv flat head wood screws	18 ea.
1 can	Carpenter's wood putty	1 can
1 gal	Heavy duty block filler	1 gal
1 gal	Acrylic latex paint (on blocks)	1 gal
1 gal	Alkyd resin coating (floor)	1 gal
1 pt	Varnish	1 pt
1 gal	Alkyd primer (primer)	1 gal
2 gal	Latex house and trim paint	2 gal
1 gal	Mineral spirits	1 gal
1 ea.	Mason blade for power saw	1 ea
1 ea.	Combination blade	1 ea
1 ea.	½-in. mason drill bit	1 ea

Rental Equipment	Duration of Rental
Cement mixer	4 days
Extension ladder	1 week
Scaffold and two planks	1 week
Mortar box (not needed if mixer is rented)	4 days

16

Trellises:
Styles, Uses, and Construction

OBJECTIVES

- Identify how the style of a trellis can accomplish a desired goal.
- Determine what a trellis is supposed to do.
- Identify technical solutions to problems encountered in building and maintaining trellises.
- Identify the dimensions of a typical trellis.
- Establish the specifications for a typical trellis.
- Define the materials required for the project.
- Identify the construction sequence needed.

STYLES CREATED WITH THE USE
OF DIFFERENT MATERIALS AND FEATURES

Trellises are closely related to arbors in that they frequently serve the same function. Therefore, the information presented in this and the next chapter can be applied to arbors as well.

In this section on creating styles, we discuss how different materials and their placement can create style and add features for the trellis.

A fundamental condition for every piece of wood used in a trellis is that it must be treated or bought already treated. This lumber and other pieces will be exposed to the weather, bugs, and fungus as long as the trellis exists. Even treated lumber should be further protected with water sealers and chemicals that inhibit the effects of fungus and ultraviolet sun on wood cells.

Oversized Timbers

The first possibility for creating style in a trellis is to use oversized timbers. These can be 6 × 6, 6 × 8, or 8 × 8 posts; 3 × 6, 3 × 8, or 3 × 10 members; 4 × 6, 4 × 8, or 4 × 10 members. These members and posts create mass and boldness. They also provide the opportunity to create large or long trellises with few pieces. Figure 16-1 provides an illustrator's rendition of this idea.

Figure 16-1 Using timbers (oversized members) for style.

Normal-Sized Lumber

Normal sized lumber is commonly used to create style in a trellis. The posts are made from treated 4 × 4s. The other members are made from treated 2 × 4s, 2 × 6s, 2 × 8s, and 2 × 10s. There are even many occasions to use 1-in. stock. The trellis shown in Figure 16-2 makes use of 1 × 2s to create the filtering pattern for sun and shade control. Normal-sized lumber can also include lattice, as we shall learn later.

Stacking Members

The fundamental design characteristic of every trellis is the method of stacking used. After the basic structural design posts and lower stacking members are placed, the remaining stacking levels and adornments are placed for effect and character. Figure 16-3 shows several adaptations of the basic design. First notice that the lowest members in any trellis design are attached to the posts. These may

Figure 16-2 Using standard-sized lumber for style.

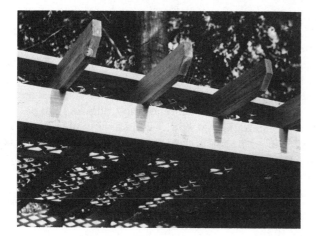

Figure 16-3 Filtering schemes for the top stacking level.

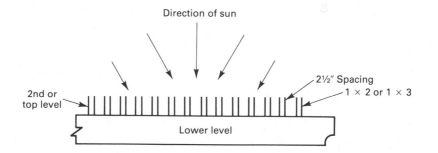

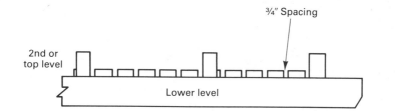

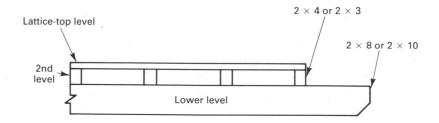

be placed to run the short length between posts, or they may be placed to run the long span between posts. Another alternative not shown is that the lowest and next stack of members may be bolted to the posts.

The number of levels of stacking and the desired sun/shade control will be the primary determining factor for use of the short or long run of the first level. Let's explain. If a fundamental purpose for a trellis is to create a shaded path between outdoor activity areas, then the direction of the trellis and the path of the sun are two factors that must be reckoned with. The shading members, usually the uppermost level, should be perpendicular to the path of the sun. In this way the sun is partially blocked by the wood. Even during the part of the day when the sun is at full height, shadows will be cast due to the thickness and the closeness of the top level of member placement.

Finishes, Protection Systems, and Added Character

Trellises can be left natural and just sealed with a wood protector of some sort. They can be stained. Most often they are painted. A very good outdoor painting system should be followed. You can refer to Chapters 13 and 15 for protection systems.

Angle bracing is usually employed in the design for stability, but these do not have to be simple 2 × 4s cut and bolted or nailed in place. Gingerbread designs using French curves are a very pleasant enhancement. We shall discuss more of this subject in Chapter 17, "Enhancing the Trellis."

Other types of additives that create character include living plants, such as grapes, ivy, such as Boston, morning glories, climbing roses, bougainvillea, and wisteria. Some people have even grown string beans up the sides of the trellis. During the growing seasons, these plants provide considerable shade under the trellis.

USES FOR TRELLISES

There are five common uses for the trellis, each slightly different.

Garden Entrance

As a pathway into a garden area, the trellis creates an opening between hedges. This application may use a flat design or may incorporate the common semicircular design. Its length probably will not exceed four feet. Its width will probably be in the range of three to four feet. However, it is possible that the length may extend partway or all the way across the garden area.

Grape Arbor

As a grape arbor the trellis may be any length but will probably be limited to four feet in width. Its height may also be lower than some other designs so that harvesting the grapes is not a real chore. One consideration that should be incorporated in the design details is the need for strength through bracing to resist the natural pull and stress of the grape vines.

Reflecting Pool Cover

A not so common use of the trellis is to fully or partially cover a reflecting pool or fish pond. The idea has merit, since many aquatic plants require filtered sun or partial shade. Where the pool is subject to very hot sun, it may be necessary to shade it during parts of the day during the summer. Yet the warming effects of the sun at other times of the year would benefit the pool and fish or plant growth.

Swimming Poolside Cover

Poolside patios are great, but sometimes it is more desirable to have a fairly large area partially shaded alongside a pool. The freedom it offers for placement of furniture, pool tools, portable barbecue, and the like is a real asset. Trellises made for these purposes would likely be made from oversized timbers due to the spans of 12 or more feet.

Pathway Between Living Areas

The fifth use for a trellis is to create a planned pathway between living areas. These paths could go from a patio to a swimming pool, from a driveway to the garden setting, from a gazebo to the main garden or lawn, or from one lawn to another through a wooded setting.

BACKGROUND

We shall design and construct a generic trellis. During the remainder of the chapter we discuss the construction conditions, which include setting posts and building the various stacking levels of horizontal members, and we show how anchoring techniques are employed.

Since some of the work is done above ground, there is a need to recognize safety and physical stress. Members are heavy when lifted above head level. Ladders are used. In addition, drilling holes for bolts and trimming post tops can be occasions for accidents to happen. So be careful. If oversized timbers are used in your own design, two people are needed to place them correctly. Also, digging post holes can be a tough job, especially in rocky or clay types of soil.

Almost all the materials we use in the generic project are purchased already treated. The wood materials not already treated are treated on site before painting or staining.

Now let's begin the generic project by establishing the specifications.

SPECIFICATIONS

The generic trellis project that we discuss and construct on paper is one designed to provide a covered pathway between the main lawn and the gardens. As you see in Table 16.1, it is designed to provide filtered sun throughout the day. Since in our project the general run of the trellis is from east to west, and the sun generally follows a close approximation of these directions, we will require only two levels of stacking.

TABLE 16.1 Specification Listing
PROJECT: *Constructing a Trellis*   **DATE:** _____

General Description

Construct a trellis 5 ft wide by 10 ft long, with 8-ft head clearance, using treated lumber and timbers as much as possible. All woods not pretreated will be treated on-site before installation. The number of stacking levels will be two, since the direction of the run of the trellis and the general path of the sun are very similar. An exterior white painting system will be used to finish the trellis. Sufficient bracing will be included to permit vines to grow over the structure without effect.

Specifications

Item	Specifications
Dimensions	5 ft wide, 10 ft long, 8 ft head clearance
Post dimensions	4 × 5 treated timbers
Horizontal members	Treated 2 × 8s, 3 × 6s, and 2 × 4s
Bracing	Double bolting and angle braces
Top stack	Will provide filtering and shading
Painting system	Exterior house and trim
Trellis floor	Natural dirt, no weeds

MATERIALS ASSESSMENT

This is one of the smaller projects that we have undertaken. But it is still a good idea to make an assessment of the types and varieties of materials we need for the project. Table 16.2 provides the information.

TABLE 16.2 Materials Assessment
PROJECT: *Constructing the Trellis*   **DATE:** _____

Direct Materials

Type or Description	Use or Purpose
4 × 5 timbers	Posts, treated
2 × 8 lumber	Horizontal members
3 × 6 timbers	Horizontal members, top stack
2 × 4 lumber	Horizontal members, top stack
Nails, lag screws, bolts	Fasteners
Angle braces (wood)	Provides support and stiffening
Wood protective fluids	Protects untreated wood
Exterior paint	Prime and final coating
Concrete (optional)	Set posts

Indirect Materials

Type or Description	Use or Purpose
1 × 4s	Temporary braces
Paint thinner	Clean brushes and sprayer
Mason line	Post positioning
Concrete mixing box (optional)	Mix concrete

Support Materials

Type or Description	Use or Purpose
Post hole digger	Prepare holes
Ladders	Off-ground work
Paint brushes	Apply preservatives and paint system
Shovel and hoe	Mix concrete and shovel dirt
Hose and water	Aids in making mud for mud set
Carpenter tools	Construction
Power saw and drill with accessories	Aids in cutting and drilling
Sawhorses and work planks	Field work station

CONSTRUCTION

There are a variety of tasks associated with the generic project of building a trellis. We list these in the general order of their accomplishment, as we have done in earlier chapters. As before, when the tasks are well discussed in earlier chapters, we reference the chapter rather than describe the process involved again. First let's look at some visual representations in the working drawings shown in Figure 16-4.

The layout shows six posts. Three are in alignment and 4 ft o.c. Since we allow 1 ft overhang on each end, the 2 × 8s must be 10 ft. Further, the posts are spaced 5 ft o.c. to create the 5-ft width called for in the specifications.

The elevation view shows the 8-ft headroom clearance height as well as the positioning of the stacking members. Make careful note of the tapering scheme used on all members.

Locate the detail about bolting the horizontal members to the posts. Notice the requirement for two bolts per post. Also notice that the post tops are capped with aluminum pieces. This is one technique for preserving the lasting quality of the columns. Another way we could do this is to taper the top.

The drawing also provides details about spacing of the top level of stacking. Notice that four 3 × 6s are spaced about every $2\frac{1}{2}$ ft, and 2 × 4s are spaced every $2\frac{1}{2}$ in. between the 3 × 6s. All these are toenailed in place.

Now the tasks:

1. Clear and level the approximate area of the trellis.
2. Set out lines for the six posts.
3. Set the posts in a mud or concrete.
4. Cut the lower stacking horizontal members, and then pretreat each with wood protector preservative.
5. Install the lower stacking members by bolting in place.
6. Cut the second level stacking members, and treat them with protective preservative.
7. Mark the first level and second level stacking members for assembly/nailing to each other.
8. Apply angle braces with bolts.
9. Clean and level the ground under the trellis.
10. Apply the painting system.

Now let's get a little technical. First, we must define the length of the posts. If the head clearance is 8 ft according to specifications, then we need a post 8 ft plus 8 in. for the first level of horizontal member and another 2 ft to $2\frac{1}{2}$ ft to go into the ground. This totals to 12-ft posts. If the ground is fairly level, we should make a mark 2 or $2\frac{1}{2}$ ft up from the bottom of each post. We dig the hole and place the post into it so that the mark is about flush with the natural level of the ground.

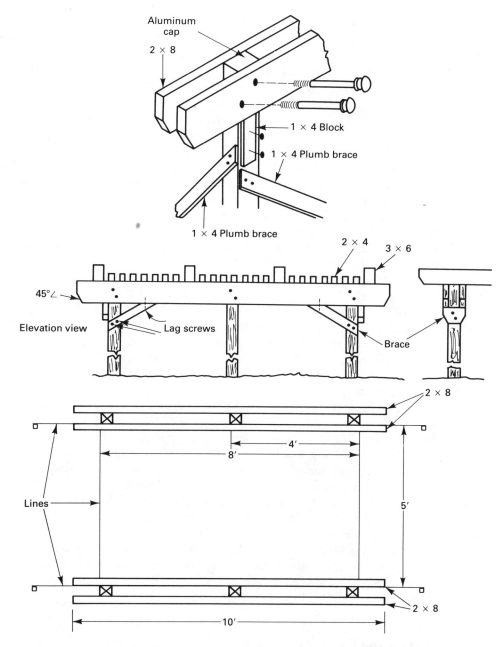

Figure 16-4   Construction details for the generic trellis.

    To install the posts with the mud technique we simply use dirt and water in the back fill. As the dirt is replaced around the post in the hole, we tamp it with a scrape of 1 × 4 and wet the dirt to make mud.

The post will stand okay, but it will not be plumb, and it may not be in line with the mason lines. We need to attach two 1 × 4 braces with nails and drive two short stakes into the ground at the other end of the 1 × 4 to act as anchors. While one of us holds the level against the post and plumbs it, the other nails the 1 × 4 to the stakes. We repeat the process five more times.

Notice in Figure 16-4 that the lower corner of each horizontal member is beveled. Let's lay out the bevel cut on each 2 × 8, making sure that the crown is *up*. Once we cut these two pieces, we must apply the wood protective coating.

Rather than work off the ground to mark the 2 × 8s for bolt holes, let's lay a 2 × 8 against the posts on the ground and position it for equal overhang on both ends. This should be 12 in. Then mark the position of the six bolt holes. Next drill these and use this piece as a pattern to make the other three.

Now we cut six 1 × 4s 12 in. and tack each on the posts. Measure up from the ground 8 ft and make a pencil mark. Tack one piece of 1 × 4 just below this mark. Use another 1 × 4 as a leveling board, and with the level on it mark the two remaining posts on the one side. Nail two more 1 × 4s below each line.

Level across the 5-ft separation to the other line of posts and tack the remaining three 1 × 4s after making level marks.

Now let's raise one 2 × 8 in place on top of the 1 × 4s, align it with the posts for overhang, and drill the bolt holes through the post. A long drill is required. Next we insert the carriage bolts and set the heads. Then we raise the other 2 × 8, slide it over the bolts sticking out, and apply washers and nuts.

By repeating the process we make the other side look the same as the one just completed.

Now let's prepare the four 3 × 6s and 26 2 × 4s that make up the second stacking level. The 3 × 6s extend beyond the outer 2 × 8s 12 in., and the 2 × 4s extend 10 in. We use 8-ft members for the project. The 3 × 6s must be 5 ft + 3 in. + 24 in. overhang = 7 ft, 3 in. The 2 × 4s are 4 in. less.

After cutting each for length, we must bevel them, as we did on the 2 × 8s, but we make a smaller cut. Then a protective coating is applied. Before trying to install each, we mark them while we are standing on the ground. The marks on the 3 × 6s are 12 in. from each end, and the marks on the 2 × 4s are 10 in. from the end.

In Figure 16-4 we see that the 3 × 6s are nailed 6 in. back from the ends of the 2 × 8s and equal distances apart for the remaining two. Nail these in place. Then measure and space the 2 × 4s at about 2½ in. separation, making any adjustments as needed. Nail the 2 × 4s in place.

Cutting and Installing
the Angle Braces

We use eight braces. These could be metal, but we will use 2 × 4s, and we will lag bolt/screw them in place. Let's cut four pieces with 45-degree angles (see Figure

16-4 again). Then we screw the lower end to the post and the upper end under the 2×8. Start with the positioning of the piece, mark it for position, and then predrill the lag screw hole. Fasten each in place after treating.

Cut the other four braces. These are shown in Figure 16-4 too. They measure 10 in. across and $5\frac{1}{5}$ in. wide. They are fastened to the post with lag bolts and screwed to the 2×8s with $2\frac{1}{2}$-in. No. 10 wood screws. Predrill angle holes through the brace into the 2×8. Then drive the screws in place.

Apply an exterior painting system.

That completes the job of building the generic trellis.

MATERIALS LISTING

Now that we have studied the building aspects of the job, let's finalize the materials invoice. Table 16.3 shows us the listing.

TABLE 16.3 Materials Invoice
PROJECT: *Constructing the Trellis*   **DATE**: _____

Quantity	Type	Total
6 ea.	4×5 12-ft posts treated pine	6 ea.
4 ea.	2×8 10-ft treated pine	4 ea.
4 ea.	3×6 8-ft treated pine or southern pine	4 ea.
28 ea.	2×4 8-ft treated pine or southern pine	28 ea.
12 bags	Ready-mix concrete (optional)	12 bags
12 ea.	1×4 12-ft pine or spruce (braces)	144 lin ft
1 ea.	2×6 6-ft pine (bracing)	6 bd ft
12 ea.	8 in. $\times \frac{1}{2}$ in. carriage bolts (galv)	12 ea.
20 ea.	$3\frac{1}{2}$ in. $\times \frac{1}{4}$ in. lag screws	12 ea.
8 ea.	$2\frac{1}{2}$ in. No. 10 flat head wood screws	8 ea.
1 ea.	$\frac{1}{2}$ in. $\times$ 12 in. drill bit	1 ea.
3 lb	12d galv common nails	3 lb
1 lb	6d common brite nails	1 lb
1 gal	Wood preservative	1 gal
2 gal	Exterior paint house and trim	2 gal
1 gal	Mineral spirits	1 gal
2 ea.	3-in. bristle brushes	2 ea.
1 roll	Mason line	1 roll

Rental Equipment	*Duration of Rental*
Post hole digger	1 day
Ladder	2 days

17

Enhancing the Trellis

OBJECTIVES

- Select the appropriate materials to finish the trellis.
- Understand how to add electricity to the trellis.
- Identify how to add wall segments to the trellis.
- How to train vines to grow over the trellis.
- Adding a floor.

ADDING GINGERBREAD

Gingerbread decorations are not added to a trellis as frequently as to a gazebo. However, there may be reasons to do it, so we discuss several possibilities and techniques.

The brace that we added to strengthen the trellis in the generic project in Chapter 16 was functional. It did not add style. However, if bracing is sculptured in French curves, it adds considerable style. Using spindles in spandrels is another way to create style.

We can illustrate many types and styles of braces and spandrels, but the key to styling the gingerbread depends on the architectural style of the property, surrounding community, and section of the country. Unless there is good reason, always keep within the regional style features.

There are some technical problems that need solutions when gingerbread is added to the trellis. First, there are not many surfaces that are in alignment for fastening the braces and spandrels. We know that posts and the lower level of stacking members are offset 90-deg angles. Second, top-level stacking members are always perpendicular to the lower ones. Recall that the braces that were installed from post to horizontal members were fastened on two different surfaces. Consequently, we need to devise some techniques to provide anchoring surfaces. Last, the braces should be placed so that beauty and style are equally evident from the inside and outside of the trellis.

One solution is shown in Figure 17-1. When the brace must be fastened to the post, that part is easy. But the upper surface floats between the 2 × 8s. We need to add a filler block flush with the lower surfaces. The piece must be fit snugly, and either nailed in place or screwed in place with general-purpose/dry wall screws. The length and placement of the block are critical, too. Sometimes

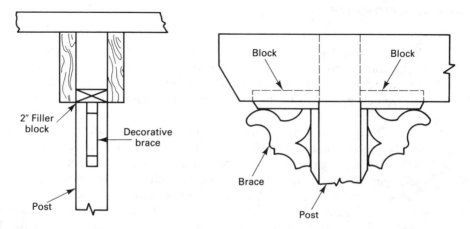

Figure 17-1 Adding blocking for decorator bracing support.

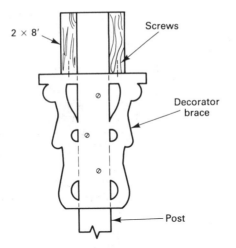

Figure 17-2 Adding decorator bracing across and under lower horizontal members.

the job looks more professional when the block is equal to the top length of the brace or 1 in. longer than the brace. The second option is to make the block long enough to provide sound anchoring but not full length.

Recall that we placed a 2 × 6 brace beneath the 2 × 8s. It was very functional, but it lacked beauty and style. Suppose that we need to add style; here is an easy opportunity. A much larger piece of 2-in. stock can be used. Figure 17-2 shows that French curves and filigree can be cut into the piece and no added blocking is necessary. The visible curves are easily seen when you enter and exit the trellis.

One caution: People must not feel that the bracing interferes with their walking through the trellis.

ADDING ELECTRICITY

When the outdoors is enhanced for living, many activities take place at night. Therefore, there is a very sound reason to install lights. The questions to be answered are: What kinds of lights? How many? How do we control them? How do we get the power to the trellis? We shall answer these questions with a few ideas.

The types of materials suited to this purpose include cabling, boxes, controls and switches, and fixtures. The cabling must be the underground variety 12-2 with ground. Figure 17-3 shows how an electrical system for low-voltage lights is arranged and wired in the trellis. The switch is a three-way variety so that the lights can be turned on and off at the house and at the trellis.

For a really sophisticated job we can add a timer so that the lights come on at dusk and turn off at ten o'clock, for example. The timer would be installed in the

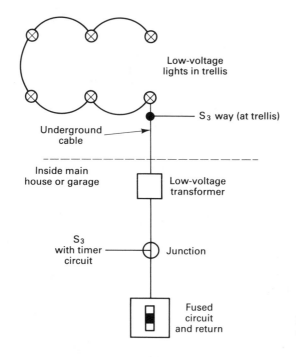

Low-voltage
lights in trellis

S₃ way (at trellis)

Underground
cable

Inside main
house or garage

Low-voltage
transformer

S₃
with timer
circuit

Junction

Fused
circuit
and return

Figure 17-3   Electrical layout for low
voltage system.

house or garage, somewhere protected from the weather and close by for easy
deactivation during parties and storms and such.

Notice that the system is connected to the fuse panel. This is absolutely
essential. If you have no skills to do this work, get help. You also need to check
your local building codes to determine if a permit is required and to learn other
particulars about the installation. These could include specifications on how deep
to bury the cable, waterproofing considerations, and types of fuse system to use.

ADDING SIDEWALLS

We discuss two approaches to making sidewalls for the trellis. There can be
several more as well as adaptations of the two. The first one is the lattice section
sidewall, and the second is the use of railings.

Lattice Assemblies

Figure 17-4 shows the style of lattice customarily used in a trellis. The details
show us that the spacing of lattice strips is 8 in. o.c. This makes an airy, open

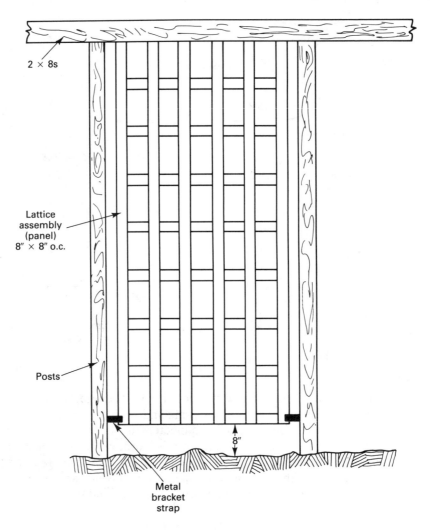

Figure 17-4 Lattice sidewall assembly/panel.

pattern. The idea is to create form but not to block the possibility of a view. Making the lattice assemblies is not a difficult job, but let's list the tasks required.

1. Measure the opening between posts for each assembly.
2. Allow at least 3 in. space on each end and 8 in. between the ground and the lowest lattice strip. Add 2 in. to the height in order to nail the assembly to the 2 × 8 horizontal member.
3. Determine the number of vertical pieces and horizontal pieces per assembly and cut these.

4. Apply a coat of wood sealer and a prime coat of paint.
5. Assemble the pieces.
6. Fasten the assembly to the 2 × 8 with nails or screws.
7. Brace the lower end with galvanized metal straps from lattice assembly to post.
8. Apply the final coats of paint.

Let's comment on assembling the lattice strips into a panel. The four perimeter pieces form the boundaries of the panel. This means that no raw ends will show, and the panel will have a finished balanced appearance. We know that the goal is to have strips at 8 in. o.c., but the likelihood of meeting this goal is slim. Therefore, we need to make fine adjustments. Measure the length of a side and divide by 8. Then divide the remainder by the total number of the first division and either add or subtract the fractional value to 8 in. This is the average o.c. separation. Repeat the process on the adjacent side. Mark off the spacings with a pencil and proceed to glue and staple the pieces into an assembly.

One of the most important concerns is to maintain a square or rectangular form. If there is a deck available, tack two 1 × 4s to the deck at 90 deg. If no deck is available, use a driveway and tack the 1 × 4s to the driveway with cement nails.

The remainder of the tasks are routine and need no further discussion.

Railing Assemblies

The patio railing assembly and the porch railing assemblies discussed in detail in earlier chapters may be used to design and construct railing assemblies for the trellis. In this section we describe another style of railing assembly that is quite open and makes a very nice addition to the trellis.

Figure 17-5 shows the details. Notice that, except for the top member of the

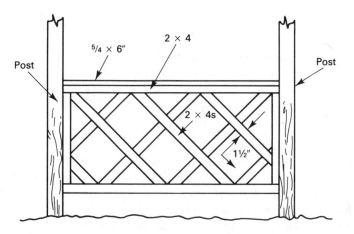

Figure 17-5 Railing assembly.

railing, all other parts are made from 2 × 4s. Once again we should allow 8-in. clearance from ground to the lower railing member. Since the railings extend from post to post, the vertical members can easily be nailed to the posts.

Another consideration is the support needed. Since the post spacing in the generic project in Chapter 16 was 4 ft, no center support is needed. But when railings extend 6 ft or more, there is a tendency for sagging. To prevent this a short 2 × 4 block of treated wood is placed under the lower railing and set on top of a brick.

PLANTING VINES AND SHRUBS (LANDSCAPING)

Recall from Chapter 16 that we mentioned the possibility of planting vines along-side the trellis and that when we did so there was a need for added structural stiffness. In this section we discuss the subject more fully. Without the added panels the only place to plant vines is at the base of the posts. But with lattice panels installed, vines can be planted anywhere along the length of the trellis. This really makes planting morning glories, pole beans, various types of grapes, and ivy possible. Some training of these plants would be required.

Planting wisteria, bougainvillea, and jasmine would still be at the base of the post, since these plants are very woody and strong and will place force against the post.

Roses can also be trained to grow within the lattice assembly. Tea roses are ideally suited for this environment.

Along the outside of the trellis shrubs selected for decoration should not reach higher than halfway up at maturity. The need for open view still remains a key aspect of the trellis.

THE FLOOR

The final enhancement for the trellis is to add a floor. Two examples are provided here, laying loose brick in a sand base and building a pine straw floor.

Paver Bricks

When we left the project of building the trellis in Chapter 16, all we did was level the dirt floor and make sure it was clean. Now we are going to add character to that part of the trellis. Paver bricks are ideal to use to create a floor. Building-supply houses sell paver brick systems that include bricks and a plastic mat with ridges that separates the bricks. After this plastic mat is laid and the bricks are set in place, washed sand is used to fill the joints. The border, if needed, can easily be made from plastic garden edge set flush with the top of the bricks.

The tasks are

1. Level the ground with flat shovel and hard rake.
2. Trench a line flush with the inside of the posts.
3. Install the garden edging and nail to the posts (optional).
4. Cut and lay the paver plastic sheet base.
5. Lay the bricks in place and cut those that need fitting with a power saw and mason blade.
6. Cover the area with washed sand and sweep clean. Add a thin film of cement on top of the sand and spray with water to keep sand in place.

Pine Straw Floor

Figure 17-6 shows how to make a pine straw floor. The depth of the pine straw should be at least 4 in. Since it will compact, more must be added from time to time. The tasks to be done are

1. Dig out the area inside the trellis about 4 in. deep.
2. Heavily treat the dug-out area with weed killer.

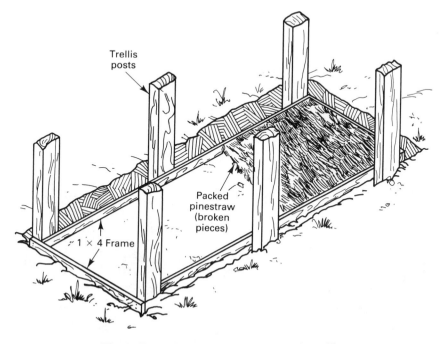

Trellis posts

Packed pinestraw (broken pieces)

1 × 4 Frame

Figure 17-6 Pine straw walkway under the trellis.

3. Cut and install the treated 1 × 4 frame.

4. Crush plenty of pine straw and lay it into the formed area. Compact it by walking on it or by using a roller.

5. Add more straw as the older straw compacts.

The job is relatively simple and includes no particularly difficult or strenuous tasks. The 1 × 4s can easily be nailed to the posts. The cross 1 × 4s should be nailed to the posts as well. Since they will be at ground level, the fact that they extend past the opening is not important.

18

Solving Landscaping Problems with Terracing

OBJECTIVES

- Identify the topography of the property.
- Understand the use of the transit.
- Identify problem conditions related to topography.
- Identify ground conditions and how these may be a help or hindrance.
- Understand the uses of terraces in urban, suburban, and country habitat.

TOPOGRAPHY

Even though a piece of property may look flat, it rarely is. Ground is almost always made up of various levels. We need to know and understand this, because decisions we make pertaining to enhancing outdoor living areas with terracing are affected by the contour of the property.

In this section we look at topographical representations and discuss some factors about the subject. We discuss the surveyors' tool called a *transit* and learn how it benefits us in making decisions about a variety of situations. Then, we show how grade stakes aid in making the planning of the landscaping solutions possible. These subjects are fundamental to dealing with terracing.

Figure 18-1 illustrates a section of a topographical map. There are grids and

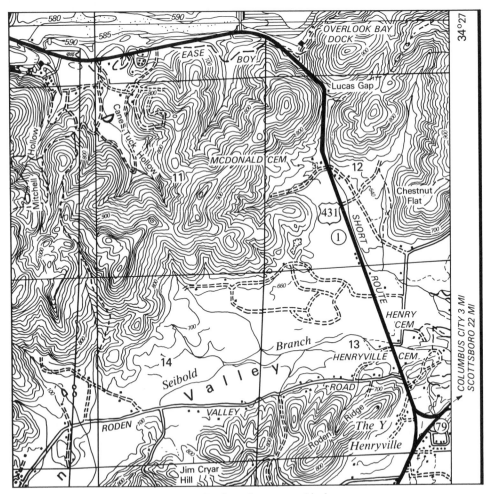

Figure 18-1 Section of a topographical map.

contour lines. The grids represent latitude and longitude markings. Latitude lines run east and west and longitude lines run north and south. Maps always contain a north-pointing arrow. The contour markings are generally irregular lines that have notations on each line. The notations represent elevation from a base line. Where the contour lines are spaced very closely, they represent a steep hill. Where they touch at a point, they represent a cliff. Where they are spaced wide apart, they represent a very gentle slope or an almost flat piece of ground.

On professional topographical maps the notations are usually referenced to sea level. For example, if you obtained a map of your property from the county it would show you the height above sea level. This information may be extremely useful if the property is on the water. Most of the time, however, the property is away from the sea, and we rarely care how high it is above sea level. We are more interested in flat ground and hilly or sloping ground on our property.

It is hard for us to estimate the slope or to make serious decisions about possible terracing solutions by using eyesight alone. We could use a line level and mason line to obtain the factors we need, but this is a cumbersome method and tends to be inaccurate. The better solution to collecting fundamental topographical data is with the use of a transit. Figure 18-2 shows a view of a transit. This instrument is built with levels and scales that are especially suited to finding the slope and contour of our individual property. With the aid of the instrument we can make a topographical map of the property.

Generally, the project goes like this. We set up the transit at a point on the property that provides us a full view of the area to be mapped. We set the instrument's levels to be perfectly level. Then we use the measurement stick usually supplied with the instrument to define the numerous heights that we will measure. We do not know what the reference is where the transit is situated, but we will find out. Stay with me on this: Next one of us paces off about five paces, and the other takes a reading by sighting through the transit and stating the measured height. Then one of us takes another five paces in the same line, and we take another reading. We repeat this until one of us reaches the end of the property.

Then we start over again at a point five paces left or right and repeat the measuring technique as often as before. On and on we go until the entire area is measured.

Next we transfer the measurements to a grid of the property which we either drew or obtained from the county assessor's office or the tax office. We add 5-pace (about 15-ft) grid lines to the drawing and then add the measurements at the appropriate points on the map. Next we connect the points that have the same measurements, using gentle curves rather than straight lines. The picture of the contour of the property will unfold as the drawing is completed.

Now if you really want to add reality to the map, get out a set of pencil colors. Use the green and yellow green for the lowest areas and light to dark browns as the elevation increases. Use blue where a natural stream or pond exists.

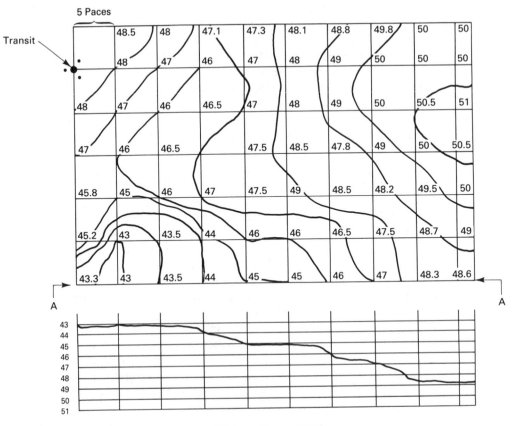

Figure 18-2 Transit tools and topographical map of a property.

With this map fairly accurately done, we have one standard to use to make decisions about terracing. To further our knowledge we can make another set of standards that will help more with our planned terracing. This technique involves the use of grade stakes. We have been using grade stakes of a sort throughout the book in the form of batter boards. Recall that in every case we established the finished floor height as the basic reference for the project. Grade stakes are similar but more advantageous for terracing.

Figure 18-3 shows a basic grade stake and another driven into the ground. Usually a 1 × 1 or 2 × 2 stake is tapered with four slopes rather than two to make driving the stake into the ground easier and more accurate. When we have decided on the solution to the terracing problem, we will drive these stakes at the

Figure 18-3 Grade stake.

appropriate points and set their height with the transit tool, as that instrument and measurement tool provides the needed height of the top of the stake.

Notice that I did not state how long to cut the stake. This would depend on the slope of the property and the target height of the final ground level. We should expect to drive every stake about 12 in. into the ground. You will have to determine the rest of the length needed.

Let's say this one time. There may be times when the grade stake will be below the present level of the property. If so, dig a hole a couple of feet across before driving the stake in place. Again, the top of the stake represents the top of finished level of the ground.

The making of a topographical map is time consuming and may seem extreme. But its use becomes very important when other factors of the project or use are considered.

SURFACE AND SUBSURFACE CONDITIONS
TO CONTEND WITH

In this section we gather factors about four soil conditions that we have to contend with when taking on a terracing project. Each of these may alter or influence the final decision about the project. In some cases we may be able to make use of the surface and subsurface conditions; in other cases we may have to remove the soil condition and replace it with clean fill.

The first of these is the *sandy soil* and the *erosion* it may cause. As a rule, sandy soil is easy to deal with. One can easily dig in it, bury posts in it, and level it. On flat surfaces these are great assets. But when it comes to terracing projects, sandy soil can be a real problem. Any rain storm will erode some soil and cause very irregular surfaces. Bulkheading must be built from materials that trap the sandy soil behind it. Bulkheads from treated timbers alone will not be suitable.

Clay presents different problems where terracing is concerned. First, it is very difficult to work with. When dry, it cracks and has to be chopped out. When wet, it is slippery and slides all over. Both conditions are tough to deal with. Clay as a surface material cannot grow grass or much else. Water must run off somewhere; if left on top, it will eventually soak in. Where clay is in the subsurface it frequently inhibits water runoff and acts to keep ground damp. Ground that stays damp may become a bog. Sometimes the only solution to a terracing problem containing clay is to dig it out and cart it off.

Rock is both an asset and a problem. *Gravel rock* is partially an asset, in that it makes an ideal watershed. Gravel rock can be worked with by mixing fill and top soil. Boulders are a different matter. A *boulder* can be a real liability if it is in the wrong place and is the wrong size. It may have to be blasted out to make the terracing project possible. On the other hand, boulders can be made a part of the terracing project. First, it is as natural as possible. Next, it may be moved to a proper location. Then too, it can be reduced in size by various means until it meets the dimensions of the project. Finally, it can be used in retaining walls. *Shale rock* at the surface is very undesirable, and the only solution possible is removal. Subsurface shale rock probably will not be a serious problem, since it can easily by cracked and moved to another location where, for example, retaining walls are to be installed. *Fieldstone* is another form of rock that is frequently used for terracing projects. Fieldstone can be any of a variety of stones, including granite and soapstone. Most of the natural ones found in fields contain a variety of minerals with iron as the most prominent one. Hence the rusty, reddish color frequently seen.

Finally, *running water* is either a problem or an asset. Surface water such as a brook or stream must be channeled into the terracing scheme. Subsurface water must be reckoned with in one of several ways, depending on the amount and kind. If it is water table runoff, we must consider where it will go after the terracing project is complete. If it is a natural spring in the subsurface, we must find another way to deal with it, such as a well point, a drain field of gravel, or a distributive drain field.

The purpose for this section was to state some of the major concerns about soils and what we may need to think about or act on when designing a terracing project.

USES OF TERRACES

In this section we explore ideas about the uses of terraces in three different habitats, urban, suburban, and country. These three areas present different situations, and the study of each may create ideas and variations that may just meet a particular set of conditions around the house.

Terraces in Urban Habitats

Let's begin with the terraces in urban habitats. Many of the areas are really small backyards, completely fenced in and secluded. The goal is to make the area appear much more than its size permits. Professional landscapers create *gardens at different levels* (Figure 18-4), and they use different types of shrubs that add color, structure, and dimension through their natural growth and flowers. Natural and man-made materials are used to create the various levels, and then the shrubs and grasses are planted. Lights placed strategically add the final touch for evening enjoyment.

The materials that can be used are bricks, natural stone, cement blocks faced with bricks or stucco, tiles, wood, and terra cotta. Underground watering systems and spraying systems are essential elements of the plan, and their parts must be included in the estimates of materials. In some cases concrete can be the best solution; it can be plastered, faced with pebble stones, or decorated with scoring. Concrete is also desirable because it can be formed into any shape. Once hard, it can be the foundation for mortaring facing brick and tile.

Figure 18-4 shows a series of gardens at different levels and a basic pathway through them. With a slight modification, a *patio* can be included in the area. The idea is to use the multilevel approach to make up for size. The patio can be on either level, but probably will be on the same level as the doors leading to the patio garden. The patio can be made from concrete or any of the various materials that we already have spoken of many times. Gardens at the second and higher levels provide the backdrop for color and harmony, disguise unsightly adjacent real property, and add color.

To add even more style and character to the small area, we can consider adding a *reflection pool*. The pool can be installed on one level, the patio slightly lower or higher, and gardens both below and above. If the pool concept is used, the water must be recycled to keep it clear and free from fungus, and to avoid its becoming a breeding place for mosquitoes. This means that water must be fed from the main house water supply, underground, with pumps while the entire project is being constructed. Provisions for draining it or heating it for winter use must also be considered. If the pool is to have a fountain or trickle-down waterfall, the water pump may serve two purposes. To operate the pump an electrical line and box must be provided to the pool.

Some form of walking access to and away from the pool must be included in the plan.

As stated earlier, it is impossible to plan for every type of urban backyard condition in this book. Yet the three ideas described in the section should stimulate possible solutions to the unique situation in the backyard. As a checklist of ideas, consider:

1. Use tall plants or evergreens to hide unsightly neighboring walls or block the view.

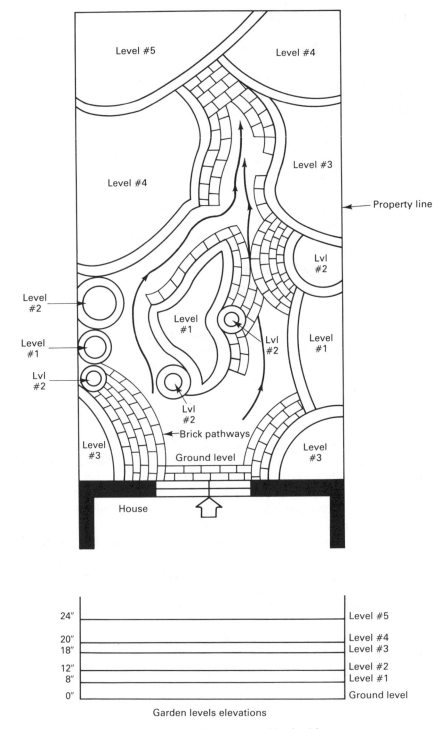

Level #5

Level #4

Level #4

Level #3

← Property line

Lvl #2

Level #2

Level #1

Lvl #2

Level #1

Lvl #2

Level #1

Lvl #2

← Brick pathways

Level #3

Ground level

Level #3

Lvl #2

House

24″	Level #5
20″	Level #4
18″	Level #3
12″	Level #2
8″	Level #1
0″	Ground level

Garden levels elevations

Figure 18-4   Urban terraced backyard.

2. Use multilevel gardens, patios, and reflection pool as an integrated approach to create the balance and harmony of peace and beauty.

3. Use concrete as a base material and face it with brick, stone, or tile.

4. Plan well when including water and its runoff, and electricity for the variety of uses that are planned.

5. Organize the selection of plants and grasses according to their mature height and color.

6. Plan for different colors to provide accents and drama.

7. Plan for the flowering shrubs to bloom at different times of the year, thereby creating changing focal points.

8. Plan for the use of annuals (flowers of one season duration) in planters, urns, or other types of containers.

Terraces in Suburban Habitats

In this section we discuss several terracing techniques different from those that were covered in urban habitat. The reasons for the differences are the dimensions of the area, which are usually much larger.

Let's start with the *berm*. Berms, which are mounds, can be made any size and any height. An excellent terracing technique can make use of a berm, where, for example, there is a need to shelter or partially hide something from general view. Figure 18-5 illustrates a berm that has been covered with shrubs and has a fairly large central shrub or tree. Most of us golfers are very familiar with these, because there is usually a sand trap lurking on the back side.

Sometimes a berm does no more than create an undulation in the terracing scheme. If so, it will probably be covered with grass or a low-growing ground cover, such as Japanese jasmine.

A second technique for the terrace in the suburban habitat is to make the house *blend in with the terrain* more fully and yet still appear natural. The specific ideas for this use are boundless. Most often terracing is used to keep the lawns from eroding where some form of bulkhead is built, and the dirt is backfilled to create the terrace. Sometimes the steepness of a sloping property can be softened by terracing.

Still the most important reason for terracing in the suburban habitat is to *create outdoor living spaces*. These include patios, swimming pool areas, ponds, gardens, waterfalls, and ways of adding pathways and sidewalks that seem to naturally fit the apparent unruly ground. The amount of movement of dirt or earth can be relatively minor if a path is to be cut into a hill. At the opposite extreme, 50 yards or more of dirt may be needed to create the terrace for an in-the-ground pool.

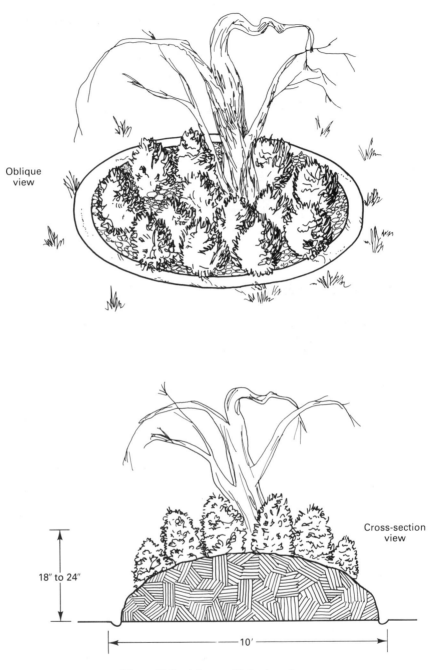

Oblique view

Cross-section view

18" to 24"

10'

Figure 18-5   A berm with landscaping.

Terraces in Country Habitats

In this setting the area is quite a bit larger than the previous two discussed. Here we may be dealing with acres of property. Four uses of terraces are the most common ones; we look at each of the four.

Since the property is large, buildings are frequently detached a few feet to many feet from the main house. These could be a garage, a barn, a workshop, a utility outbuilding, or something similar. Where the ground slopes radically at the place where it is most advantageous to place the building, terracing solves the problem. First a terrace is built, and then the building is erected. A few to many yards of fill dirt could be required. Or bulldozing a hill to a terrace-like plateau could meet the initial requirements.

A second reason for terracing is to control the natural flow of springs, ponds, or waterfalls. Terracing may include bulkheads, dikes, sluices, and importation of boulders and fieldstone to cause the running water to travel in a certain predetermined way.

A third use for the terrace in this habitat is to prevent erosion due to wind and weather. Many times the use of a berm of rather long dimensions will cause the wind to deflect above the ground level and thereby reduce erosion. Heavy rains always cause erosion unless specific action is taken to prevent it. Terracing can solve many problems with rain runoff. The flatter the ground, the more slowly the water runs away. Further, each level of the terrace can be designed to retain its measure of rain. This will nurture the ground and make it productive rather than devoid of nutrients carried away by the runoff.

Which brings us to the final use, making ground useful to grow edibles. If we can reclaim the ground by building one or more levels of terraces, they can be turned into vegetable gardens, fruit groves, or orchards. In these cases we would probably need to use bulkheads, since the object is *not* to grow grass or ground cover. Bulkheads keep the shape of the terrace and thus permit us to make use of the terrace with little or no maintenance.

In summary, terracing is a technique that has many applications where enhancing outdoor living areas is the goal. The solutions may be all similar in function, yet their specific applications may range from several square feet in the urban environment to several acres in the country environment. A plan must be made that includes all that is known about the problem to be solved and the goal to be achieved. In the next two chapters we deal with the use of materials to solve these problems.

19

Single-Material Approach to Terracing

OBJECTIVES

- Identify the effect of terracing with a single material, such as wood, brick, or fieldstone.
- Understand some of the surface and embankment concerns when terracing with wood, brick, or stone.
- Identify some of the techniques used to hold the building materials in place.
- Understand how differently treated lumber extends the life of wood.

TERRACING WITH BRICK

General Approach

Generically, a brick wall used in a terracing plan is called a *retaining wall*. Its purpose is to create a level or almost level surface at one height and another one at a lower level. How high and how long it will be is a function of the topography and plan. How thick it will be and what type of cap it will have are also elements of the plan. How it will be reinforced and anchored are also functions of the plans.

The work begins with locating the wall with grade stakes and lines. Then earth must be removed to permit footings, drain pipes, and backfill of gravel. Additional earth may need to be removed if anchors are to be installed below ground level. Then footings are formed and poured. Frequently these are graduated in steps to reduce the number of bricks used. Then the brick wall is raised, using one of many bricklaying patterns. Figure 19-1 shows a half brick overlay pattern. Notice the capping technique. Irrigation drain pipes are placed behind the wall and gravel is laid around them, as we see later in Figure 19-4. Then the dirt is backfilled against the wall and the surface is landscaped. The lower side facing the wall is landscaped next; a pathway could be made, as shown in Figure 19-1.

Figure 19-1 Terracing with brick.

Specifications

We build the generic brick terracing wall 10 ft long, curved, with double thickness brick. Table 19.1 provides the exact specification.

Materials Assessment

In keeping with earlier chapters, we look at a materials assessment of the generic project. Table 19.2 provides us with a quick guide to the variety of materials we need.

Construction Sequence

Let's start with several views of the project, as shown in Figure 19-2. The retaining wall is made of common brick, double wall thick and capped. We can see that the upper level is partly a garden and that the lower level is a sidewalk and lawn. Further, we see where the anchor is located and how the footings extend 4 in. wider than the wall and longer than the wall. The tasks to be performed are

---

TABLE 19.1 Specification Listing
PROJECT: *Brick Terracing Retaining Wall*   **DATE:** _____

General Description

Build a 10-ft curved brick retaining wall to provide a smoother gentler sloped path way. Make the wall from dark red brick, using $\frac{1}{2}$ lap pattern and cap it with the same brick, using lay-down soldier course. Strike the joints with a concave tool. Where possible step the footings to save on bricks. No footings are to show. Place one anchor midway along the wall and ensure that the rebar is embedded into the center of the double brick wall. Place drain pipes and gravel behind the wall prior to backfilling. Landscape and then install sidewalks.

Specifications

Item	*Specifications*
Footing	16 in. W × 6 in. D × 10 ft 8 in.
Wall	Double thickness brick, $\frac{1}{2}$ overlap; only face or end will show
Mortar	Standard mortar mix and sand
Anchor	Mortared bricks and $\frac{1}{2}$-in. rebar 4 ft back from the center length of the wall, rebar anchored to wall one course down from top course

TABLE 19.2 Materials Assessment
PROJECT: *Brick Terracing Retaining Wall*   **DATE**: _____

Direct Materials

Type or Description	Use or Purpose
Brick	Basic retaining wall material
Mortar and sand	Cement bricks in place
Concrete	Footings
½-in. rebar	Reinforcing footings
Gravel	Water shed fill
4-in. perforated pipe	Water shed
Steel rod	Earth anchor

Indirect Materials

Type or Description	Use or Purpose
Forms	For footings
Mortar board	Aids in bricklaying
Mason line	Aids in bricklaying
Batter boards (optional)	Aids in defining the location of the retaining wall
Stakes	Hold forms and pinpoint location of footings and heights
Nails	Fasteners

Support Materials

Type or Description	Use or Purpose
Power concrete mixer	Aids in making concrete and mortar
Mason tools	Construction
Carpentry tools	Construction
Transit and measuring rod	Establish references
Shovel and rake	Moving dirt, concrete, and mortar
Bolt cutters	Cut rebars
Power saw and mason blade	Cut bricks

1. Remove earth and prepare the natural form for footing where possible.
2. Locate and install the grade stakes.
3. Trench out behind the wall for the brick anchor.
4. Pour footings and screed flush with top of form or grade stakes.
5. Lay bricks for the anchor and embed rebar.

6. Lay wall bricks and install rebar; strike joints.
7. Lay perforated pipe behind wall and backfill with gravel.
8. Replace dirt and topsoil.
9. Landscape upper and lower levels.

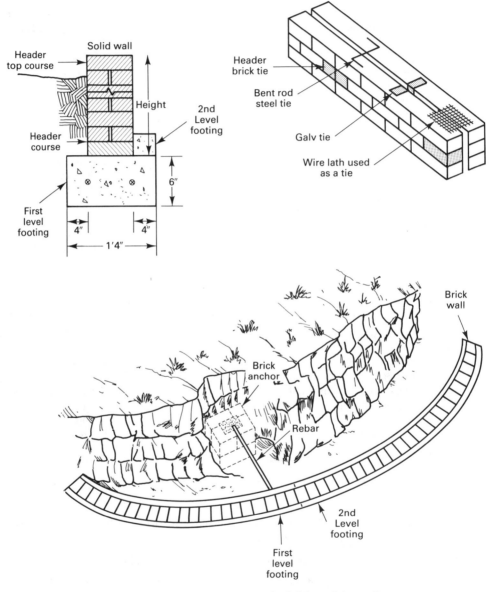

Figure 19-2   Construction details for brick retaining wall.

A review of Figure 19-1 shows a curved retaining wall with several courses of brick showing. To the right the ground rises, and fewer courses are visible. To the left two more courses show. If we take a cross-sectional view, the construction details become visible. In part of Figure 19-2 we see a footing and brick wall. Notice the header course on top of the footing. This is the standard way to begin. Then the wall courses are laid up. Whether or not the courses touch in the middle depends upon the width and length of the brick. Use Figure 19-2 to see this. If a gap exists between inner and outer bricks, a tie of some sort must be installed every few courses and about 4 ft o.c. throughout the length of the wall. The top course of brick is laid as a lay-down soldier course to finish the job and add the support needed to make the final tie.

Generally the footing is 8 in. deep and about 8 in. wider than the length of the brick. In a retaining wall this requirement may be used, though a 6-in.-deep footing can be used when the number of courses is few. Normally, the brick wall and footing carry the loads of the house and therefore need the heavy footing. Here there are no loads save the dead load of the wall.

The type or pattern of bricklaying shown in Figure 19-1 is called *running*. Since each brick is overlapped half its length, we have a half overlap running design. Figure 19-3 shows it and six others. These patterns have unique characteristics:

1. The *running* pattern consists of stretchers only. The vertical joints are centered above and below the middle of the alternate course.

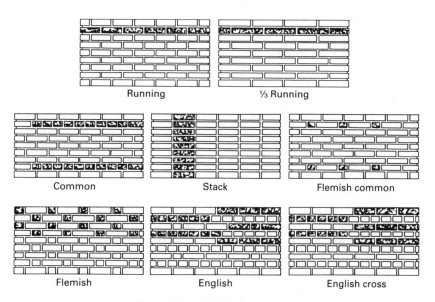

Figure 19-3 Bricklaying patterns.

2. The *one-third running* pattern uses only stretchers, but the vertical joints fall one-third of a brick's length away from its end.

3. The *common* pattern consists of a first course of continuous full headers, followed by five courses of stretchers and another course of continuous headers.

4. The *stack* pattern has the least strength and as a rule cannot be used as a load-bearing wall. All vertical joints are aligned.

5. The *flemish common* pattern consists of a course made up of alternate stretchers and headers, followed by five courses of stretchers and another course of alternate stretchers and headers.

6. The *flemish* pattern differs from the flemish common in that each course has a repeat pattern of a header and a stretcher. Further, each header is centered above and below the middle of the stretcher brick.

7. The *english* pattern consists of alternate courses of headers and stretchers, where the headers are centered over the stretcher joints. Every fourth vertical joint alignment is made on the stretcher joints only.

8. The *english cross* pattern is similar to the english, except that all stretcher joints line up vertically.

Trenching for the footing, watershed pipe, and a foot of gravel must be adequate to the needs. Then the form, either natural or man-made, is installed with its top equal to the tops of the grade stakes previously driven in the trench. Backfilling is done to make the depth of the footing correct and even with the bottom of the form, or 6 in. down from the top of the grade stakes.

We need an anchor. We use 12 bricks as the anchor and a piece of rebar as the link between wall and anchor. We place the brick about 4 ft back of the wall and 2 feet below the finished height of the wall. Once it is in place, we fill the center with mortar and embed the rebar in the fresh mortar. The rebar runs perpendicular to the wall, as shown in Figure 19-2, and the other end of the rebar is bent parallel with the wall and laid on top of the next-to-top course. Once the mortar hardens, the dirt can be backfilled over the anchor unit.

With the wall finished, we must prepare the back side of it to permit water to shed along the wall and leach into the ground; see Figure 19-4. First we place a thin layer of gravel along the wall. Then we cut the perforated 4-in. pipe for length and lay it against the wall and on top of the gravel. Then we place about a foot of gravel over the pipe and replace the dirt removed earlier. Finally, we grade the dirt and topsoil.

After cleaning the face side of the wall and ground of construction debris, we landscape the lower area. Finally, we must clean all tools and put them away.

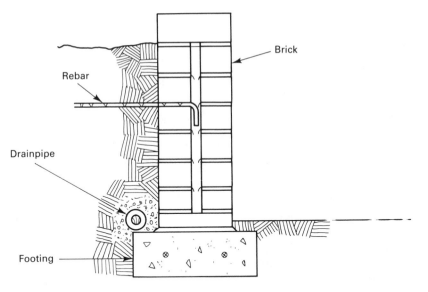

Figure 19-4 End view of wall with drain system in place.

TERRACING WITH WOOD

One of the most commonly used informal materials for terracing in suburban and country habitats is treated wood. The two kinds most often used are garden landscape timbers, which measure $3\frac{1}{2}$ in. × 5 in. × 8 ft long, and railroad ties, which measure about 6 × 8 in. × 8 ft long. Both are pressure-treated, but with different chemicals. The garden landscape timbers are treated with some form of phenol, and the railroad ties are treated with creosote. Creosote is dangerous to handle and burns the skin. Long-sleeved shirts and gloves are used when these timbers are handled.

Before we start with the project, let's establish several ideas concerning the use of treated ties in terracing. Fundamentally, ties provide a rustic appearance. They are an informal solution, whereas brick and stone are formal. When new ties are first installed, they look very nice, but as they age they bleach, as the tar and creosote leach out and into the ground. They also split and readily accept seeds from the wind, which mature into grass and weeds. These ties will never have the added-value quality compared to brick.

The treated landscape timbers are not suited to terracing over four to six timbers high. They do not possess the substance necessary to retain the earth behind the wall. When they are used even four high, steel rods must be used behind them and anchors will be required. These members also leach the preservative over time and turn gray. They will rot and sometimes split. They too will provide habitat for blown seed and mature grass and weed.

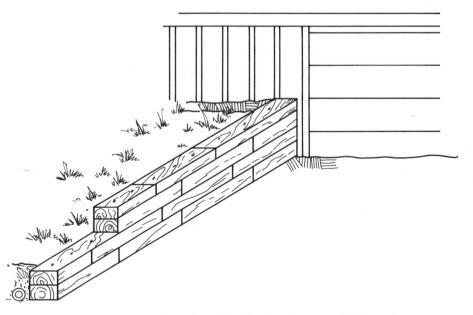

Figure 19-5   Treated wood wall for left side of a proposed driveway.

Our generic project is made from the railroad tie. Its purpose, as shown in Figure 19-5, is to provide a retaining wall to the left side of a proposed new driveway. The ground slopes steeply, approximately 18 in., and if it is just tapered, the erosion caused by repeated rainfall would fill the driveway with dirt and sand. The wall will prevent this. One added requirement is to prevent leaching of dirt from between the rows and ends of the ties onto the driveway.

Specifications

The driveway will slope down and the earth against the house will slope away from the house so that the maximum height of the retaining wall will be 18 in. graduating down to 6 in. high about 30 ft from the foundation of the house. Table 19.3 provides the exact specifications.

Materials Assessment

At first glance there would seem to be very few requirements for materials to complete this generic project. However, we need to take a closer look. Table 19.4 (see page 268) shows us that not only do we need ties but quite a bit more.

TABLE 19.3 Specification Listing
PROJECT: *Terracing with Wood*   DATE: _____

General Description

The ties will have offset end lap not less than 3 feet. The ties will be linked together with ⅜- or ½-in. rebars at not less than 4 ft o.c. spacing. Plastic sheeting not less than 8 mm thick will be placed behind the wall before backfilling. Backfilling will be held 4 in. below the top of the ties before seeding.

Specifications

Item	*Specifications*
Ties	6 × 8 8-ft treated new railroad
Tie placement	On solid soil or brick or rock
Ties overlap	Not less than 3 ft
Ties united	⅜ or ½ in rebar @ 4 ft o.c.
Polyvinyl	8 mm minimum thickness, no joints
Pipe	Perforated 4 in.
Gravel	Washed not larger than 1 in. average

Construction

We have the specifications and materials assessment; now let's get to building the wall. Since the length is 30 ft, we know that it will take four ties to reach full length. Further, we know that the slope toward the street means that the third and fourth rows or courses will not reach to the street. We also know that we have to cut away the ground at least 12 in. back from the finished line of the wall to allow for placement of the ties, pipe, and gravel.

The tasks we must complete are

1. Establish the finished line of the wall with grade stakes and/or batter boards.
2. Remove the earth to 12 in. back from the line and to the grade depth.
3. Lay in stone or brick as a base to set the first row of timber optional: lay in a bed of concrete about 4 in. thick).
4. Beginning at the street, set the first course of ties in place end to end.
5. Cut the first piece of tie for the second course and install it by alignment and drilling for rebar. Insert the rebar.
6. Drop back and install the last or top course of ties.
7. Install the 4-in. perforated pipe on a shallow bed of gravel and then cover with several inches of gravel.
8. Backfill with dirt and topsoil to within 4 in. of the top of the wall.

TABLE 19.4 Materials Assessment
PROJECT: *Terracing with Wood*   DATE: _____

Direct Materials

Type or Description	Use or Purpose
½-in. rebars	Used to tie each level of wood together
Polyvinyl	Isolates wood from earth
4-in. perforated drain pipe	Permits water shed
Gravel	Water shed
Treated wood timbers	Basic retaining wall member
Nails	Fasteners

Indirect Materials

Type or Description	Use or Purpose
Mason line	Establish references
Grade stakes	Establish reference heights

Support Materials

Type or Description	Use or Purpose
Carpentry tools	Construction
Shovel and rake	Moving dirt
Wheelbarrow	Moving dirt
Sledge hammer	Drive stakes and ties
Power saw and drill	Aids in cutting and drilling
Transit and measuring rod	Establish grades
Chain saw or tree saw	Cutting wood ties
Bolt cutters	Cut rebars

The tasks are not difficult to understand. A lot of hard work is involved, since shoveling dirt is hard work and lifting the heavy ties is strenuous. We describe some of the more technical details associated with this project.

Establishing the grade for the first row or course of ties takes some work, since the earth must first be removed. Recall from the previous chapter that sometimes we need to dig a hole to establish the finished grade. In this project the finished grade will be above the present level of ground, and we must work down from there. Since there must be 4 in. of wood above the natural height of the ground and the slope is about 18 in., we need 22 in. of height at the house. The ground slopes toward the street, so we do not need to extend the top course of ties all the way to the street. The ties are 6 in. thick; therefore, we need four courses (6 in./22 in. = 3.67). Part of the first course will be below the driveway level, which is all right.

After removing the earth to the established level of 24 in. below the top of the grade stakes and leveling the trench, we must make a decision concerning the substrate for the first course of ties. If the ground is firm, the ties can be placed on it, but if the ground is not firm, some sort of materials must be added. To firm the ground, brick or stone may be placed at the proper ground level. A simpler solution is to fill the area with washed sand and wet it well to compact it.

To aid in setting the first course of ties, establish a line at the top of the course and along its driveway side with a mason line. Then place the ties one at a time alongside the line. As each is placed, use the electric drill and drill several holes through the tie. Cut rebars about 2 ft long and drive these through the holes into the ground until they are flush with the top of the tie. This will hold the tie in place.

When setting each of the remaining courses in place, make sure that the offset of joints is 3 ft or more. Drill holes for the rebar deep enough to penetrate at least well into the lower course. It is possible to drive the rebar into undrilled wood, but do not drive it too far; splitting may result, or the rebar may bend and throw the wall out of alignment.

After the courses are laid, cut a piece of 6-ft-by-30-ft polyvinyl sheeting from the roll, double it, and staple it to the back side of the ties. It should be trimmed just about 2 in. below the top of the tie so that it does not show.

The remaining tasks of placing the pipes and gravel and backfilling do not need further explanation. Just be sure that the pipe slopes toward the street and not toward the house. About $\frac{1}{4}$ in. per 10 ft of run is adequate.

The project described in this section can be employed with slight modification wherever it is deemed practical.

TERRACING WITH STONE

Terracing with quarry and fieldstone can be made formal or informal, as shown in Figures 19-6 and 19-7. In Figure 19-6 notice how the stone has been mortared in place alongside the stairs. This finished appearance is as formal as stone can get. In contrast Figure 19-7 shows how stone can be used informally to solve a terracing situation. Here the idea is to protect the tree from erosion of its root soils, yet still contour the surrounding ground.

Have you driven in the countryside and noticed the separation between fields? Often the fieldstone extracted when land was cleared and plowed has been used to build divider walls. These informal uses of fieldstone or rubble stone, as they are sometimes called, serve that purpose very well. Figure 19-8 shows two different arrangements of this kind of stone. In Figure 19-8a a random rubble-stone pattern is used. In this method stones are laid in any pattern that seems to fit well. Header stones are placed at random as well to unite the wall, but they should be placed approximately one each every 2 to 4 ft. Chips and small stones

Figure 19-6   Formal terracing with stone.

Figure 19-7   Informal terracing with stone.

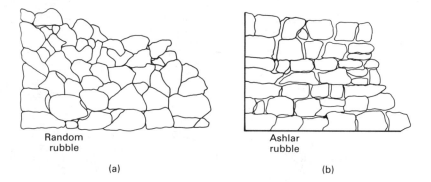

Random
rubble

Ashlar
rubble

(a)   (b)

Figure 19-8 Laying stone in a retaining wall. (a) Random rubble; (b) Ashlar rubble.

are used as fillers and wedges. In contrast, Figure 19-9b shows rubble stone laid in courses. To do this means that the stones must be shaped with a brick hammer and chisel to approximate rectangles before they are laid. This technique is called *ashlar rubble*.

Quarry stone is made from stone cut in a quarry. These stones are relatively square and rectangular. They are approximately the same color, and of course they are the same kind of stone. These make excellent retaining walls for terracing situations. They can be laid in ashlar pattern very well and can easily be mortared.

Our generic project is to build a retaining wall from rubble or quarry stone. We assume that the purpose for building this wall is the same as for the railroad-tie wall (previous section). To preclude your having to read the earlier section: The project was to build a retaining wall about 22 in. high and 30 ft long in order for a new driveway to be built leading to the garage. Our options for the wall are

1. Poured concrete footing/foundation.
2. Natural stone footing/foundation.
3. Random rubble pattern of stone laying.
4. Ashlar pattern of stone laying.
5. Mortarless stacking.
6. Mortared-in-place stone.

For this generic project we use a poured concrete footing and an ashlar stone-laying pattern, and we mortar the stones in place. This combination of characteristics meets the basic requirement to prevent soil erosion onto the new driveway. Figure 19-9 shows both arrangements that are included in the list above. We use the one on the right.

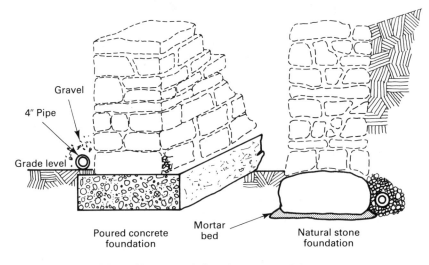

Gravel

4″ Pipe

Grade level

Poured concrete
foundation

Mortar
bed

Natural stone
foundation

Figure 19-9 Foundations for stone retaining walls.

Specifications

Table 19.5 provides the specifications. Besides being 30 ft long and about 22 in. high, the wall will be at least 12 in. thick, and it may slope back, away from the driveway side, slightly but not more than 2 in.

TABLE 19.5 Specification Listing
PROJECT: *Terracing with Quarry or Rubble Stone*   **DATE**: _____

General Description

The wall will be about 30 ft long and about 2 ft high, and 12 in. thick at the top, made from quarry or rubble stone mortared in place on top of a concrete foundation. Ashlar rubble pattern will be used. Drain pipe and gravel will be installed behind the wall before backfilling.

Specifications

Item	*Specifications*
Stone	Varied sizes and generally square or rectangular, free from all forms of vegetation, approximately the same color and type
Mortar	Commercial mixture with lime
Concrete	2500 psf quality
Rebar	$\frac{1}{2}$-in. diameter, 2 abreast
Drain pipe	4-in., perforated
Gravel	$\frac{1}{2}$–$\frac{3}{4}$-in. dimension

Materials Assessment

Quite a few materials and considerable equipment are required for this job. It would be a good idea to rent a mixer for both the concrete and mortar. Table 19.6 lists our needs.

Construction

The project begins with setting grade stakes to establish the references. This, in some ways, simplifies the removal of earth. Then a footing form, natural or man-made, is established and the concrete poured. It should be reinforced with rebars. Then the stone is laid in mortar. Here is the hard work. First, the stones

---

TABLE 19.6 Materials Assessment
PROJECT: *Terracing with Quarry or Rubble Stone*   **DATE:** _____

Direct Materials

Type or Description	*Use or Purpose*
Stone	Basic wall material
$\frac{1}{2}$-in. rebar	Reinforces footing
Concrete	Footings
Straps (strap steel)	Tie rebars together
4-in. perforated drain pipe	Water shed
Gravel	Water shed
Mortar and sand	Mortar stone together

Indirect Materials

Type or Description	*Use or Purpose*
Mason line	Establish references
Grade stakes	Establish heights
Mortar board	Aid in laying stone

Support Materials

Type or Description	*Use or Purpose*
Mason tools	Construction
Shovel and hoe	Dig dirt and mix mortar
Power mixer	Aids in mixing mortar
Transit and measuring rod	Establishes references
Sledge hammer	Drive stakes and break up stone
Stone-cutting chisels	Aids in cutting stone
Bolt cutters	Cut rebars

must be laid out on the ground to sort of make the first course. Several stones should be installed as headers, while the rest can be laid serially as stretchers. Overall the first course should be a bit wider than 12 in.

The upper courses are laid as a patchwork of stone with the aim of retaining the ashlar pattern. Mortar beds are laid and stones are set into the mortar. A clean job minimizes the splashing of mortar on the face of the stone.

Mason line stretched along the driveway side of the retaining wall aids in maintaining course alignment and overall wall alignment. So far we have used the following tasks:

1. Locate the retaining wall and establish the grade stakes.
2. Remove the earth, including the area for the footing.
3. Build the footing and pour it full of concrete; add rebars.
4. Lay the first course of stone in a mortar bed.
5. Lay the remaining stone courses, maintaining the ashlar pattern.

Now let's list the remaining tasks:

6. Place the drain pipe in place behind the wall accurately.
7. Place gravel over the pipe.
8. Backfill with dirt, and terrace.

RETAINING WALL VARIATIONS

The walls we selected for the generic projects are not very high, and therefore the amount of pressure against them is moderate. Even so, we did add an anchor to the brick wall. In this section we describe several techniques that do specific things for the retaining walls.

A technique that adds some strength to a retaining wall is the inclusion of double curves. The concave part, as we look at it, acts like a keystone to soil pressure. The convex distributes the force against the curves at different pressures.

Sometimes the inclusion of a pilaster in the retaining wall is needed to add stiffness. Pilasters are columns with considerable strength, since they are usually well anchored in the footing area. Sometimes the footings are considerably deeper than those for the retaining wall. Once the pilasters are in place, the retaining wall members, stone, bricks, and even wood timbers are installed between and tied to the pilasters.

It is not absolutely necessary to make a retaining wall vertical. In fact, where wood and stone are the basic materials used, sloping them back several degrees aids in wall design and strength. The idea is that the first course is wider than the final or top course. Slopes should not exceed 5 to 8 deg for appearance's sake.

Although the generic projects in this chapter are very plain, this does not have to be the case. The brick wall can be made with one of the more distinguished patterns. The wall may have light fixtures. Planter boxes can be built into the design. For example, the stone retaining wall could easily have a round planter at or near the street. It could be filled with dirt, or a half keg could be set into it and filled with flowers.

Finally, finishes can be added to preserve the color and texture of the wall. Protective sealers, painting systems, and even stucco or facing tile may be added to enhance the appearance of the wall.

20

Different Construction Techniques for Terrace Stairs

OBJECTIVES

- Identify the construction techniques applicable to building terrace steps.
- Understand the conditions where a gentle or steep slope stair design is useful.

GENTLE SLOPE STAIR DESIGN

In Chapter 19 we discussed, designed, and built on paper a retaining wall that allowed for a curved sloping walkway. The slope was only a foot to 18 in. Therefore, the idea of using gentle-slope stair design was really not justified. Where we would be restricted from using the design of the retaining wall due to the distance of the sloping ground, the slope might warrant the use of a gentle stair design. More probably, the slope will be several feet back or a relatively long way—20 ft or more.

The idea of using the gentle slope stair design solution to making an access from one level to another means that the usual "rule of 17" in step design is set aside. We substitute a deep tread area and limit the step rise to a maximum of 8 in. high. With careful design planning the tread depth will be established in increments of usual paces.

Most people have a pace whose distance is approximately 26 to 28 in. Let's assume that the above measurement is a standard. Figure 20-1 shows that a normal person stepping down from one level or step to another lands on the lower level about 4 to 5 in. from the riser. Added to this is the average 27 in., which places the toe near the 32-in. mark. Therefore, the edge of the next riser should be about 32 to 34 inches from the last one. For an even more gentle slope, the depth of the tread area can be increments of 32 in.

Horizontal Stringers

Under normal circumstances a stringer is used in step design and construction. But in the construction of the gentle slope design landscape stairs, normal stringers are not used. Rather, *horizontal stringers*, as shown conceptually in Figure

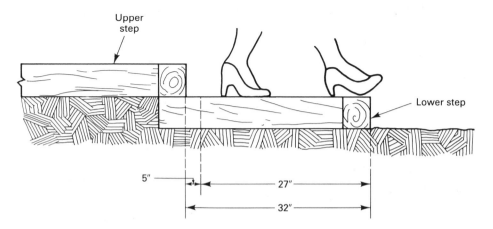

Figure 20-1 Dimensions for the tread for a gentle slope stair design.

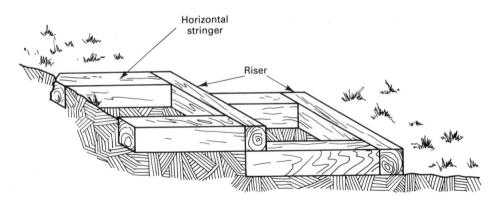

Figure 20-2   The use of horizontal stringers in a gentle slope stair design.

20-2, are used. These stringers may be made from natural materials, such as stone or ties, or they may be formed and poured with concrete or made from steel. Then the tread surface can be made from a variety of materials, which include slate, thin stone, bricks, treated lumber, gravel, and even sod.

Where ties are the stringers, no special footings need to be used. A level surface area of virgin soil will support the ties, and their sides will remain in place laterally with the natural sloping ground at their outsides. But, for example, where stones or bricks are the stringers, footings are needed; they are usually made from either natural stone or, more commonly, concrete.

Once the stringers are in place, the risers are installed. The installation technique depends upon the materials selected for the risers. If wood is used, spiking the risers to the stringers is appropriate. When stone or brick is used, mortar must be used to hold them in place.

Now the tread surface materials must be installed. If it is treated lumber, the first piece will overlap the riser by $1\frac{1}{2}$ in. All other pieces are installed behind this piece, and the last piece is cut to fit against the next higher riser.

When the stringers and risers are made from stone or brick, the tread area must be backfilled with clean fill and compacted with water spray and tamping. Then the tread materials are installed. A mortar bed about 2 in. thick in the filled area and about 1 in. thick over the stringers and riser prepares the surface for the brick or stone tread materials. Even in this situation there can be a slight bullnose over the riser.

When natural sod or pine straw is the tread material, two slightly different approaches are used. For the sod, topsoil is the appropriate filler. Then the sod is placed within the boundaries of the stringer and riser. When pine straw is the tread material, first a coating of weed killer is sprayed within the areas. Then polyvinyl is cut to fit in each area. Finally, crushed pine straw is installed.

Building the steps with a gentle slope design is physically difficult. It can be complex if concrete forms are required and bricks are mortared in place. It is equally taxing to make the stairs from stone. It is less taxing to make them from treated lumber and timbers.

STEEP GRADE STAIR DESIGN

A steep slope presents us with different problems to solve compared to the gentle slope. In this section we examine several conditions and possible solutions and begin with several fundamentals of stair design.

Fundamentals

Steep stairs used in the garden or yard area should follow the design rules used for residential stairs, which include limitations on the total number of steps between landings, inclusion of landings, angle of inclination limits, the rules of "17 and 25" and the use of the handrail.

Stairs in residential homes are limited to 13 risers. Property that slopes no more than about 8 to 9 ft would fit the requirements very well, since the height from floor to floor is also about 9 ft. Naturally, sloping ground that is less high than these maximums would use fewer than the maximum number of risers.

Where the total rise is above the 9-ft amount, a landing must be installed. This breaks up the climb and provides a resting space for the person using the stairs. The landing in this situation should be about halfway up, but again not more than 13 risers.

Several other reasons make the use of the landing a good idea. There may be a situation where the ground flattens out partway up the hill. Here a landing would be a natural solution to bridge from one set of stairs to the next. A second reason for including a landing is to change direction. If the stairs must turn partway up the slope to allow the top step to meet a path, sidewalk, or patio, the landing is used to permit the turn. This is the safest method, and it eliminates the curved step design, which is not a safe design. Finally, the landing in a steep stair design reduces or eliminates the fear of falling from a height. Some people have fear of falling, but the landing somehow reduces the fear.

Inclination of the stairs is another important principle in the design. Figure 20-3 shows three inclinations, and these are the extremes and mean angles for the design of stairs. All are obtainable when the rules of "17 or 25" are used. The angles range from 30 deg, which represents the least amount of steepness, to 40 deg for the steepest stairs. The dimensions provided are for a total rise of 105 in.

The rules of "17 or 25" mean the following:

1. The rule of 17 means that sum of the depth of the tread + the height of the rise = 17 in.
2. The rule of 25 means that the sum of two risers and one tread = 25 in.

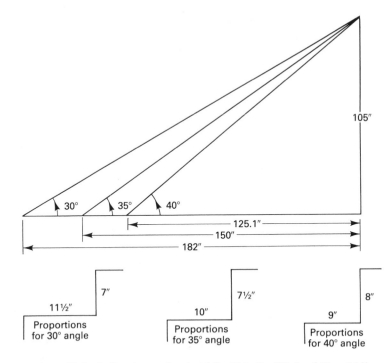

Figure 20-3   Inclination angles that fall within the "Rule of 17 or 25."

The use of a handrail is mandatory in steep stair design. It may be installed on either side of the stair. It should be 30 to 34 in. high and well anchored. Where there is a falling away of the ground on one side of the stair, thus exposing people to falling, the railing assembly must be installed to provide protection. Where the ground is even on both sides of the stairs, a railing on the side that provides the most esthetic appearance is appropriate. When there is no other reason for inclusion of the railing, then place it on the right side as one would descend the stairs, since most people are right-handed.

Stringer Design and Installation

The idea of using a 2 × 12 treated member for a stringer is a possibility with the steep design. If the conditions of slope permit its use, a footing should be established from stone, brick, cement blocks, or other materials not likely to rot. The upper end or top of the stair should likewise have a sound anchoring system for the stringer. Then a trench should be dug behind the area for the stairs so that the stringers can be installed with relative ease.

When a wood stringer is made, it should be laid out and cut following the rules for stair stringer design for basements. This is the simplest design possible. Figure 20-4 shows the details. The tasks are

1. Determine the total rise and inclination of the stringer.
2. Transfer the dimensions to the 2 × 12 or plan, if used.
3. Determine the number of rises, using mathematics.

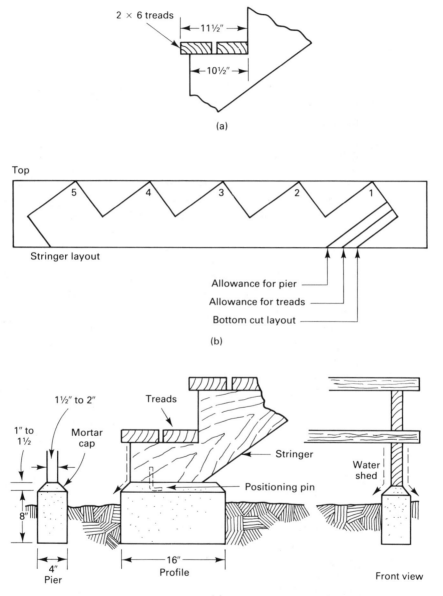

Figure 20-4 Stringer layout for a steep slope stair design.

4. Use the framing square and step off the runs and rises on the 2 × 12.

5. Cut away the unwanted wood.

6. Build the anchor footing and top header if not already done.

7. Try the stringer for fit and make adjustments.

8. Cut the second and, if needed, the third stringer, using the first for the pattern.

9. Install the stringers.

10. Cut the risers and nail in place.

11. Cut the treads and nail or screw in place.

12. Build the handrail with posts anchored to the stringers with bolts.

13. Landscape around the stairs.

The more difficult activities within the list are determining the slope and rise, determining the number of rises, and laying out the stringers. The other tasks are not difficult to perform. We discuss these three aspects more fully.

The rise and slope can be found with the use of a long 1 × 2, a level, and a tape measure. Two people are required. Fasten the tape measure to the side of the 1 × 2 and hold the 1 × 2 plumb and even with the point on the ground where the stringer will set. The second person on the top of the slope reads the distance on the tape. Next, determine the height. The person on the top of the slope lays the 1 × 2 out over the slope and, placing the level on top of it, levels the board. The person at the lower end measures the distance on the tape. With the slope defined, the stringer can be laid out with the framing square. Figure 20-4 shows the parts of the layout. Notice that the lower end is trimmed to make the top of the tread the desired height. The top is trimmed to fit against the foundation installed at the top of the slope.

Anchoring at top and bottom is essential for safety. A concrete footing with anchor bolts "J-bolts" simplifies the problem. Likewise, a concrete footing at the top of the slope with bolts projecting from the side makes anchoring the top of the stringer simpler. These anchors should be formed with 1-in. stock, accurately positioned.

Completing the Stairs

When the stringers are leveled and in place, the treads are cut and installed. Next, the handrail should be mounted as follows. First cut several 2 × 4s and bolt them to the stringer with lag bolts. Then stretch a line from the bottom one to the top one at 34 in. high measured from the edge of the tread. Mark the posts with a bevel square set to the angle created with the string. Mark and trim the posts. Last, install a rail or 2 × 4 on top of the trimmed ends of the posts. Then trim off both ends plumb with the leading edge of the lower step and the back edge of the top step.

Using the Cut-In Technique
for Steep Stair Design

A second solution to making stairs into a slope is to cut-in the steps and then build them with natural materials. Figure 20-5 highlights some of the following ideas. The tasks are as follows:

1. Define the height and slope of the incline where the steps will be built.
2. Using the rule of 17, determine the best rise and tread dimensions for the situation.
3. Make a story pole or layout pole with increments equal to the rise of each step.
4. Beginning at the base of the hill, carefully cut-in the first step.

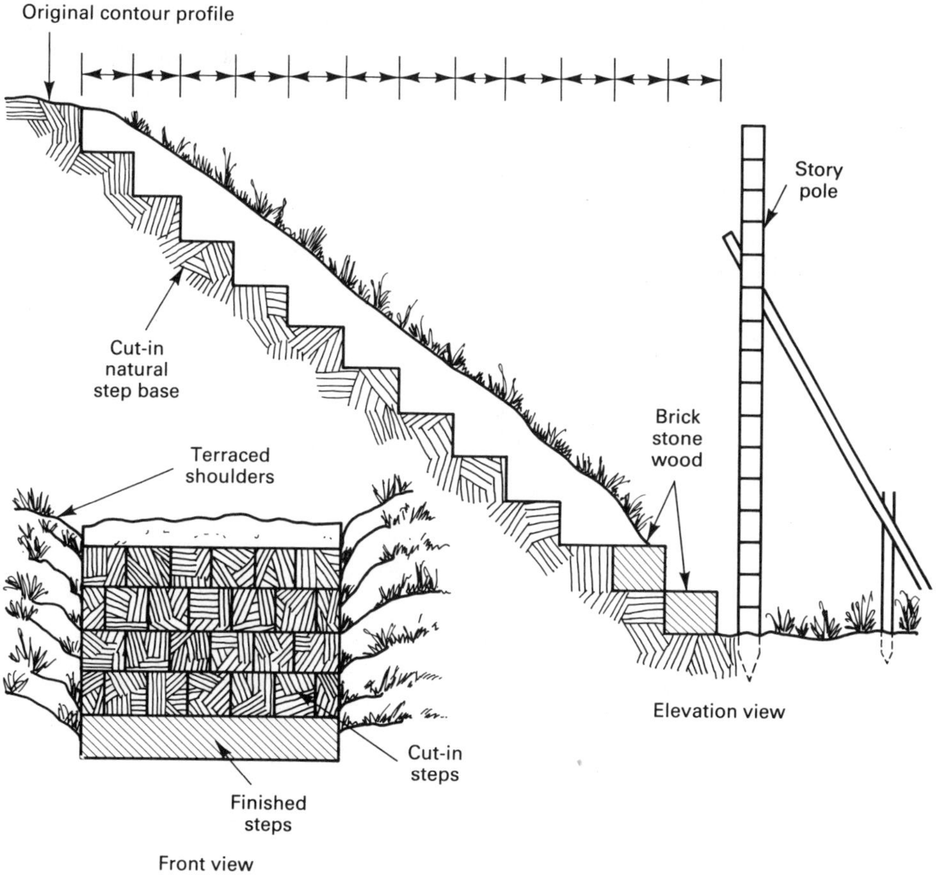

Figure 20-5 Cut-in techniques for the steep slope stair design.

5. Set the natural material in place along the face and on top of the cut-in.

6. Proceed with the second and subsequent steps, using the same technique until the stairs are completed.

7. Terrace the ground around the stairs.

There are numerous decisions implied in the short seven-step list. The one that causes most concern and the one that must be decided on first is the type of natural material to use for the step. You see, if bricks are selected, footings must be laid first. Some forming is required. If wood ties are used, the work is simplified, since these are placed quite easily. If natural stone is used, it may need to be set in mortar, so mortar must be made. Further, stone may need cutting.

Another consideration is the tread materials. These will affect the riser height, as well as the installation technique most appropriate. All of these decisions affect the marking on the story pole, and, in turn, affect the cut-ins made.

These two treatments of the steep sloping grade that needs stairs cover about all situations. Careful study of the discussions will provide you with the fundamental understanding from which you can adapt to the specifics of the problem.

21

Wood Fences

OBJECTIVES

- Identify design characteristics in wood frame that affect their appearance.
- Understand the construction techniques of building wood fences.

BACKGROUND

Fences definitely improve the outdoor living area. They provide dimension to the places where they are used. In this chapter we discuss several types of fences, and later we complete a generic fence project.

The styles of wood fences vary as greatly as any possible combination of materials can. The simple picket fence is still in use today. More common is the 6-ft-high privacy wood fence made from treated lumber. Then there are the fences that use the basic fence boards, but carpenters modify the design, as seen in Figure 21-1. Another simple variation in the wood privacy fence, shown in Figure 21-2, includes 6 × 6 posts that have been trimmed with brick molding. In this figure the gate is fastened to one of the white painted 6 × 6 posts and is locked to the other one. The painted posts provide a significant accent to a common fence. In yet another situation the wood sections are placed between brick columns; this is the subject of the next chapter. We have already identified pickets and treated boards as the vertical boards on the fence and posts made of wood or brick. There must be horizontal members; these are usually treated 2 × 4s.

The way in which vertical members are installed on the fence definitely adds style. Pickets are usually installed every other picket width. Treated 1 × 6 or wider boards can be installed in ways shown in Figure 21-3. The details are provided there.

Now let's shift our attention to the ways in which posts are generally installed. Two techniques are the *mud-set* and the *concrete-set*. Post holes are dug with a post hole digger, and the post is placed into it. For the mud-set dirt is

Figure 21-1   Wood fence made with treated materials.

Figure 21-2   Gate in a fence with 6 × 6-in. posts.

backfilled and water is added. The mud is tamped until the air is all removed. When the mud hardens, the post will be rigid. For the concrete-set the post hole is filled with either wet or dry concrete after the post is placed in the hole. When dry, this technique produces a rock-solid post.

Generally, a fence is laid out along a predetermined line with a mason line. A measure stick is used to space the holes where the posts will be installed. After the posts are in place, are spaced correctly, and are plumb, the horizontal members are cut and installed. Finally the vertical boards are installed. After this the gate is built and installed.

It sounds easy to do and for the professional carpenter, fence building is fun, since it is one of the simplest jobs. However, there are considerations and we need to identify several now. First, fences *sag* if they are not built correctly. The span between posts must be limited to some length. The horizontal 2 × 4 members can carry very little weight when installed the flat way; they can support somewhat more when installed the edge way. If the post spacing is around 6 ft, there is little sagging when the 2 × 4s are installed edgewise. When the post separation is greater, some provision must be made midway between posts to prevent sagging. The usual solution is to block the lower horizontal member with a short 2 × 4. The next most serious problem is *warping*. Warping happens after the fence has been built for a while and is usually caused by the prevailing wind, by weathering forces, or by pressure on the posts and vertical members.

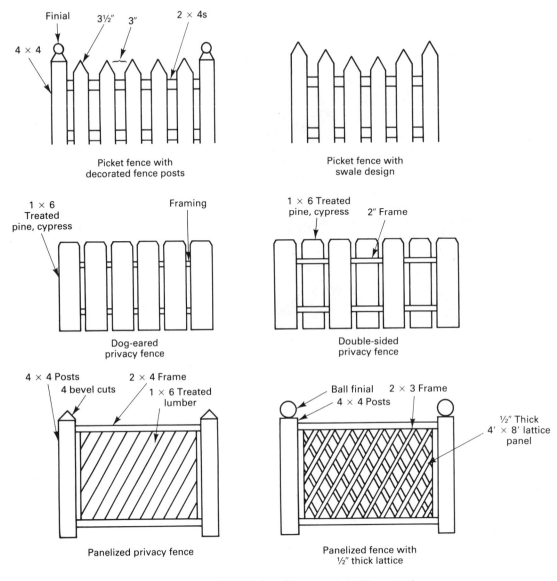

Figure 21-3 Styles of fences using different designs.

Almost every fence needs a gate. Gates made from wood are notorious for sagging because most are built incorrectly. In this chapter we design one that will resist sagging for a long time.

For the generic project we shall construct a 6 ft high by 30 ft long fence with a gate.

This project incorporates the basic and advanced design and construction techniques that can be adapted as needed. Now let's begin with the specifications of the first project.

SPECIFICATIONS

We use the standard convention of listing the specifications in Table 21.1. They are very simple for the generic project, but they could be much more complex if the fencing had more character and style and included sloping ground and other problems to solve.

TABLE 21.1 Specification Listing
PROJECT: *Constructing a Wood Fence with Gate*   **DATE**: _____

General Description

Using all treated lumber, construct a 30-ft-long, 6-ft-high fence. Make the posts from 6 × 6s and trim these with brick molding. Use the mud-set technique to set the posts 2 ft in the ground. The gate will be made from treated lumber as well.

Specifications

Item	*Specifications*
Posts	6 × 6 treated pine timbers, beveled ¾ in. on all four sides, trimmed with brick molding according to plans. Laminated with 2 × 4s to anchor the horizontal 2 × 4s
Horizontal fence members	2 × 4 treated pine, fastened to posts with *top one flat* and *bottom one edge up*
Fence boards	1 × 6 treated pine nailed with galv 6d common nails
Dimensions	30 ft long by 6 ft high with a 4-ft gate at one end.
Fence board spacing	About ½-in. separation
Ground clearance	Maintain about ½-in. clearance between the ground and bottom of fence boards and 2 in. beneath gate and ground
Gate	Use lap joint for stiles and rails; use X bracing for stability
Fence board design	Use S design on fence boards next to posts

TABLE 21.2 Materials Assessment
PROJECT: *Constructing a Wood Fence with Gate*   **DATE:** _____

Direct Materials

Type or Description	*Use or Purpose*
Posts	Provide the vertical support and anchor the fence in the ground
Treated 2 × 4s	Form the horizontal fence members and gate frame
Treated 1 × 6s	Fence boards
Nails, 12d and 6d common, 6d fin	Fasteners, all galvanized
Galvanized hinges	Used on the gate
Gate latch	Secures the gate to the post
Brick molding	Trim used on the posts

Indirect Materials

Type or Description	*Use or Purpose*
Mason line	Establishes the fence line
Grade stakes	Establishes the center positions on each post
1 × 4 or 1 × 2	Braces to hold posts plumb and tamp mud

Support Materials

Type or Description	*Use or Purpose*
Carpenter tools	Construction
Post hole digger	Prepare post holes
Shovel and rake	Clear ground and move dirt
Transit (optional)	Sight fence line
Power saw	Bevel post tops, cut lumber
Garden hose	Supply water to the holes for mud

MATERIALS ASSESSMENT

Table 21.2 lists the materials assessments we can expect to employ in building the 30 ft of fence, which includes a gate.

CONSTRUCTION SEQUENCE

In Figure 21-4 we see the plan and the details for the construction project. The 30-ft fence is designed, according to the specifications, with four 6 × 6 trimmed posts

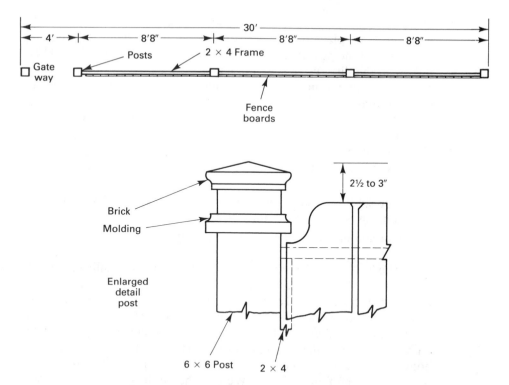

Figure 21-4 Generic project fence plans and details.

spaced approximately 10 ft apart with the last one separated about 4 ft. To perform the related tasks we must do the following:

1. Install a line along the proposed fence line.
2. Place grade stakes where the center of each post will be placed.
3. Dig the post holes.
4. Prepare the trim and install it on the posts.
5. Using the *mud-set* technique, set the post—plumb and in line.

Identify the ends of the fence placement along the property line. We stretch a mason line a little longer than 30 ft and along the inner or outer line of the final post positions. Then after cutting the five grade stakes, we drive them into the ground with one at each end, one at 4 ft and two interior posts at 8 ft 8 in. o.c.

Since we plan to trim out the tops of the 8-ft posts before we install the posts, each post hole must be dug to exactly the proper depth. Here's how we do this. The fence is to be 6 ft high. Therefore, the post must be 6 ft out of the ground. That means we need to make a mark about 2 ft up from the bottom of the post.

Next we check the hole with a 2-ft stick to see if its top is even with the ground. If it is too deep, place a brick or some stone in the hole until the height is right. Carefully set the post in the hole and align it with the fence line. Then backfill the hole with the dirt and water. Poke a stick into the mud until there is no air left. Tack 1 × 2 braces on two adjacent sides and plumb the post. Repeat the process with the four remaining posts.

If time permits, wait several days to continue with the fence. This permits the mud to harden and stiffens the post. If not, brace each post securely on the side opposite the fence boards.

Next are the tasks of placing the horizontal members. The tasks are

6. Cut six 2 × 4 supports and install these on the four posts that will have fencing boards (see Figure 21-4).
7. Cut and install the horizontal members.

The 2 × 4s can be anchored to the posts with toenailing alone. But we add a piece of 2 × 4 to the post to provide added support, as shown in Figure 21-4. Notice that this 2 × 4 piece is notched at the bottom in the exact dimensions of a 2 × 4. The horizontal 2 × 4s are installed one edge up for added strength (the lower) and the other flat (the upper). Both are cut to fit between the posts and within the notch of the 2 × 4 pieces nailed to the posts. In the detail in Figure 21-4 notice that we must keep the 2 × 4s back from the 6 × 6 edge by $\frac{3}{4}$ in. (the thickness of the fence board). We can then either drive drywall or general-purpose screws through the 2 × 4 horizontal members into the 2 × 4 piece nailed to the post, or we can nail each 2 × 4 with 12d galvanized common nails.

Now we are ready to prepare the fence boards and install them. Look at the plan in Figure 21-4 and carefully note the double S curve on the end pieces. The tasks are

8. Lay out and cut the curve into six pieces.
9. Install a line 1 in. down from the tops of the posts.
10. Install the pieces, allowing a $\frac{1}{2}$-in. space between post and board.
11. Lay out the remaining boards and spaces and install them.

Since we know that the top of the post is 6 ft high and that the boards are 1 in. lower, we may need to trim the bottoms of all pieces before cutting the curve and installing the pieces. When laying out the spacing, we divide the total length by 6 in. for a start. Each board is about $5\frac{1}{2}$ in. wide plus a $\frac{1}{2}$-in. space, which equals 6 in. Then we can make adjustments to the spaces when the division does not exactly come out even.

Now let's install a mason line 1 in. down from opposite posts. This line will guide us while installing the boards.

Once we know the separation, we mark off the spacing on the top 2 × 4. As each board is nailed in place, a level is used to ensure that it is plumb as it is being nailed.

Building the Gate

Now let's build the gate. Figure 21-5 provides the detail. But first let's list the tasks:

1. Measure and cut the two stiles and two rails that make up the frame.
2. Make the half-lap joints in the four pieces.
3. Screw the four pieces together, making sure that the frame is square.
4. Cut and install the cross bracing.
5. Install the fence boards, first the outer ones and then the inner ones, spaced evenly.
6. Install the hinges on the gate.

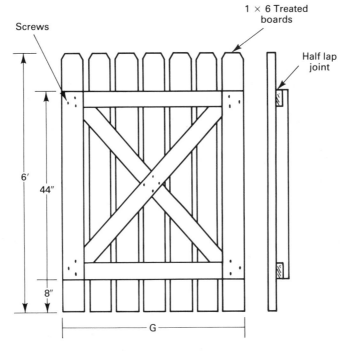

G = Gate width

Figure 21-5 Generic project gate plans and details.

7. Position the gate and screw the hinges to the post.

8. Install the *stop* to prevent the gate from swinging too far closed.

9. Install the gate latch.

We use 2 × 4s for the frame. The four outside pieces are joined with a half-lap joint. Then they are fastened with screws. Next the brace marked *a* is installed from the bottom of the hinged side to the opposite top corner. This brace will resist the force that usually causes sagging. Finally, two short pieces of 2 × 4 are cut to complete the cross bracing.

When we install the fence boards onto the gate frame, the first pieces are the outer ones. But to know where they go we must make a decision about where the frame is in relation to the 6-ft height of the boards. Let's assume that we want 2-in. clearance between the ground and bottom of the boards for swing clearance. Further, we know that the total height is 1 in. less than the 6-ft total height. This translates to trimming the boards 3 in. Next we need to make the S curve on the two outer ones. Now we are ready to position the end boards on the frame. For looks as well as strength, let's have 8 in. of fence board extend below the lower rail and use this as a standard. Position the outer boards accordingly and screw them to the frame (see details in Figure 21-5). Then lay more boards between these two and space them, to arrive at about ½-in. gap between boards. Align the lower ends and nail in place. Trim the tops if not already done. (*Note*: Some people precut all pieces at the same time.)

While the gate is still on the bench, it is a good idea to screw the gate hinges in place. Have each one extend into the rail.

The easiest way to install the gate is to tack two pieces of 2 × 4 on opposite posts about 10 in. above the ground. Next, drive two nails partway into the posts about 2¼ in. back from the post edge. This forms a condition that positions the gate correctly for installation. Slide a 6d common nail between the gate and post on the hinge side to create clearance, thus preventing binding. Next screw the hinges to the post. Open the gate and remove the 2 × 4s and nails on the hinge side.

Cut a 2 × 4 the height of the rail with a beveled top end, and install it where the two 6d common nails are. Then remove the nails.

Finally, install the gate lock or hasp that will secure the gate.

MATERIALS LISTING

With the tasks completed for the generic project, we need to proceed with the actual materials used in the projects. For this we use Table 21.3. Only quantities and identities are provided. Pricing is omitted because of the constant price fluctuation in materials.

TABLE 21.3 Materials Invoice
PROJECT: *Constructing a Wood Fence with Gate*   **DATE**: _____

Quantity	Type	Total
5 ea.	6 × 6 8-ft treated pine timbers	5 ea.
6 ea.	2 × 4 10-ft treated pine	60 lin ft
1 ea.	2 × 4 12-ft treated pine	12 lin ft
8 ea.	2 × 4 8-ft treated pine	64 lin ft
60 ea.	1 × 6 6-ft dog-eared treated pine fence boards	60 ea.
1 pair	Garden gate galv hinges, 4 in.	1 pair
1 ea.	Gate latch	1 ea.
5 ea.	1 × 4 12-ft pine or spruce	60 lin ft
1 roll	Mason line	50 lin ft
1 lb	12d galv common nails	1 lb
6 lb	6d galv common nails	6 lb
1 lb	6d galv fin or casement nails	1 lb
1 box	$1\frac{5}{8}$-in. drywall screws	1 box
1 gal	Wood protector	1 gal

Rental Equipment		*Duration of Rental*
Transit (optional)		4 hr
Post hole digger		4 hr

22

Brick Columns in a Wood Fence

OBJECTIVES

- Identify where brick columns may be used in wood fences.
- Understand the construction of brick columns and how to anchor wood members to them.

BACKGROUND

In this chapter we design and construct a section of a fence that includes a brick column between sections of wood. The brick column in this fence would be the same whether it were used for the corner, in-line, or on either side of a gate. The dimensions would be the same, and so would the construction techniques. The differences would be where the anchor bolts are installed that support the fence section or gate. The anchor bolts for the in-line columns would be on opposite sides; that way wood fence sections would be secured in-line with the column. Anchor bolts in the outside and inside columns would have to be installed 90 deg. to each other. That way wood sections anchored to the adjacent sides form the corner in the yard. Anchor bolts need to be installed opposite each other in the columns that frame-in the gate opening. The 2×4 pieces bolted with these bolts allow hinging of the gate on one side and installation of the gate lock on the opposite side.

There are several critical elements of design that should always be employed. The most important is the mass of the column. A column as small as one used as a pier under a porch would look skimpy and out of place. On the other hand, a brick column too massive dwarfs the fence and uses too much yard space. The one we shall design and construct in the generic project has some mass but not too much.

Another critical element in the design is the bricklaying sequence and the methods used to tie the courses together and strengthen the column. We could fill the center of the column with brick or leave it hollow. We leave it hollow, but we use screen mesh to bind every fifth course. We also embed bolts, which will be used to anchor wood fence sections.

We also examine a couple of column crowns. One is the concrete cap. It looks nice, but it requires either preforming and pouring, and when set it is mortared in place on top of the last course of brick. The other crown employs the technique of *corbelling*. Corbelling is the bricklaying technique where each of the top three courses extend outward about $\frac{1}{2}$ in. to $\frac{3}{4}$ in. wider than the column.

Wood sections are built between the columns. The end 2×4s must be bolted to the column. Then the horizontal members are fastened to these pieces; finally the fence boards are nailed in place.

Let's begin with the specifications.

SPECIFICATIONS

We assume that we already know how to build wood fences with wood posts. This generic project differs in that the wood sections are not continuous. This construction situation simplifies the overwork with wood. Our main concern is specifying the column construction and the 2×4 connector pieces. Table 22.1 provides the specifications.

TABLE 22.1 Specification Listing
PROJECT: *Constructing Brick Columns*
in a Wood Fence   **DATE:** _____

General Description

Construct a brick column 16 in. square on a footing that is 4 in. wider on all sides. Have the footing surface one course of brick below ground level. Use common brick, standard joint thickness, and strike all joints to seal them. Wash bricks with acid to clean the surface after the mortar has set several days.

Specifications

Item	Specifications
Dimensions	16×16 in. $\times$ 6 ft $3\frac{1}{2}$ in. high from the footing
Footing	$24 \times 2 \times 8$ in. concrete
Joint striking	Concave
Connectors for wood	$\frac{3}{8}$-in. bolts projecting out $2\frac{1}{4}$ to $2\frac{1}{2}$ in.
Screen mesh	$\frac{1}{2} \times \frac{1}{2}$ in.
Common brick	$3\frac{5}{8} \times 7\frac{5}{8} \times 2\frac{5}{8}$ in.
Mortar joints	$\frac{3}{8}$ in.
Column crown	$3\frac{1}{2}$-in.-thick concrete sloping $\frac{3}{4}$ in. to a peak, mortared to top course

MATERIALS ASSESSMENT

We list the direct, indirect, and support materials in Table 22.2. These are our best guess of all the materials required for the construction of *one* column.

CONSTRUCTION SEQUENCE

The tasks we are to accomplish in this generic project are

1. Locating the position of the column and its footing.
2. Forming the footing and pouring the concrete.
3. Forming the cap and pouring the concrete.
4. Raising the column with the brick.
5. Striking the joints.
6. Washing the overspill of mortar from the brick surface.
7. Installing the 2×4 member of the fence.
8. General cleanup.

TABLE 22.2 Materials Assessment
PROJECT: *Constructing Brick Columns*
              in a Wood Fence   **DATE**: _____

Direct Materials

Type or Description	Use or Purpose
Bricks	Basic item of the column
Mortar mix and sand	Cement bricks in place
Concrete	Footing and crown
Bolts	Anchors for wood fence
Screen wire	Header/tie every fifth course
2 × 4 treated pine	Fence members

Indirect Materials

Type or Description	Use or Purpose
Mortar board	Eases brick laying
1 × 8 treated pine	Footing form
2 × 4 treated pine	Form for cap
2 × 2 stakes	Secure the footing form
Mason line	Locate the footing and column positions
Nails	Used in building the form

Support Materials

Type or Description	Use or Purpose
Carpentry tools	Construction
Mason tools	Construction
Transit (optional)	Locate the column
Sawhorses	Aids in construction
Planks	Set bricks on and work from while bricklaying
Mortar box	Mix concrete and mortar

We use Figure 22-1 as an aid in describing the more difficult aspects and tasks of this project. But first let's discuss several ideas about positioning the fence. Since the fence is expected to be located along the property line, we must make sure that the footings do *not* extend across this line. Second, we will need to trim grass on the outside. Therefore, some consideration about setting the fence back several feet from the property line should be made. However, this is part of the adaptation to the generic project and we cannot answer this question here.

For our generic project we establish the reference line at 12 in. back from the property line. This line represents the outer side of all brick columns, not the footing. When the line is positioned, the center of each column is established with

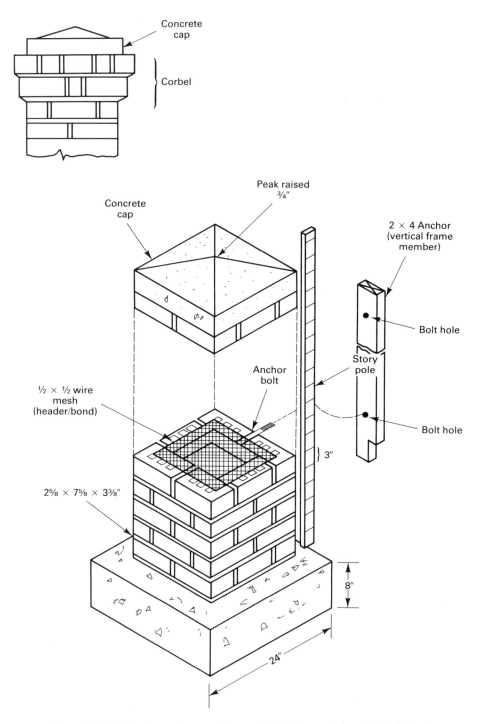

Figure 22-1 Brick column in a wood fence, details, story pole, and alternate cap showing corbelling.

the grade stake, as we did in Chapter 21. We also set the stake for the height of the footing form.

In step 2 we build the footing form from 1 × 8 by cutting two pieces 24 in. long and two others $25\frac{1}{2}$ in. long and then nailing them to make a 24-in.-square form. See Figure 22-1. Following this we must dig a hole large enough for the form and deep enough to set the form to the height of one course of brick below ground level. Then set the form in the hole and align it 4 in. outside the line and centered over the grade stake.

While we are making the form for the footing, let's make the form for the cap as well. It is 16 in. square inside the form. We use the 1 × 4 for this form, since the height of the cap is $3\frac{1}{2}$ in. With this form nailed together, we place a piece of polyvinyl or tar paper on level ground. Then position the form over the paper and stake the form to the ground.

With both forms ready, let's make some concrete. For this single-column project, we use bags of premixed concrete. If there were many columns to do, we would call for concrete to be delivered. For our generic project we need about $3\frac{1}{3}$ cu ft of concrete. At $\frac{1}{2}$ cu ft per bag, we use seven bags for both the footing and cap.

After the concrete sets in the cap form, we must make sure that there is a peak or hip style $\frac{3}{4}$ in. higher than the edge of the form. Also we should use an edger tool and round off the edges of the concrete and smooth the slopes with a metal trowel.

Now let's turn our attention to bricklaying. Figure 22-1 shows that no bricks need to be cut for the job. In every course there are six bricks; two full faces show on two opposite sides and one face side and two ends of bricks. Since these bricks are $7\frac{5}{8}$ in. long and the joint is $\frac{3}{8}$ in., the total length is $15\frac{5}{8}$ in. on the face side. On the adjacent sides the dimensions are two mortar joints at $\frac{3}{8}$ in. plus one brick $7\frac{5}{8}$ in. and two ends at $3\frac{5}{8}$ in. each for a total of $15\frac{5}{8}$ in. (Note that these dimensions are slightly less than the final width of the cap. Therefore, the cap will overlap all edges about $\frac{3}{16}$ in.

We mix mortar from mortar mix, sand, and water in batches of a bag at a time. Then we need to make a story pole with marks every 3 in. ($2\frac{5}{8}$ in. thick brick plus a $\frac{3}{8}$-in. mortar bed/joint. After five courses we place the first square of screen wire mesh cut about 14 in. square. We also install the first of two long bolts. We also strike these joints when the mortar is stiff enough. If it is not, then we can wait and lay several more courses before striking the joints. Every fifth course we lay another piece of wire in place. The second bolt needs to be placed about 3 ft higher than the first one.

After completing the final course, we place mortar around the top course and then carefully lay the cap in place. Finally, we strike all remaining joints.

At 3 in. per course we complete our height with 24 courses. Then with the cap in place we will have achieved our desired height of 6 ft $3\frac{1}{2}$ in. This places the column slightly above the height of the wood sections.

Finally, we prepare the 2 × 4 with a notch in the bottom and drill holes to slide it over the bolts. See the details for aligning the 2 × 4 and mark it for boring the holes.

After the mortar has set for a week or so, we should wash the bricks with muriatic acid and water to rid the faces of the bricks of cement.

MATERIALS INVOICE

With the construction effort for the generic project complete, let's make a materials invoice that identifies all the materials actually used. Table 22.3 shows the information.

TABLE 22.3 Materials Invoice
PROJECT: *Constructing Brick Columns in a Wood Fence*   **DATE:** _____

Quantity	Type	Total
1 ea.	1 × 8 10-ft pine	10 lin ft
1 ea.	1 × 4 8-ft pine	8 lin ft
1 ea.	1 × 2 12-ft (stakes)	12 lin ft
7 bags	Premixed concrete	7 bags
$\frac{1}{4}$ yd	Washed sand	$\frac{1}{4}$ yd
1 bag	Mortar mix	1 bag
144 ea.	Common brick	144 ea.
2 ea.	$\frac{3}{8}$ in. × 6 in. galvanized bolts	2 ea.
6 pieces	12 × 12 × $\frac{1}{2}$ in. wire mesh	12 sq ft
1 ea.	2 × 4 4-ft	4 lin ft
$\frac{1}{4}$ lb	8d common nails	$\frac{1}{4}$ lb
1 ea.	Mortar board	1 ea.
1 ea.	Mortar box	1 ea.

Rental Equipment		*Duration of Rental*
Transit (optional)		2 hr

REFERENCES

BYRON W. MAGUIRE, *Carpentry Framing and Finishing,* 2nd ed. Prentice-Hall, Englewood Cliffs, New Jersey 07632.

BYRON W. MAGUIRE, *Carpentry for Residential Construction*. Craftsman Book Co., 6058 Corte del Cedro, P. O. Box 6500, Carlsbad, California 92009.

BYRON W. MAGUIRE, *Masonry and Concrete*. Prentice-Hall, Englewood Cliffs, New Jersey 07632.

Painting and Coating Systems for Specifiers and Applicators. The Sherwin-Williams Company, Cleveland, Ohio 44101.

Southern Pine Maximum Spans for Joists and Rafters. Southern Forest Products Association, P. O. Box 52468, New Orleans, Louisiana 70150.

Thompson's Water Seal Brand Concrete Protector, Wood Protector, 825 Crossover Lane, Suite 240, Memphis, Tennessee 38117.

Victorian and Country Gingerbread. Vintage Wood Works, 513 S. Adams, Fredericksburg, Texas 78624.

INDEX

A

Abrasion, 108
Acid cleaning, 55
Acrylic latex, 190
Acrylic latex system, 189
Add-on-railing, 117
Add-on-seating, 117
Add-on-stairs, 117
A-frame, 134
Aggregate, 33
Airless spray, 190
Alkyd paints, 190
Alkyd paint system, 188
Alkyd primer, 189, 223
Alkyd resin enamel, 190
Aluminum flashing, 149, 156
Aluminum flashing, 16″ wide, 224
Amount of decking required, 76
Anchor, 84, 260
Anchoring technique, 82
Angle braces, 236
Angle bracing, 230
Angle iron, 84
Arbors, 227
Ashlar rubble, 271

B

Backfilling, 45
Backing cut, 218
Baluster, 83, 84
Balustrade, 200
Base design, 159
Basket weave, 61
Basket weave brick, 62
Basket weave pavers, 63

Batter board(s), 2, 6, 8–10, 17, 27, 38, 39, 40, 51, 67, 119, 122, 123, 124, 125, 205, 207, 208, 224
Berm, 255–56
Biological damage, 109
Biological rot, 107
Bird's mouth cut, 218, 219
Block laying, 43, 44, 72, 209
Block pier, 84, 124
Blocks, 45, 204
Block wall needs, 38
Border bricks, 62
Border pavers, 63
Borer damage, 110
Bottom rail, 176
Boulders, 252
Box, 127
Brace(s), 236, 240
Bracing, 28, 47
Bracket(s), 84, 199
Brick, 26, 141, 192, 261, 267, 269
Brick border, 25
Brick column(s), 297–99, 300, 302
Bricklaying, 26, 119, 301
Bricklaying pattern, 124, 263
Brick partitioning, 27
Brick patterns, 64, 263–264
Brick pavers, 61
Bricks, 28, 261
Brick slab, 24
Brick terracing retaining wall, 260
Brick tie, 262
Brick wall, 259, 274–75
Bridging, 67, 74, 75, 106, 108, 111, 112, 121, 127, 210
Bridging stiffened, 78
Broom finish, 36

Building the porch floor assembly, 121
Bulkheading, 251
Bulkheads, 257
Bullnose, 278
Burlap, 58, 60
Burlap bags, 59
Butt joint, 169

C

Cape cod house, 182
Casing, 159, 161, 164
Casing materials, 159
Ceiling, 151, 154
Ceiling joist, 132
Cement blocks, 51
Center rail, 176
Ceramic or clay tile, 57
Chair rail, 212
Chalkline, 144
Chord, 132, 134
Clay, 252
Clean fill, 46
Cleaning, 31
Cleanup, 16, 50, 155, 165, 223–24
Colonial, 182
Coloring agents concrete, 35, 36
Column(s), 158, 159, 160, 161, 162, 163, 164, 165, 186, 213
Common brick, 260
Common moldings, 184
Common truss, 133
Concrete, 124, 206, 220–24, 252, 255, 273, 278, 301
Concrete blocks, 210
Concrete finishing tasks, 38
Concrete footing, 271, 282

Concrete foundation, 272
Concrete mix, 224
Concrete mixture, 4, 39
Concrete patio, 2, 32
Concrete protective coatings, 52
Concrete ready mix bags, 72
Concrete requirements, 43
Concrete sealer, 55
Concrete-set, 286
Concrete slab, 3, 26, 54, 192
Concrete slab patio, 20, 57
Constructing a gazebo, 205
Constructing a trellis, 232–33
Copper naphthenate, 98, 99
Corbelling, 297, 300
Core materials, 159
Cornice, 132, 134, 136, 140, 141, 146, 151, 152, 200
Cornice fascias, 149
Cove, 128, 162
Cove molding, 210, 224
Creosote, 98
Crown and base molding, 178
Crown design, 159
Crown molding(s), 177
Crown(s), 160, 161, 162
Cubic yard, 16
Curing, 2, 3
Curing requirements, 4
Cypress, 20

D

Dadoing, 83
Darby, 8, 15, 17
Dead and live load of 40 psf, 67
Deck, 111, 112, 113
Decking, 108–17
Decking wood deck, 75
Decorator blocks, 221
DFT, 187, 188
Direct materials, 5, 6
Distributive drain field, 252
Divider members, 21
Door, 178

Dowel centering tool, 173, 174
Dowel holes, 173
Dowel-centering pin, 173
Dry-film thickness, 186
Dry rot, 106, 110

E

Edger tool, 30
Electrical layout, 241
Electrical service, 221
Electricity, 240
Elevation, 119, 121
Elevation drawing, 6
Equally-pitched valley, 148
Erosion, 251, 257
Estimate of direct and indirect materials, 116
Estimate number of bricks, 63
Estimating muriatic acid requirements, 57
Evergreens, 253
Expansion joint(s), 5, 16
Exposed aggregate, 32, 33
Extent of repair, 116
Exterior latex, 178
Exterior latex solid-color stain, 189
Exterior painting, 188
Exterior varnish, 190

F

Fan, 60 cycle, 201
Fascia, 134, 137, 140, 141, 151, 152
Fasteners, 112
Felt-#15, 140, 149, 155
Fence, 286–87, 291–92, 297, 299
Fence board(s), 289, 290, 293, 297
Fence plans, 291
Fieldstone, 252, 257
Finish coats, 222
Finished floor, 38

Finished floor height, 21, 39, 40, 87, 123
Finished lumber, trims, railing assemblies, 189
Finishing techniques for wood decks, 103
Flashing, 137, 224
Flat stain systems, 189
Floating the slab edges, 48
Floor, 222
Floor assembly, 210
Floor framing, 211
Flooring, 119–21, 126–28
Floor plan, 119, 124
Flush form, 47
Fly rafter, 138, 146, 147, 152, 156
Footing forms, 209, 273
Footing line, 41
Footing(s), 16, 26, 28, 30, 38, 39, 43, 44, 70, 78, 120, 209, 259–61, 271, 278, 282, 301
Form(s), 38, 40, 41, 46, 51, 71–72, 301
Foundation, 41, 45, 122, 204–5
Foundation walls, 40
Frame for the deck, 73
Frame for the floor, 125
Framing, 117–21, 138
Framing square, 88, 210, 218, 282
Freeze line, 120, 123
French curves, 197, 198
Fretwork, 194
Frieze board, 134, 141, 151–53, 156
Fungi, 107
Fungus growth, 109

G

Gable end, 136, 138, 152, 153
Gable end fascia, 151
Gable end overhang, 146
Gable end studs, 133, 139
Gable end truss, 146
Gable roof, 132–33

Gardens at different levels, 253
Gate, 193–95, 287–90
Gazebo, 192–205, 198, 200–204, 207–8, 220–21, 239
Gazebo roof, 196
Geometric shapes, 22
Gingerbread, 183–84, 196–97, 205–6, 230, 239
Girder, 119, 121, 125–27, 129
Gloss alkyd, 222
Gloss clear alkyd, 189
Glue, 169, 173
Grade stakes, 250, 259, 261, 264, 267, 274, 290–91, 301
Grape arbor, 231
Gravel, 252
Grinding slab, 54
Grooving (concrete), 15
Grout, 57, 58, 59, 60

H

Half-lap, 293
Half-lap joint, 294
Handrail, 280, 282
Header, 68, 73, 74, 106–8, 110, 112, 113, 120–21, 125, 127, 128, 132, 134, 137–43, 147, 154, 161, 176, 206, 211, 225, 274
Head rail, 173, 176, 178
Heavy-bodied stain, 101
Hexagon, 21
Hip rafters, 216, 217
Hip roof, 134, 214, 216
Hip truss, 133
Homes, 182
Horizontal stringers, 277, 278
House jack, 165

I

Indirect materials, 6
Inspection of wood decks, 115
Irrigation drain pipes, 259

J

Jack trusses, 133
J-bolts, 67, 68, 71, 73, 78, 124, 210, 282
Joist hangers, 68, 73, 78, 111, 113
Joists, 67, 68, 106–8, 110, 112–13, 121, 124–27, 128, 206, 212, 224

K

Kiln-dried lumber, 119

L

Landing, 279
Landscape, 262
Landscape timbers, 265
Landscaping, 16, 50, 193, 244, 256
Lap-joint, 109
Lap-siding, 178
Latex (paint), 190, 223
Lattice, 170–71, 177–78, 185, 196, 212, 224, 243
Lattice assemblies, 241
Lattice designs, 183
Lattice panels, 119
Lattice sidewall, 242
Latticeworks, 193, 197
Layout for footings, 42
Layout stick, 41, 43, 72, 80
Ledger, 125–26
Line level, 2
Lookout, 134, 146, 153
L-sill, 67, 73, 74, 78, 210, 212

M

Mason line, 7, 11, 14, 40, 41, 274
Masonry, 119, 123
Masonry anchors, 67
Materials assessment, 5

Materials invoice, 16
Materials listing, 51, 60, 61, 77
Mineral spirits, 104, 190
Miter box, 212
Mix concrete, 71
Modern house, 182
Molding(s), 128, 162, 183
Mortar, brick, 26
Mortar bed ($\frac{1}{2}''$), 61
Mortar bed(s), 274, 278, 301
Mortar(ed), 24, 29, 43, 57, 58, 113, 210, 220, 260, 264
Mortar joints, 24, 28, 39
Mortar mix, 51, 59, 87, 121, 299, 301
Mortise and tenon, 168
Mud-set, 286, 291
Muriatic acid, 28, 59, 60–62

N

Nailing sequence, 76
Naphtha, 190
Newel (post), 80, 82, 84, 88, 108, 111
No. 15 felt, 156
Normal-sized lumber, 228

O

Oil-modified, alkyd flat stain, 188
Order of repair, 117
Overbricking, 61, 62
Overhang, 140, 144, 147–48, 151, 218
Overhang $1\frac{1}{2}$-in. form, 46
Oversized timbers, 227, 231

P

Paint, 101–2, 121, 128, 186, 223
Painting, 178, 187
Painting system, 222
Panel, 169
Panel design, 170
Panel installation, 176

Panel stile, 178
Pathways, 255
Patio, 32, 33, 253, 255
Patio slab, 4, 5, 11, 12, 17, 26, 62
Patio slope, 11
Pattern of bricklaying, 263
Paver bricks, 244
Pentachlorophenol, 98, 99
Perimeter seating, 90, 91, 109, 111, 114, 200
Picket fence, 286, 288
Pier, 74, 87, 120, 123, 138
Piers, 68, 69, 71, 119, 124, 159
Pilaster, 274
Pine straw floor, 245
Pitch, 134, 136, 196
Plate, 134
Plumb bob, 11, 16, 41
Plywood, 132, 140–41, 149, 153–56, 188, 206, 216, 219, 222
Plywood sheathing, 148
Polyvinyl, 269, 301
Pool, 253
Pool-Side cover, 231
Porch, 120, 183, 186
Porch columns, 159
Porch floor, 121, 138, 188
Porch floor assembly, 119, 122
Porch floor elevation plan, 120
Porch roof, 132, 134, 136–37, 148, 164
Porch roof assembly, 136
Post(s), 80, 82–83, 114, 138, 141, 177, 183, 185–86, 192, 228, 230–31, 234, 235, 236, 239, 244, 282, 286–87, 292
Pouring concrete, 14, 42, 48
Preventing decay, 102
Prime coat, 187, 222
Primer, 189
Privacy fence, 288
Privacy wood fence, 286
Protective coating, 52, 77

Pythagorean theorem, 10, 142

Q

Quarry stone, 271
Quarter round, 128, 170–71, 177–78, 222

R

Rafter end, 140
Rafter tail, 205, 218
Rafter(s), 132, 140, 196, 200, 218, 219, 221
Rail, 111
Railing assemblies, 183, 193, 243
Railing(s), 80–82, 88–89, 109, 114, 200, 206, 280
Railroad tie, 265
Rails, 168, 170, 173
Ranch-style homes, 182
Random rubble, 271
Rebar, 2, 4, 5, 14, 17, 25–26, 41–43, 51, 206, 262, 264, 269, 273
Redwood, 20
Reflecting pool cover, 231
Reflection pool, 253, 255
Reinforcements, 39, 42
Removing the forms, 48
Repair of deck surface materials, 113
Repair of framing section, 111
Retaining wall, 259–60, 265, 274–75
Ridge, 148
Ridge board, 134
Ridge vents, 149
Riser(s), 88, 277–79, 282
Rock, 252
Rock salt slab, 34, 35
Roof, 135, 137, 144, 192, 196, 220
Roof assembly, 144
Roof construction, 132, 214
Roof design, 132

Roof framing, 216
Roof pitch, 205
Roof style, 195
Roof trusses, 155
Rot, 106, 109–10
Rough-sawn lumber, 189
Rubble stone, 271
Rule of 17, 283
Rules of "17 and 25," 279–80

S

Safety 155, 165, 223
Salt preservatives, 99
Saturation, 33
Saw horses, 68
Scaffolds, 132
Scoring (concrete), 15
Screed(ing), 2, 30–31, 48, 124
Screen door, 169, 171, 174
Screen door hinges, 179
Screen door lock set, 179
Screen molding, 169, 170, 173, 178
Screen panel, 172
Screen wire, 168–79
Screened porch, 168–70
Screening, 174
Scrollwork, 197
Sealing agent, 56
Seat brace, 94
Sectionalizing, 26
Semitransparent stains, 101, 181
Serrated trowel, 60
Shale rock, 252
Sheathing, 136, 138, 140–41, 144, 146–47, 149, 155–56, 196, 219, 221
Sheathing plywood, 224
Shed roof, 133
Shellac, 180
Shields, 106 (*see also* Termite shields)
Shingles, 196
Shingling, 149

Ship-lap, 89
Ship-lap joint(s), 91, 92, 93
Sidewalks, 255
Sidewalls, 241
Siding, 140, 153
Sills, 68, 73, 106, 112, 121, 127, 206, 211, 224
Sill (sole plate), 74
Slab, 40
Slab above ground level, 38
Slab patio, 6, 60
Slate, 30, 31, 32
Slate slab, 30
Soffit, 134, 136–37, 141, 151, 153, 185
Soffit vents, 136
Soldier course, 61
Southern colonial, 182
Spalling, 54
Spandrels, 194, 197, 199, 239
Specification listing, 4
Specification, 3, 38, 67–68, 136
Spindles, 183, 184, 200, 212, 239
Stain, 101, 186, 190
Staining, 100
Staining systems, 188
Stair design 277–83
Stairs, 87, 90, 109, 279, 282
Stair stringer, 114
Stapling, 176
Step construction, 220
Step treads, 222
Steps, 111, 221
Stiles, 168, 170, 173
Stone, 267, 269
Stone foundation, 272
Stop, 128
Story pole, 300
Stretchers, 274
Strike the joints, 124
Striking mortar joints, 45, 63
Striking tool, 24
Stringer layout, 85
Stringer(s), 84, 87–88, 109, 277, 278, 280–82
Strip shingle(s), 134, 150, 151, 224

Suburban and country habitats, 265
Support materials, 6
Swimming pool, 255

T

Termite shield(s), 67–68, 71, 97–98, 125, 210
Terrace, 284
Terraces in country habitats, 257
Terraces in suburban habitats, 255
Terraces in urban habitats, 253
Terracing, 250, 251–52, 263, 265, 274
Terracing with quarry or rubble stone, 272, 273
Terracing with stone, 269
Terracing with wood, 267, 268
Thermal hydraulic action, 34
Ties, 278
Tile(s), 30, 58, 59, 60
Tile slab, 29
Tiling a sound concrete patio slab, 67–68
Toenailing, 128
Tongue and groove flooring, 119, 127–28, 210, 212
Top chord, 144, 147
Top coats (paint), 187
Topographical map, 248–49
Topography, 2, 6, 7, 248
Top plates, 215
Transit, 248
Treads, 84–88, 221, 271, 282
Treated pine, 20
Treated wood, 97, 266
Trellis, 227–28, 230–32, 235, 240–41
Trenches, 28
Trenching, 41, 42, 264
Trim, 119
Trimmer board, 210, 212
Trowel, 30, 36
Trowel, power, 17

Truss, 132–56
Truss chord, 141

U

Ultramodern, 183

V

Valley, 135, 147, 149, 151–52
Valley extension, 148
Valley lines, 144
Valley trusses, 144–45
Varnish, 180, 222
Vents, 151
Vinyl acrylic flat stain, 188

W

Wall, 260
Wall construction, 212
Wall panel, 214
Wall/panel design, 213
Wall plates, 138, 214
Warping, 287
Water-borne salt solutions, 98
Waterproof, 135
Weathering, 36, 108–9
Wire mesh (6 × 6), 4, 5, 14, 17, 26, 51
Wood borer, 107, 109
Wood deck, 80, 106, 195
Wood deck patio, 68, 69, 77
Wood deck perimeter seating, 89, 92
Wood deck steps, 84
Wood fence(s), 286, 289, 290, 295–96, 302
Wood patio deck, 67
Wood preservatives, 98
Wood protector, 68, 189, 230
Wood screen door, 179
Wood sealer, 128
Wood stringer, 280

X

X-bridging, 210, 212, 224